W9-AFK-179

THE GAY '90s

Disciplinary and Interdisciplinary Formations
in Queer Studies

GENDERS

GENDERS 26

THE GAY '90s

Disciplinary and Interdisciplinary Formations
in Queer Studies

Edited by Thomas Foster, Carol Siegel, and Ellen E. Berry

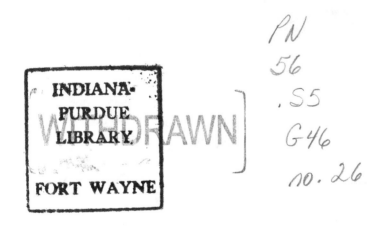

NEW YORK UNIVERSITY PRESS
NEW YORK AND LONDON

NEW YORK UNIVERSITY PRESS
New York and London

ISBN 0–8147–2672–0 (clothbound)
ISBN 0–8147–2673–9 (paperbound)

New York University Press books are printed on acid-free paper,
and their binding materials are chosen for strength and durability.

Manufactured in the United States of America

10 9 8 7 6 5 4 3 2 1

ftw
A JK 9034

Contents

PART ONE

Disciplinary Reflections

Queering the Academy

Robyn Wiegman

Each fall, my institution, like many others, honors newly tenured faculty by holding a reception. ("Celebration" would be too energetic a word to use here.) These receptions usher faculty into the privilege of a seemingly permanent job and can entail institutional gifts, such as the transgender corsage. (At Indiana, for instance, we each received a rosebud nested in baby's breath.) While I have no scorn for allowing boys and girls at the end of the twentieth century to wear the same flower in public, there is little to recommend the rosebud when attached to this: the culminating moment of the event when the Dean of Faculties asked us to join her in toasting "our marriage to the institution." At the time, I nudged the newly divorced woman next to me and stared quietly at my shoes.

The politeness of my response is only one of the many ways in which tenure as a structured process of employment betrays itself as a disciplining system and one so deeply mystified that referencing tenure as marriage can seem to so many people both "normal" and "real." For this Dean of Faculties, in fact, the collapse of two modes of production—the intellectual and the social—enabled a jaunty and compelling analogy: tenure equaled marriage. (Perhaps she was thinking about how long-term commitments tend to be most productive and interesting in their formative years. . . .) As someone who has learned to be wary if I find myself suddenly married with no memory of a proposal (or a spouse, or being heterosexual in the first place), I found the equation offered here scary.[1] On one hand, it reiterates the structural dynamics of the patriarchal family, presenting gender difference and reproduction as covert ideals. On the other hand, it fuses the public and the private, revealing the way that the disciplinary structure of tenure has a governing logic that over-

3

sees not simply intellectual production but the libidinal and affective economies of our social intimacies as well.

There is a great deal that needs to be said about what precisely tethers the intellectual to the social mode of production in the contemporary academy and why any political project articulated under the sign of the queer must attend, institutionally speaking, to both. But before I rush into this, before I satisfy any institutionalized desires for a disciplined, perhaps even disciplining thesis, let's linger over the scene being described.

Tenure, after all, is no minor institutional moment but a lengthy and cunning seduction, one through which we learn to read the "work" that is extracted and required of us as the measure of both our personal and intellectual self-worth. This process, which is central to the production of intellectuals as bourgeois subjects, usually seems fine as long as the institution supports us. When it doesn't, individuals tend to abject themselves as the institution's excess. In these and other ways, the institution's disciplining codes discipline our affect to stunted, standardized modalities, thereby condemning political rage to the individual level ("I wasn't good enough") where it can be dismissed (as sour grapes or a refusal to "fit in"). Most crucial, it is this regulated and polite individualism—the protocol of a certain bourgeois sociality—that comes to shape the political imaginary we share as intellectual workers in the academy.

In making this critique of tenure as disciplinary, I am of course risking far more than bad timing, given the current efforts at the University of Minnesota and elsewhere to erode the employment protections that tenure offers.[2] Certainly there are many, graduate students and adjuncts in particular, who would like the opportunity to be abused by the practice of being tenured. From the position of the radically un- and underemployed, and in the context of a nearly nonexistent job market, being tenured is the imagined nirvana, if not the pot of gold at the end of the rainbow, at least the end of paying the institution for the privilege of laboring within it, not to mention the possibility of dental care and a future unfettered from the terror of student evaluations. Many scholars rightly worry about the fact that the "benefits" of being an emergent academic in America at the end of the twentieth century include downsized health care, increased teaching loads, and the loss of job security altogether. In such a climate, tenure now more than ever represents the academy's version of the American dream: hard work can set you free. Our attraction to this representation—as with the American Dream more generally—lies in its suggestion that individuals control their own destinies. Self-discipline, in other words, is the disciplinary scheme. Such a scheme functions ideologically to produce a class of intellectuals who not only fail to perceive themselves as a class but who rarely see themselves as employees.

The point here is not that we should be idle in the face of the attack against tenure but that we fail if we assume that the defense of tenure is adequate to the labor issues of the contemporary academy, especially if we consider that these issues are not just about job security but about the bodies, ideologies, and social subjectivities being secured through academic jobs. The tenure system is, after all, panoptic and disciplinary. It transmutes the labor issues of the academy into the language and ethos of individualism, which means that the systemic effects of that transmutation—discrimination against people on the basis of group characteristics (race, gender, sexuality, religion)—are and continue to be registered in individual terms.[3]

The issues I am pointing to (about the class status of intellectuals, their working conditions, their subjective internalizations, their ideological formation) form the backdrop to the political project I call queering the academy. By exploring the modes of production, both social and intellectual, that now wed sexuality and sexuality studies to the institution, this paper invests in the political contestations that the concept of the queer has and continues to raise—about sexual practices, the couple and family form, and postidentity knowledges.[4] In my title, you will note, the term insists on being an activity, queering the academy, and its usage is geared toward exploring a new political imaginary in which various alliances might be made—among nonreproductive people, for the gender eccentric, the bisexual, gays and lesbians, the nonmonogamous—alliances that can begin to reshape the academy's forms of social and intellectual discipline.[5]

THE BOURGEOIS SUBJECT

In thinking about sexuality and institutional modes of production, I am assuming a certain Foucauldian function for the university, one in which education serves not to liberate the individual into enlightened citizenship but through which the individual is tied to the economic and political forms of the nation-state.[6] While the popular rhetoric of public education since the Enlightenment has stressed the academy's function to preserve and distribute democratic equalities among citizens—if not to produce citizenship itself—Foucault's work encourages us to read the school as part of the broader apparatus of modern governmentality.[7] For him, the end of monarchical power in the West was effected by the emergence of what others have called the "constitutional state" and its referential reliance on its citizens for legitimation.[8] Through various "technologies" of power (from the school to the prison to the military and the law), the new citizen took his place as part of a corporate social body, one defined by the state and governed less by direct force than by the self-regulation achieved through the internalization of disciplinary discourses and routines. This self-regulation, or internalized surveillance, is the cornerstone of Foucault's theory of modern power, a noncoercive but wholly disciplinary regime.

To think about the academy in this light is to confront the legacy of humanism that has governed the founding and growth of the modern university. I don't simply mean the historical emergence of the humanities as a set of professional knowledges about the human being and his (and more recently her) cultures and social systems (psychology, sociology, literature, political science, and so on) but also the Enlightenment legacy of humanism that links democratic entitlements to a public sphere of literacy and rational debate. It is this latter sense of humanism that governs the contemporary academy, revealing itself in the rhetorical move to defend tenure as "free speech" and in the new critical emphasis on the role and responsibility of the "public intellectual," as well as in the long line of educational reform discourses from Wollstonecraft's argument for women's inclusion to contemporary "multicultural" challenges to Eurocentric and Anglophilic curricula.[9] Humanism has served, rhetorically and epistemologically, to ground much of what now passes under the rubric of "progressive" institutional politics.

But as postmodern theory has been quick to tell us, the humanist legacy is deeply contradictory, being culturally and corporeally bound to the specificities of Western and white male bodies. As Michael Warner and others have discussed, the corporate social body, in the United States in particular, has been compromised from within, serving to define the heralded democracy of American exceptionalism while clearly relying on exclusionary assumptions about the bodies able to achieve the seemingly universal abstraction of citizenship both promised and demanded by entrance into the public sphere. "The bourgeois public sphere has been structured from the outset by a logic of abstraction that provides a privilege for unmarked identities: the male, the white, the middle class, the normal," Warner writes.[10] It is for this reason—that citizenship abstracts and universalizes the particularity of bourgeois (literacy, property) white masculinity—that identity politics have so profoundly shaped the political imaginary of the twentieth century and likewise been so profoundly undermined in recent years (think here of the legal retreat from school desegregation, affirmative action, and aid to the poor).

This does not mean that identity politics will soon be gone from the scene of national struggle but rather that the universalizing abstraction of citizenship is reformulating its precedence over collective "minoritized" identity claims for inclusion. In this climate, educational reform efforts such as Women's Studies and various identity-based ethnic studies that have been tacitly aimed at the exclusions underlying the historical formation of the social body, forging recognition of certain identities as "persons" in the individualist legal sense, are now heralded as bastions of exclusions. Critics of what have been called, inadequately, "the PC Wars" attack identity-based discourses as "ideology," with the clear assumption that "knowledge" can somehow be without politics.[11] Most commentators are bent on proclaiming the university a neutral zone. As the authors of *Professing Feminism* put it, "Academe is ... a sheltered arena in which ideas ... can be developed and thrashed out largely unconstrained by the world outside."[12]

The point here, of course, is that education in general and the academy in particular serve a particular function in the social formation of capitalist democracies, being simultaneously minipublics for the transmission and debate of ideas and training ground (as well as holding pen) for the bourgeois social subject. By "bourgeois subject" I mean the social subject produced out of the contradictory tie between a capitalist economic order and the political philosophy of democratic citizenship—that subject who is able simultaneously to insist on its own willful self-creation and maintenance while being disciplinarily tied to the economic and political hierarchies intrinsic to capitalism. Most crucial, the contemporary bourgeois subject is literate in practices of consumption and in the technological languages of capitalism, able to take his or her place in the expanding managerial network of transnational information and commodity flows, and an expert at the compartmentalization of pleasure and desire and the fetishistic care of the body. The university serves a primary institutional function in the construction and protection of this subject, regardless of the extent to which we pedagogically invest in a critical thinking practice that seeks to counter dominant economic and political formations. (It is, after all, the bourgeois subject who has historically been licensed to both self-contemplation and critical thought.)[13]

When we talk about educational reform efforts as quests to extend the conditions of democratic citizenship to those historically excluded, it is this production of the bourgeois subject that often goes unnoted.[14] But in failing to reference this production, we underplay the function of education as an institution, that is, as a disciplinary structure that performs, through the very myth of free and open citizenship, the crucial service of interpellating social subjects into the ideological and materialist modes of capitalism.[15] To speak of any identity-based incursion into the academy's formation of knowledge (the disciplines) or its social body (administration, faculty, students, and staff) requires, then, a certain kind of attention to the role and function of the university.

How might we imagine the university in ways that would challenge instead of retain "faith" in the public function and ideological productions of the bourgeois subject? And why is such a challenge necessary to the political project I call "queering the academy"? My speculations on these questions will take a seemingly circuitous route, considering, first, the way Gay and Lesbian Studies models itself on other identity-based rhetorics, primarily that of black civil rights, before returning to reassess my opening scene of institutional marriage. Rather than conceiving of the academy as outside or adjacent to the political, we need to read it as a deeply political arena in which a normative bourgeois subject is most consistently produced. To intervene in that production as part of the project of queering the academy means examining the ways in which both Gay and Lesbian Studies and gay, lesbian, and bisexual people are being integrated into the institution's social and intellectual modes of production today.

IDENTITY PRACTICES

In focusing on the way that specific social identities have been denied democratic access to enlightened citizenship, educational reform efforts since the middle of the twentieth century have forged disciplinary knowledges in which the object to be studied was the very social subject that had been historically excluded. What I call the academy's intellectual mode of production—its formations of disciplinary or interdisciplinary knowledges—was thus politically linked to, at times indistinguishable from, the social mode of production—those practices through which the diversity (or lack thereof) of the social body has been both defined and regulated. In arguing for the necessity and the specificity of the study of sexuality and sexual identity *and* for the transformation of the social forms and practices of the institution, Gay and Lesbian Studies has modeled itself on the activist institutional agendas that have accompanied insurgent race and gender struggles in the twentieth century. Like Women's Studies and various identity-based ethnic studies, it has forged a new disciplinary identity and raised issues concerning both the diversity of the social body (in student, faculty, and administrative ranks) *and* that body's citizenship needs (child care, spousal health benefits, student and faculty housing, and family leave). In this multiple focus, Lesbian and Gay Studies (and the student unions, research agendas, and out faculty groups that either precede or accompany it) hopes to challenge, as do all identity-based disciplinary formations, the myth of the academy's political neutrality (of its separation from public political culture), while bringing to the foreground the exclusion not only of knowledge about specific sexual identities but also of gays and lesbians from the benefits of democratic citizenship.

The violences that have met these challenges—hate crimes, firings, roadblocks to curricular change, public ridicule, suspensions—demonstrate the inelasticity of liberal humanism's own commitment to democratic equality. One cannot underscore strongly enough the difficulty facing those engaged in rebuilding a world in the context of political, social, and psychic oppressions. At the same time, a more careful examination of the relationship between the academy's two modes of production, the intellectual and the social, is demanded, not only because of the legacy of bourgeois humanism that underlies the expectation that interventionist disciplinary knowledges take shape as identity configurations but also because of the incommensurabilities between various identity formations. In particular, I am struck by the inability of race and gender, specifically of blacks and women, to adequately serve as frameworks for the social production of sexuality or its institutional disciplinary construction. It is toward thinking beyond the habit of analogizing sexuality to race and gender that the conversation in this section turns.

In "Pedagogy in the Context of an Antihomophobic Project," Eve Sedgwick has remarked that "[t]he most dramatic difference between gender and sexual orientation—that virtually all people are publicly and unalterably assigned to one or the other gender, and from birth—seems if anything to mean that it is rather sexual orientation, with its far greater potential for rearrangement, ambiguity, and representational doubleness, that would offer the apter deconstructive object."[16] For Sedgwick, the deconstruction of sexual orientation goes beyond the expected revelation that homosexuality is the necessary binary term upholding the normative function of heterosexuality by demonstrating that neither sexual orientation nor sexual identity can adequately conceptualize the broad and fluid terrain of sexuality itself. The critical association, sometimes the very conflatability, of Sedgwick's work with queer theory emerges from this kind of deft deconstructive maneuver, which does not abandon the struggle to forge identities in the face of homophobic and heterosexist social practices but fundamentally questions the elision between sexuality and identity—and, especially for my purposes, identity understood as a distinct corporeality along the same lines as race and gender.[17]

There are a number of good reasons why Lesbian and Gay Studies in the academy and the homosexual liberation movement outside it have relied on analogies to race and gender. The long history of locating difference in bodily economies, both biological and psychological (even the antidote to discrimination figured in the "discovery" of the homosexual brain) have established an easy working hypothesis that sexuality is kin to race and gender. Studies of human anatomy in the nineteenth century spawned the growth of various disciplines through which the cultural predisposition that the body speaks the truth of its interior moral and emotional being moved from race to gender to sexuality as critical foci.[18] And of course, feminism's long standing conversations about sameness/ difference and essentialism/constructionism have dovetailed with the cultural debate about homosexuality as choice or fate, at the same time that homosexuality has been mistaken for failed normative gender roles and relations.

Since the mid-1980s, however, the popular imagination has been fixed most strongly, it seems to me, on homosexuality's analogy with African American social identity, partly because of the shared historical construction of each as deviant sexualities and partly because of the overwhelming effect of civil rights rhetoric on the political imaginary of twentieth century America. The 1993 Lesbian, Gay, and Bisexual March on Washington for "equal rights and liberation," for instance, overtly relied on civil rights history and discourse to create a public image and political rhetoric for challenging heterosexual norms. The televisual staging of the March featured footage from the 1963 civil rights demonstration at which Martin Luther King Jr. delivered his famous "I Have a Dream" speech, and speakers repeatedly invoked the language of minority that has been so powerful in the assault against segregation. In these and other ways, the March manifested what has long been the practical and theoretical gestures of "gay liberation"—that is, its desire to secure an identity discourse that could harness, like black liberation, the collective energies of a specified group of people on the basis of that group's claim to both a common identity and a shared "minority" status.

But the analogy between blackness and homosexuality is not as easily forged as the March would have it. In fact, we might read the overdetermined use of black liberation discourses at the March as evidence of the *crisis* of identity within the lesbian and gay movement, the difficulty it has had, historically speaking, to define itself within the prevailing terms of corporeal visibility that underwrote "minority" identity movements for equal rights in the twentieth century. There has been no homosexual "face," no familiar visage, no corporeal specificity that identifies gay identity. Without the corporeal logic that attends race and gender significations—that logic through which the body is cast as the definitive "sight" of difference and against which and through which black and feminist resistances have been formed—homosexuality as an identity-based movement has rather desperately sought a corporealizing specificity. Here, I am thinking of the gay and lesbian culture of performance, from camp styles of butch-femme and drag to the more mundane identifications found in hair, handkerchiefs, and other aspects of adornments and apparel. The controversial practice of political "outing," where gay and lesbian groups reveal the homosexuality of well-placed political and cultural figures, evinces this crisis of corporeal identity, challenging the body's inability "to tell the truth" of sexuality by forging visibility via the representative publicity of homosexual people. These practices collectively demonstrate the willful production of a body to serve as the recognized referent for the truth that the identity of "homosexual" supposedly names.

From a Judith Butler point of view, this production of the referent is just another reason to think of sexuality as performative, and it is an analysis that can lead us to the quite necessary conclusion that race too is founded on a performative and not a corporeal "real."[19] While I agree with this conclusion, the inability of the performative model to discuss the distinct cultural semiotics, historical conditions, and epistemological assumptions that frame white racial supremacy on one hand and compulsory heterosexuality on the other is more than disturbing. Race and sexuality operate differently, and while the postmodern dismantling of identity has given rise to an antiessentialist theory of performance, that theory is not adequate to talk about the ways in which differences are culturally produced and maintained.[20] Whether in the popular political sphere or in the academy, the analogy between race and sexuality reveals less about the way white supremacy and heterosexuality function as forms of difference and disempowerment than it does the fact that the black liberation struggle has offered the most successful articulation of identity-based resistance in U.S. culture in the twentieth century as well as in the nineteenth.

What the adoption of the discourse of minority has meant for gay and lesbian politics in the academy has been double edged. At times, it has worked to help create and build Lesbian and Gay Studies programs and student groups. At other times, it has faltered precisely because conservative forces have argued that homosexuality is a lifestyle choice and not an essential corporeal difference along the lines of race and ethnicity. To choose a difference would somehow negate the democratic right to minority protection. When claims to minority status via corporeal specificity are not made, the political argument tends to eschew difference altogether, positioning homosexuals as members of the generic human family and its smaller nuclear units as well: "we are one of you," or so the deeply humanist rhetoric goes.[21]

While the analogy between blackness and homosexuality has its roots in the history of anatomization of the human being that has accompanied the work of knowledge in modernity, the demand that the disciplinary formation of sexuality follow the lead of African American Studies may well come at too high a political cost. Sexual minorities and minoritized sexualities, as well as a whole host of practices, desires, and queer political affiliations are rendered excessive to such a formulation or else established in codified identity form as bedfellows to gays and lesbians (Lesbian, Gay, Bisexual, and Transgender Studies, for instance). Most crucial, like the analogy between blacks and women, the analogy of homosexuality to blackness racially bifurcates Lesbian and Gay Studies as an identity formation, rendering it most responsive to those primarily white (and too often male as well). This is the case, in part, because of the discourse of injurious inequality that now governs our political imaginary, whereby legal protections and recriminations are sought as substitutes for freedom, with both the state and capitalism, as Wendy Brown explains, being of "relatively unproblematic instrumental value . . . in redressing such inequalities."[22] In the context of the preceding anatomization of knowledge along racially minoritized and gendered lines, Lesbian and Gay Studies risks appealing most intensely to those who experience injury primarily, if not solely, through sexual identity.[23]

Because of this, and because sexuality is itself more complex, fluid, and critically volatile than the identity configuration on its own can evince, it is necessary to differentiate, at least provisionally, issues of disciplinary formation (or the intellectual mode of production) from the social (equality in protections and benefits for sexual minorities as well as admittance to the various avenues of leisure life created and sustained by the university as a local community). To be sure, gay and lesbian research agendas must be vehemently protected, but it is not clear that a disciplinary identity in the same name is the primary means of doing so, nor is it likely that the identity structure can accommodate the contemporary demand for subtle renderings of the complex interplay of the multiple categories defining social and subjective being.

These are not the only reasons, however, to question identity as the privileged mode of disciplinary formation. As I mentioned earlier, one of the primary characteristics of the contemporary bourgeois subject is consumer literacy, a literacy so profoundly tied to the production of a bourgeois "self" that social identities have now been rendered cultural products. Citizenship as a definable set of practices, in other words, has shifted to consumer practices. As David T. Evans writes, "[t]he modern citizen's prime rights are to have the freedom to make a well-informed choice of high-quality commodities and services in public and private sectors."[24] For sexual minorities, gays and lesbians in particular, a culture of identity-based consumption has emerged as the index of social transformation. From pink triangle credit cards and phone services to music, resort facilities, counseling, and clothing, "gay products" beckon the homosexual as consumer, while the gay press eagerly promotes the representation of gays and lesbians as middle class, mobile, and cash fluid. This new found consumer "visibility" made a mainstream media splash in the early 1990s as evidence of a new political identity.

While there is enormous power in a consumer society for collective economic engagement, the reliance on the commodity as a form of political representation underscores the bourgeois components of citizenship (leisure time as well as cash and credit mobility) while simultaneously outfitting a despised minority in the trendy products of lifestyle chic. The problem here is not that new social spaces emerge for sexual minorities, thereby enabling for the first time in history a kind of publicity and minipublic sphere, but that, as Evans discusses, significant proportions of incomes are spent "on gay commodities in pursuit of distinguishable gay and lesbian lifestyles in segregated specifically gay social and sexual territories . . . [with little] citizenship advance beyond the limited constraints of permitted legal participation in [these] privatized social and economic" settings (7, 8).

The social subject produced from this formulation of "sexual citizenship," to use Evans's term, is one quite smoothly assimilated into first-world capitalist economies where identities of all kinds are bought and sold in consumer markets.[25] For this reason, various critics have expressed concern about the political power and the significatory potential of identity-based knowledge formations, since they threaten to confirm instead of interrupt the interpellation of the bourgeois subject as one for whom knowledge gains value in a circuit of self-production and consumption.[26] In other words, the focus on a discrete identity that lies at the disciplinary heart of Gay and Lesbian Studies threatens to replicate the logic of the market, packaging knowledge as a special product designed for students as well as scholars whose social formation demands that we consume themselves.

Given the violent force of homophobia in our society and the difficulty with which young people are able to gain knowledge about sexual desires and practices, the critique of the commodity form that accompanies identity today is not, let me be clear, a call for the dissolution of courses that focus on gay and lesbian subjects. It's the broader conceptualization of the field of sexuality studies that is at stake here, requiring us to think more creatively about disciplinarity, curricular development, and both our own and our students' institutional security.[27] We are facing the distinct possibility that disciplinarity cannot and will not adequately answer the political needs of gay and lesbian people in the academy, unless we are willing to limit those needs to the terms of presence and identity licensed by capitalism and the state in the formation of today's bourgeois subject.

NOT YOUR WIFE

It seems that I have moved a long way from my initial narrative of marital institutional nonbliss in which I left that projected fragment of myself staring at her shoes. She's been waiting nervously throughout. The academy, after all, has required her to be its bride; it wants her to believe in her own suitability as a regular member of the family. And often, because it is so psychically tiring not to, she wants to believe in that suitability, too. She wants the benefits, psychic as well as economic, of being an acceptable academic subject. At the same time, however, she's a bit tired of the academy's ability to absorb so much of her labor. What was once considered the quantity of a life's intellectual work is now required for tenure; what was once a tenure dossier is now an assistant professor application. In cultural studies, in particular, graduate students are the primary producers of gay and lesbian intellectual work, and it is a production for which there are few gay/lesbian/or even queer defined jobs.

What propels this hyperproduction? One explanation must turn toward the increasing privatization of the academy and its emphasis on technical/administrative knowledge and the celebration of knowledge for profit and only profit's sake. Hyperproductivity, especially in the humanities, legitimizes academic work by presenting it in commodity form, and it does so in a political climate in which the "work" of academic labor is being called consistently into question. At the same time, hyperproduction speaks specifically to transformations in the professional/managerial class, whose public and private are being conflated as the family formation in first-world economies becomes ever more in conflict with capitalism. Mobile workers are the PMC's necessity (and, not surprisingly, the newest class formation in the academy). Home has been rapidly reconfigured as work station, as has the automobile, airplane, and commuter train—nearly every space one moves through can now be accessed by technological feed (e.g., cellular phones, fax machines, laptops, on-line coffeehouses).

For gay and lesbian academics, whose seeming mobility and middle-class affluence dovetail with qualities sought for the worker of the twenty-first century, these transformations in the PMC bring into stark relief the complexities of the academy's social mode of production (its practices, that is, of defining and regulating private intimacies and community bonds). In a perverse and ironic way, reproduction, whether biological or adoptive, becomes a means for gays and lesbians to carve out a life distinct from the workplace, one evocative of the culturally desirable "private." Of course, given the historical legislation of sexuality, both legally and in popular discourses, there is really no private realm, but the fantasy of its possibility has an ideological hold on everyday life that is nonetheless profound. The baby boom among bourgeois homosexuals is a case in point, as the production of children now offers what symbolically and affectively can mean a reprieve for gay bourgeois subjects from the force and domination of the workplace.

At least this is one way to think about the increasing inclination toward reproduction of lesbians and gays, academics included, but there are others. In the academy especially, the family form serves as a primary means for the articulation of social bonds, shaping a host of activities and services provided by the institution and offering temporal and spatial opportunities for community outside work. Many colleges and universities, for instance, run child care programs, even elementary schools for the children of their workers; house organizations devoted to family fun (picnics, plays, holiday festivities, vacations); build faculty and student residence communities designed for children; and provide newsletters for newcomers that detail the area in terms of the specific needs of families. Accompanying these are nonuniversity sponsored but family-related rituals of community: confirmations, bar mitzvahs, graduations, weddings, baby showers. To be outside these modes of social engagement—to be uncoupled, nonreproductive, nonmonogamous (and to be so especially when taking one's first job) is often a deeply alienating experience, whether or not one is heterosexual. In this context, the hyperproduction of the queer intellectual might be read as an expression of this alienation, since the family formation is nearly the only visible and sanctioned alternative to work identity in the academy. (What aspect of the academy's social mode of production attends to identifications and practices that place sexuality and pleasure outside the bourgeois family form?)

To queer the academy's social mode of production entails reconsidering how the structures and practices of community, which turn repeatedly to monogamously coupled, reproductive, heterosexual norms, have been historically identified as the "civil rights" needed to undo the various oppressions facing gays and lesbians (i.e., marital rights, spousal insurance, child care). This is not an argument for abandoning the liberal agenda of minority inclusion, but it is to say that the project of queering the academy cannot be accomplished by reconvening the determinants of a bourgeois subjectivity as the horizon of our political hopes. After all, allowing lesbians to receive the material benefits of het repro normativity will not undo the couple form as the institution's primary means of social legitimacy, even if its exclusive gender binary will be forced to yield.

A queer political imaginary thus envisions modalities of affect, of sociality and community, that exist in contradiction and without comfort with the standardized features of the bourgeois couple and family form. This is no easy task, to be sure, but queering the academy demands the rearticulation of its social practices as well as its disciplinary formations, and in ways that challenge our individual and collective aspirations and ideals.

NOTES

Numerous readers have offered critical commentary on this paper; my thanks especially to Tom Foster, Judith Halberstam, Lauren Berlant, and Dennis Allen.

1. Some readers might want to argue here that I am reinscribing the heterosexism of marriage by assuming its displacement, if not elision, of homosexuals. Certainly a great deal of political energy has been devoted in the 1990s to securing for lesbians and gays the "right" to marriage, and we may find it politically enabling to forge narratives that place us on the inside of such cultural practices. But I am critical of the normative function of the marital scenario as it privileges couple formations and an ethics of property as the legitimate affective economy for human relationships. Gay and lesbian participation in this privilege is indeed an incursion into the exclusionary practices of the bourgeois marital form, but while extending the practice through a different performance of bodies, certain features of the normative—coupledom, monogamy, sexuality as a property relation—are not undone. This is not to say that Bill Clinton and other contemporary politicians should be forgiven for their election-year support of the right of states to refuse recognition of homosexual marriage, but it is to mark the complexities and complicities of queer politics in the 1990s when everyday protections (tax shelters, death and insurance benefits, child custody) are continually set against broader political challenges to the institutions of heterosexual power. For a related conversation about the politics of "family" in the context of homosexuality, see Eve Sedgwick, "Tales of the Avunculate: Queer Tutelage in *The Importance of Being Earnest*," *Professions of Desire: Lesbian and Gay Studies in Literature*, ed. George E. Haggerty and Bonnie Zimmerman (New York: Modern Language Association of America, 1995), 191–209.

2. In the outpouring of concern over the threatened elimination of tenure, I think we should be cautious not to take tenure as the most critically symbolic labor issue in the contemporary academy. I say this partly because of the way that the situation at Yale in 1995–1996 has been less generative of critical commentary than the issue of tenure—and further because of the way that intellectual labor in general is being feminized at the end of the twentieth century, which means that the attack against tenure is a consequence of the privatization (and service sectoring) of education in our increasingly transnational economy. To address these issues—of capital's transformation and of the "work" of intellectual culture—will require attention to the relationship between tenure and other forms of employment in the academy, especially the expanding "migrancy" of adjunct

positions. For related conversations about general issues of labor in the contemporary academy, see Michael Berube and Cary Nelson, eds., *Higher Education Under Fire: Politics, Economics, and the Crisis of the Humanities* (New York: Routledge, 1995).

3. In the current social climate that privileges the resentment of people variously privileged (the white, male, heterosexual, U.S.-born, wealthy, educated), it is perhaps just more whining from the margins to note that "standards of excellence" continue to function the way they always have: whereas those outfitted by social categories of acceptance are passed through unscathed as the various institutional, "others" seem never to be as "excellent," as truly "ground breaking" in their scholarship, or as compelling to students. While departments of every discipline can offer narratives about the specific inadequacies of individual scholars denied tenure, the systemic effect—in which white women and scholars of color are denied tenure in disproportionate numbers—should draw our continued attention.

4. Since the late 1980s, "queer" has been in tension, at times in overt conflict, with the terms "gay" and "lesbian" to define the political horizon of sexuality studies in the academy. For some critics, including myself, queer references sexual practices, social forms, and knowledge formations that do not arrive at identity as an ontological or epistemological destination. See especially Eve Sedgwick, *Tendencies* (Durham, N. C.: Duke University Press, 1993) and Judith Butler, *Bodies That Matter* (New York: Routledge, 1993). For others, however, queer threatens to erase the specificity of same-sex desires and identity formations, especially the legacy of lesbian-feminist critical theory and political culture. Bonnie Zimmerman, for instance, writes, "It is curious indeed to find Queer Nation—even a totalizing Queer Planet—emerging to replace a discredited Lesbian Nation" ("Introduction," *National Women's Studies Association Journal* 7 (1) [Spring 1995]: 4). For a crucial counterpoint to the critical divide that separates lesbian from queer, see Lauren Berlant's "lesbian/queer challenge to the sexual imaginaries of feminist and gay politics" in " '68 or the Revolution of Little Queers," *Feminism Beside Itself*, ed. Diane Elam and Robyn Wiegman (New York: Routledge, 1995), 301.

5. This paper moves across a variety of topics concerning the contemporary academy in ways that do not constitute, by any stretch, a coherent argument. Its provisional nature is linked, I'd like to think, to its utopian gesture, even as the rhetorical paths I take are almost paranoid in their citing of the possibilities of political containment.

6. John Champagne also takes a Foucauldian perspective in *The Ethics of Marginality: A New Approach to Gay Studies* (Minneapolis: University of Minnesota Press, 1995).

7. See Michel Foucault, *Discipline and Punish: The Birth of the Prison*, trans. Alan Sheridan (New York: Pantheon, 1977).

8. For a discussion of the complexities of the state very different from the formulations of power found in Foucault, see Jurgen Habermas, "Struggles for Recognition in the Democratic Constitutional State," Amy Gutmann, ed., *Multi-*

culturalism: Examining the Politics of Recognition (Princeton, N. J.: Princeton University Press, 1994), 107–48.

9. I think we should be cautious about the way that "free speech" seems to hold a privileged position in arguments defending tenure. "Free speech" forgets, if you will, the way that the years of graduate and postdoctoral training have a panoptic disciplinary effect on a scholar, and it underplays how tenure functions as a hierarchical system of employment that demands various and unequal productivities from workers, depending on their rank (and race and gender). Coupled with the way that salary and performance are most often judged and adjusted—through ill-defined merit systems applied in closed committee settings—we might begin to weigh the myth of "free speech" against the practices enfolded in tenure as a system of employment.

For critical conversation about the public intellectual, see Bruce Robbins, ed., *Intellectuals: Aesthetics, Politics, Academics* (Minneapolis: University of Minnesota Press, 1990). On the complexities of multiculturalism, see especially Gutmann, ed., *Multiculturalism*; Jeff Escoffier, "The Limits of Multiculturalism," *Socialist Review* 21, nos. 3/4: 61–73; Gayatri Spivak and Sneja Gunew, "Questions of Multiculturalism," *The Cultural Studies Reader*, ed. Simon During (London: Routledge, 1993), 193–202; and Henry A. Giroux and Peter McLaren, eds., *Between Borders: Pedagogy and the Politics of Cultural Studies* (New York: Routledge, 1994).

10. Michael Warner, "The Mass Public and the Mass Subject," *Habermas and the Public Sphere*, ed. Craig Calhoun (Cambridge, Mass.: MIT Press, 1992), 383.

11. See Paul Berman, ed., *Debating P.C.: The Controversy over Political Correctness on College Campuses* (New York: Dell, 1992); and Paul Lauter, " 'Political Correctness' and the Attack on American Colleges," *Higher Education Under Fire*, 73–90.

12. Daphne Patai and Noretta Koertge, *Professing Feminism: Cautionary Tales from the Strange World of Women's Studies* (New York: Basic Books, 1994), xvii. Koertge and Patai read the current crisis in higher education as a result of the ideological bulldogging of identity-based discourses, with Women's Studies as head pit bull. A more useful analysis would examine the postindustrial imperative that accompanies the "work" of knowledge under capitalism in the contemporary West, especially the privatization of the U.S. economy generally and the university specifically. For further discussion about academics, intellectuals, and the professional-managerial class, see Barbara Ehrenreich and John Ehrenreich, "The Professional-Managerial Class," *Beyond Labour and Capital*, ed. Pat Walker (Montreal: Black Rose Press, 1979); and B. Ehrenreich, "The Professional-Managerial Class Revisited," *Intellectuals*, 173–85.

13. It's interesting to note that the earliest Gay and Lesbian Studies department emerged at a community college, San Francisco City College, while more recent programs have tended to be established in elite institutions, which says a great deal about the student population currently being served in the classroom by the field. While I don't mean to underestimate the fiscal constraints facing those who struggle—anywhere—to found lesbian and gay studies programs, we

need to pay attention to the way that the privatization of education has rhetorically worked by establishing students as consumer markets and pitching both courses and programs to their articulated needs. The insistence on studying oneself is part of the enduring legacy of humanism and one of its most incisively bourgeois characteristics.

14. In this context, it is perhaps no surprise that one of the disappointing effects of identity-based struggle in the academy (and elsewhere) has been the tokenizing of "minoritized" individuals who function representationally to ward off the critique of exclusion while stalling the move toward proportional equality. These "exemplary" Others offer the "face" of inclusion while institutional practices seem more rather than less based on the implicit constructs of humanism's historical political identity.

In his recounting of the organizational struggles of the first group of gay academics in the United States, the Gay Academic Union, John D'Emilio describes the debate in 1973 concerning proportional equality for women (who numbered six while men numbered more than 40). Women's votes, some members proposed, should constitute 50 percent of all decision making. While the proposal lost after vigorous debate, the narrative D'Emilio tells importantly demonstrates the conflict within majority-ruled democratic practice for those in minority positions. See "The Universities and the Gay Experience," *Making Trouble: Essays on Gay History, Politics, and the University* (New York: Routledge, 1992), 117–27.

15. The incorporation of women into public citizenship in the West, for instance, has served a critical function in the postindustrial proliferation of capital. As Maria Mies discusses, the redistribution of the sexual division of labor *within* the West has had a global economic effect: the third world has become a domestic industrial service sector to the first world's global management class. It's a heterosexual economy on a world scale, with white women in the United States, straight or lesbian, serving as the newly "masculinized" labor force for the professional management of global capital. See Mies, *Patriarchy and Accumulation on a World Scale: Women and the International Division of Labor* (London: Zed Press, 1986), and *Woman: The Last Colony* (London: Zed Press, 1990).

16. Eve Sedgwick, "Pedagogy in the Context of an Antihomophobic Project," *The Politics of Liberal Education,* ed. Darryl J. Gless and Barbara Herrnstein Smith (Durham, N. C.: Duke University Press, 1992), 147.

17. Let me make clear that I am not supporting the cultural taxonomies of race and gender as distinct, essential, or irrefutable corporeal differences. Current critical focus on passing on one hand and transgender and transsexuality on the other radically challenges the ease with which we can read either race or gender as natural bodily scripts. My point is rather that continued analogies between sexuality and either race or gender may sacrifice the most decisive threat that sexuality holds.

18. See especially Sander Gilman, "Black Bodies, White Bodies: Toward an Iconography of Female Sexuality in Late Nineteenth-Century Art, Medicine, and Literature," *"Race," Writing, and Difference,* ed. Henry Louis Gates Jr. (Chicago: University of Chicago Press, 1986), 223–61; Londa Schiebinger, *Nature's Body:*

Gender in the Making of Modern Science (Boston: Beacon Press, 1993); and Robyn Wiegman, *American Anatomies: Theorizing Race and Gender* (Durham, N. C.: Duke University Press, 1995).

19. See especially Judith Butler, *Gender Trouble: Feminism and the Subversion of Identity* (New York: Routledge, 1990).

20. In discussing the limitations of the performative model for thinking about race, Yvonne Yarbro-Bejarano suggests that the answer to current critical difficulties is not about "evolving a parallel theory of the performance of racial identity vis-à-vis a phantasmatic racial ideal analogous to gender but, rather, one of reading race, and political movement as well, into Butler's performative model." See "Expanding the Categories of Race and Sexuality in Lesbian and Gay Studies," *Professions of Desire*, 129. For a critical analysis of the imbrications of race and sexuality that purposely avoids the analogical gesture, see Lindon Barrett, "Black Men in the Mix: Bad Boys, Heroes, Sequins, and Dennis Rodman," *Callaloo* (forthcoming) and "Identities and Identity Studies: Reading Toni Cade Bambara's "The Hammer Man," *PMLA* (forthcoming).

21. At the March on Washington, in fact, the second most popular rhetorical tactic was that of the "family"—gay people are part of *your* family, and they have families as well. While the language of minority produces an ontological category, which means that its borders do not leak (one *is* either a homosexual or one is not), the difference that is finally not a difference envisions homosexuality's seamless assimilation; the family, in other words, is healed.

22. Wendy Brown, *States of Injury: Power and Freedom in Late Modernity* (Princeton, N. J.: Princeton University Press, 1995), 10.

23. For different purposes but in importantly linked ways, Leo Bersani explores the relationship between whiteness and gay male identity in *Homos* (Cambridge, Mass.: Harvard University Press, 1995).

24. David T. Evans, *Sexual Citizenship: The Material Construction of Sexualities* (London: Routledge, 1993), 5. Further citations from this text will be included parenthetically in the text.

25. For other conversations about sexual identity and consumption, see Sue Ellen Case, "The Student and the Strap: Authority and Seduction in the Class-(room)," *Professions of Desire*, 38–46; and Arlene Stein, "Style Wars and the New Lesbian," *Out/Look* 1, no. 4 (1989): 34–42.

26. See Champagne, *The Ethics of Marginality*; and Judith Roof, "Buckling Down or Knuckling Under: Discipline or Punish in Lesbian and Gay Studies," *Who Can Speak? Authority and Critical Identity* (Urbana: University of Illinois Press, 1995), 180–92.

27. In this context, something needs to be said about practices of evaluation governing scholarship, teaching, and service in the academy. Disciplinarity brings with it specific kinds of measurement and assessment as avenues of institutional legitimacy, but rarely are these modes of evaluation called into question. Queering the academy in this register would mean challenging the evaluation and assessment of "good" teaching and the ways in which standards of academic "excellence" police the study of sexuality. Further, it would mean resisting the seduction of the star system, since it is through the bourgeois production of star academics

that the political aspirations of a new knowledge formation have historically been translated into the academy's commodity ethos. Most important perhaps, it would mean developing pedagogy for challenging students (and administrators) to think beyond the bourgeois consumption of an identified "self" (or identifiable student market) as the necessary knowledge of sexuality studies.

Lesbian and Gay Studies
A Consumer's Guide

Dennis Allen

The first time that I taught an introductory class in Lesbian and Gay Studies, a course overtly predicated on the examination of a particular set of identity categories, what was striking was the way in which these categories soon proved themselves to be thoroughly inadequate. The problem was not so much that, as the students quickly realized, the list of possible designations currently available (straight, gay, lesbian, bisexual) is far too rudimentary a taxonomic system to describe the sexual field. Rather, the difficulty seemed to lie in assigning individuals their place in the system. In part, of course, this was the familiar problem of determining who was what, since, despite the fantasies of some heterosexuals, gay or lesbian or bisexual identity is not always immediately evident. Far more intriguing, however, was the fact that, even as the vast majority of the students argued that sexual orientation was innately determined, not at all a matter of choice, the self-designations of several of them changed in the course of the semester. Thus, not only did one of the straight men ("Matt") came to the conclusion that he was "really" bisexual, but one of the bisexual women ("Chrissie") decided that she was "really" straight. Now, if the first of these metamorphoses is familiar enough that it has become naturalized as the classic coming out narrative, the second story becomes, following the same logic, intensely problematic. If the underlying assumption of Matt's narrative is that he has acknowledged his "true" sexual identity by throwing off the misrecognitions induced by compulsory heterosexuality, then Chrissie's story must be read, using the same valuations, as a descent into méconnaissance. Following the popular be-

23

liefs that, for certain individuals, lesbigay desire is "authentic," heterosexuality merely a cultural imposition, and that, in a heteronormative society, only lesbigays experience (or need to experience) a process of discovery of their "real" sexuality, Chrissie's self-recognition has to be seen as inauthentic: as a personal regression or as an effect of internalized biphobia or as an enslavement by the dominant ideology or as all of the above. Implicit in this logic, then, is the assumption that "genuine" sexual self-discovery can "really" move only in one direction.

I suppose that what concerns me here is the lack of other interpretive options. If Chrissie's story is not read as a minor, "tragic" exemplum in the Divine Comedy of Queer Liberation, then it becomes, simply, incomprehensible, and this poverty of interpretive possibility persists if we turn from popular understandings of sexual orientation to current academic thinking on the subject of sexual identity. While one of the cardinal tenets of Queer Theory is the necessity of voiding such labels as "lesbian" or "bisexual" or "gay" of any determinate content, this very process works to deflect attention from the persistence within the field of certain residual, hegemonic assumptions.[1] Thus, even as much of Queer Theory calls identity categories into question, the performative conception of identity so often used in these arguments is itself often implicitly reinscribed within a nineteenth-century teleology, a logic of progress, whether this is seen as the freeing of the individual from the "regulatory effect" of the category or, more generally, as a step toward lesbigay "liberation" in the culture at large. One problem with this is that these two conceptions of progress are at odds with each other, if only because the notion of a progressive liberation, the implicit rationale for the very existence of Queer Theory itself, implies, as an inherent corollary of its political vision, the existence of something like lesbian or gay "identity" (as categories of oppressed persons) that performative conceptions of the self are supposed to shatter. In addition, the ideology of progress that is inherent here sketches out a sort of eschatology for both the individual and society: an irreversible "coming out of" a hegemonic heterosexuality and into the social possibility of a recognizable (albeit "indeterminate") lesbian or gay or bisexual identity. As such, most Queer Theorists, I would argue, implicitly subscribe to the notion that lesbigay identities have an authenticity that heterosexuality lacks, whether the latter is considered as a cultural norm or as the sexual identity of certain people (like Matt and Chrissie). In other words, they assume some version of the popular beliefs that make Chrissie's narrative so problematic. Simply put, while the current interrogation of categories of sexual identity allows Eve Sedgwick to claim that she is a gay man, an announcement by, say, Leo Bersani or Elizabeth Meese that he or she is "really" straight would be, if not exactly a cover story for the *National Enquirer*, considered scandalous in certain circles.

Important in and of themselves, these limitations in current thinking about the nature of sexual identity take on added urgency within the literal and figurative space in which my opening anecdote takes place: the progressive institutionalization of Lesbian and Gay Studies in the academy. The issue here, I would argue, is not simply how we might better understand the concept of "identity" but also how we can explain the fact that there is a classroom in which such issues can be raised in the first place. Why have Lesbian and Gay Studies courses begun to be incorporated, albeit slowly and sporadically, into university curricula? [2] Or, to put it another way, what is the institutional and cultural significance of the development of Lesbian and Gay Studies as an academic discipline? [3] To answer such questions, we have to begin by looking (yet again) at the definitions of "lesbian" and "gay" that provide the basis for such "identity courses." I will argue that our notions of these identities need to be reconceived by supplementing the current Foucauldian paradigm for conceptualizing identity with a renewed attention to the ideological implications of postindustrial capitalism, specifically its shift in emphasis from production to consumption. As I hope to show, a postindustrial economy based on consumption has not only radically affected contemporary processes of identity formation but has been highly influential in the development of Gay and Lesbian Studies as an academic discipline, a discipline that is designed to fit the increasingly consumerist structure of higher education and that is, itself, thoroughly imbued with the ideology of consumption. Not entirely incidentally, as we will see, the analysis of these phenomena also provides a better framework for understanding Chrissie's story.

"IS THERE A SUBJECTIVITY IN THIS CLASS?": POSTINDUSTRIAL CONSUMPTION AND THE FORMATION OF IDENTITY

Much of contemporary Queer Theory follows Foucault in seeing our current idea of sexual identity as the result of an epistemological shift that took place in the nineteenth century, the migration from an understanding of sexuality as a set of external acts to a notion of it as an internal state of being, an identity.[4] The problem here is less the validity of this assumption than the explanation of the causality behind this shift, for Foucault attributes it, somewhat notoriously by now, to the disciplinary mechanisms inherent in "power," a concept that, even seen as the independent (if often convergent) operations of a variety of institutions and domains of knowledge, serves simply to reify "power" as a sort of transcendental first cause that, itself, operates outside the constraints of historical determination.[5] A Foucauldian analysis of lesbigay identity cannot, then, stand entirely by itself, and some clue to what might profitably be added to it is provided by Judith Roof's assessment of the introduction of Gay and Lesbian Studies into the academy. The major argument of "Buckling Down or Knuckling Under: Discipline or Punish in Lesbian and Gay Studies" is a compelling analysis of the ways in which the institutionalization of Queer Studies allows for the regulation and control of sexuality and sexual excess in general within the disciplinary structures of the university. Yet Roof goes even further, suggestively noting, in passing, "the surfacing of the link between knowledge and capital," the connection between identity-based academic disciplines and larger economic trends. Thus, Roof argues, such areas of study follow a postindustrial consumer logic in which "identity courses" allow the participants to consume themselves.[6] Unfortunately, Roof does not elaborate on this link between late capitalism and the formation of (queer) identity, a link that must be explored further if we are to understand both our conceptions of sexual identity and the emergence of Lesbian and Gay Studies as an academic discipline.[7]

Rosemary Hennessy's "Queer Visibility in Commodity Culture" can be helpful here, since Hennessy's primary aim is to demonstrate that the current focus of much of Queer Theory on the discursive construction of the subject works to elide or ignore the materiality of social life and the ways in which late capitalist consumption shapes subjectivities.[8] While being careful to note that economic factors are only part of the larger complex of institutions and practices that constitute the social, Hennessy identifies the impact of late capitalism on identity formation as part of a process that she terms "the aestheticization of daily life." Predicated on the increasing significance of the sphere of consumption, the "aestheticization of daily life" includes the reconceptualization of identity as a "lifestyle," according to Hennessy, in which advertising's saturation of the quotidian with images and signs works to promote a conception of the self as a malleable, self-fashioned identity. As Hennessy makes clear, such an identity is created by purchases, rather than generated by moral codes or social rules or by one's place in "gender and racial hierarchies."[9] This new sense of self is, in part, deceptive, for such an identity cannot be quite as de-centered or porous or postmodern as it first seems given the fact that it is still inserted into a hierarchical social structure. Nonetheless, Hennessy notes, the aestheticization of daily life and the reconceptualization of identity as a lifestyle does, after all, reflect a reworking of the processes of identity formation: "Concern with the stylization of life suggests that practices of consumption are not merely a matter of economic exchange but also affect the formation of sensibilities and tastes that in turn support more flexible subjectivities" (58). The problem, however, is that, following the logic of the commodity fetish itself, in which the value of the commodity is an illusion (because it is divorced from the creation of surplus value through the labor that produced it), this process of aestheticization serves to obscure not only the existence of social hierarchies but to mystify the social relations, specifically the exploitation of labor, that produce the commodities in the first place (Hennessy's examples are sweatshop laborers in the South Bronx and migrant farm workers in California). As such, Hennessy argues, the new gay/lesbian/queer identity that has emerged under late capitalism is a class-based subjectivity that actually prevents an examination of the social relations (such as hierarchies of gender and class) on which it depends.

Hennessy's analysis leads to some important insights. She is able, for example, to identify the current trend toward performative conceptions of identity in Queer Theory as, itself, a reflection of the material practices of identity construction that she discusses. Moreover, Hennessy's willingness to discuss issues of class exploitation is crucial to an understanding of how identity formation works under late capitalism (as well as a refreshing change from the current academic tendency to analyze issues of "raceclassgender" in such a way that attention to race and gender work precisely to metonymically stand in for, and hence erase any reflection on, issues of class). Yet Hennessy's essay requires a closer look, if only because certain of its presuppositions actually foreclose a more complete reading of the relation of late capitalism to identity (and hence, for the purposes of this essay, to the formation of Gay and Lesbian Studies as a discipline). By examining three problematic assumptions underlying Hennessy's argument, we can, I think, further our understanding of the interrelation of consumption, identity, and disciplinarity. These assumptions can be summarized as: a conceptualization of identity that serves, implicitly, to erase lesbians and gay men; a catachrestic (mis)understanding of consumption as production; and, as a consequence, a misreading of the social contradictions at work in the commodification of (queer) identity.

"IN THE LIFE(STYLE)"? IDENTITIES, AUTHENTIC AND OTHERWISE

We can begin with Hennessy's conceptualization of identity. It is somewhat alarming that, in an essay ostensibly devoted to addressing "queer visibility," the final emphasis invariably falls on nearly every "identity category" *but* lesbians and gay men. Thus, the exploitations that are concealed by (queer) self-fashioning through consumption are variously identified by Hennessy but are never really identified as the exploitation of queers. Take, for example, Hennessy's assertion that queer consumer visibility "keeps invisible the capitalist divisions of labor that organize sexuality and in particular lesbian, gay, queer lives" (66). Aside from the fact that lesbigays are forced to bear the entire burden of contemporary consumerism here, Hennessy's emphasis falls on divisions of labor, rather than on organizations of sexuality, so that queer visibility is read as itself oppressive to those (i.e., the working class) on whose "invisible labor" the production of consumer goods rests.[10] Hennessy's continual erasure of lesbigays is thus due, in large part, to her allegiance to a particular model of Marxist feminism that leads her to take class (and, to a lesser extent, gender) as the primary categories of analysis. As a result, the essay demonstrates a continual tendency to posit a group (lesbigays) as an analytic category and then to argue that the historical and material production of that category diverts attention from more "authentic" social groups (the working class, women). Thus, the social exploitation detailed in the final third of the essay, when Hennessy moves beyond class issues to discuss gender oppression, is seen to consist largely of the structures of patriarchy, and the negative effects of heteronormativity are subordinated to gender issues. As a result, Hennessy's critique of heterosexism is reduced to the assertion that heterosexuality is integral to patriarchy because it identifies woman as both property and exploited labor, an analysis that, while certainly true, is not perhaps the most direct way to approach the oppression of lesbians and does little to explain the oppression of gay men (65).

If this were merely a question of emphasis, yet another instance of the differences in the ways that various strands of feminism hierarchically rank the analytic priority of various oppressed social groups, then we could simply acknowledge those differences.[11] We could note in passing that, like Tolstoy's unhappy families, each oppressed group is oppressed in its own way and that arguing over degrees of victimization is unprofitable, and proceed to do what Hennessy does not really do: analyze the particularities of lesbigay oppression and discern the structural links to other categories of oppression (class, gender, race, and so on). Yet, Hennessy's implicit sense that lesbigays do not constitute a properly Marxist analytic category is important precisely because it subtly shapes her whole analysis of lesbigay identity, causing her to project the issue of authenticity onto that identity itself, producing an idea of "identity" that requires further analysis.

This idea is signaled by Hennessy's use of the term "lifestyle" as the label for a consumerist lesbigay identity, a singularly unfortunate choice given the current appropriation of the word by the radical right, for whom the phrase "homosexual lifestyle" encodes an entire set of assumptions: that homosexuality is a(n immoral) choice; that it is superficial, if not depraved; and that it is inauthentic in comparison to heterosexuality (i.e., a real life based on "values").[12] While Hennessy's perspective is certainly distinct from that of the Christian Coalition, her characterization of consumer self-fashioning as "aestheticization," hardly an inevitable label, resonates against the now fading stereotype of gay men as Wildean aesthetes to suggest, in conjunction with the word "lifestyle," that post-industrial lesbigay identity is precisely a superficial focus on style. This impression is compounded by Hennessy's use of a quote from Foucault (about "making one's life a work of art") to argue, not surprisingly, that such a "stylization of identity" conceals the fact that not everyone (read the workers who produce consumer goods) can do so (59), and it is here that Hennessy invokes the sweatshops of the South Bronx and the migrant tomato harvesters of the San Joaquin Valley. The problem with this argument is not simply that it radically misreads the idea of a technology of the self in Foucault's later work.[13] Rather, it is here that Hennessy's leftist critique aligns with rightist diatribes against homosexuality so that her implicit charge that lesbigays are politically superficial meshes perfectly with the Christian Coalition's insistence that we are morally superficial. As I have already suggested, this alignment is not entirely accidental since, despite their very different conceptions of what would constitute it, both positions refuse lesbigays the status of an authentic identity. In

Hennessy's case, this derives from the use of a traditional (rather than "Neo-") Marxist paradigm that contrasts the "real" identity of the "worker" (an identity literally produced, as it were, by labor) with the "inauthentic" role of the consumer, a position that is occupied primarily by lesbigays in Hennessy's argument (even before the choice of that particular "lifestyle" compounds this inauthenticity).[14] As such, Hennessy misrepresents, I will argue, the processes of postindustrial identity formation. To understand this, however, we have to turn to the second problem in Hennessy's essay: her tendency to analyze an economy of consumption in terms more suited to an economy of production.

MATERIAL (BOYS AND) GIRLS: POSTINDUSTRIAL
CONSUMPTION AND THE FORMATION OF IDENTITY II

This misreading is apparent in Hennessy's identification of the groups that are exploited by the ideal of making one's life a work of art. While the sweatshops of the South Bronx can be clearly linked to the production of clothing that could be purchased to create a "personal style," it is difficult to see how consumer self-fashioning is related in any direct way to the situation of migrant farm workers (tomatoes playing little or no role, that I know of, in contemporary lesbigay self-constructions). Let me be careful not to misread Hennessy here. Certainly migrant workers are economically exploited, and it is equally true that a consumer economy as a whole distracts attention from such exploitation. However, the juxtaposition of (lesbigay) postindustrial consumption with industrial and agricultural labor categories itself works to (mis)articulate the nature of postindustrial capitalism in ways that are not particularly helpful. By implicitly defining labor throughout her essay as the production of material goods, Hennessy blocks an analysis of the processes of both production and consumption in an economy of consumption. The problem is less that self-fashioning, in a postindustrial economy, is based as much on the consumption of services as on goods and that not all workers in all service industries can be said to be exploited (fast food employees—yes, lawyers—no). Rather, by treating an economy of consumption as if it were an economy of production, Hennessy restricts her analysis of exactly how identity is produced in such circumstances. If we return to Hennessy's characterization of postindustrial "aestheticization," we note that she herself stresses that much of what is produced takes the form of signs or images rather than of material goods (57). Further examination of this recognition about postindustrial production can lead us to a clearer understanding of the nature of identity in a consumer society.

It is at this juncture that Baudrillard's analysis of the workings of a society of consumption proves useful. Rejecting standard economic theory centered on the assumption that consumer needs are based on the relation of the individual and an object, Baudrillard argues that the society of consumption is merely an extension of the forces of production, a mutation in the previous system rather than a radical break from it.[15] As such, consumer needs must be understood as the created product of the system of production (rather than as arising spontaneously from individual desire), with the further implication that such needs, as elements of that larger system, must be seen as collective rather than individual. As a result, Baudrillard argues, consumption as a whole is based not on the object's ability to perform a function or satisfy a defined need but derives instead from a general system of exchange and coded values. In Baudrillard's view, these coded values are the production of "social meaning," in other words the creation of "difference," social categories. Thus, although, as Baudrillard points out, consumption is primarily organized as "a discourse to oneself" (*Selected Writings* 54), what this discourse says is not that one's "identity" is an isolated entity but that "identity" is a locus, the site where one's patterns of consumption place one within the entire system of differentiated, overlapping niches that are the social meaning of the goods and services one consumes.[16]

As such, to extend Baudrillard's analysis, we might consider the following: even if we agree that certain identity categories derive from a variety of organizing discourses, such as the corporeal taxonomies of race or gender or the psychologized division of sexual orientations, when they are filtered through the system of consumption such identity categories can be best understood as semiotic relay points where "identity" is constituted through the consumption of particular sets of signs, including, of course, the consumption of the idea of a particular "identity" itself. This is to say, of course, not that gay men and lesbians would not exist without rainbow flag bumper stickers, Melissa Etheridge CDs, or movies featuring Brad Pitt or Jodie Foster but that these identity categories must now be understood not as the inevitable outcome of individual (sexual) desire but rather as the insertion of that desire into a differentiated structure of social signs that defines identities through consumption.

If we use Baudrillard's analysis to refine Hennessy's understanding of consumer identity, then, what we realize is that a reading of consumer self-fashioning that posits it as merely an efflorescence, as a superstructural stylization of the self, misunderstands several crucial points. Rather than seeing lesbigay consumption as the "aestheticization" of an implicitly preexisting self, it might be more profitable to view the constitution of identity through consumption as the process by which individuals are interpellated into identity in a postindustrial society. In other words, consumption is not merely a surface "stylization" of the self but rather a continual process, both conscious and unconscious, of defining an identity by associating the "self" with the (differentiated) signifiers of (the various aspects of) that identity. While identity is thus inscribed externally, on the surface of the body or in one's surroundings or through one's actions, this does not necessarily mean, as Hennessy implies, that it is superficial. Rather, one might argue that what is going on here is an ideological shift in our notion of identity itself. If Foucault is right in noting that the nineteenth century is the period at which sexual identity is implanted in the body, migrating inward as the conception of an inner core of "self," the construction of the self through consumption might represent another historical shift, a reexteriorization of identity. This exteriorization cannot simply be thought of only as the ownership or display of particular consumer goods, however. If consumption as identity formation is the association of various signifiers of identity with a "self" that is thus always under construction, this process must be seen finally as a complex set of actions (including the purchase and consumption of both goods and services) that in turn depends on and reflects the consumer's (and the culture's) conception of the meaning of those actions. As such, what is finally being consumed here is not "materiality" in the limited sense of physical objects but rather "materiality" in the broader sense of a socially produced, reified identity itself. Thus, although the reexteriorization of the self depends precisely on the conspicuousness of the consumption, we should not confuse it with an oversimplified sense that such an identity is a (literally) superficial style.

An example should help to clarify the process at work. For reasons far too overdetermined to address here, the majority of gay male homepages on the Internet contain a "gallery," usually a collection of commercially produced pictures of male models or still images taken from videos that are reproduced in violation of copyright. The link between such galleries and the construction and display of individual identity on the homepage itself is perhaps best suggested by one particular instance. In the fall of 1995, as a tribute to a man who had recently died of AIDS, several of his friends produced a memorial gallery for him. This gallery did not consist, as one might expect, of pictures of the individual thus memorialized, however. Instead, it was composed of scans of part of his collection of soft-core porn. If such a tribute is incomprehensible when seen in light of essentialized views of identity (since it does not include representations of the person himself), from Hennessy's perspective the gallery is even more pernicious since it has to be understood as an appalling reification: a display of the dead man's possessions that substitutes for, and thus erases (again), the (dead) self of which they are merely the detritus. The memorial thus could be said to be, really, an unwitting tribute to the bad faith endemic to a particular lifestyle, in which commodities and self-stylization substitute for "identity."

Seen another way, however, such a memorial is both perfect and intensely "real." If the site focused on one aspect of the individual's identity, his sexuality (as opposed to, say, his gender, race, class, or age), the gallery successfully materialized the signifiers of the desire that most people would agree forms the basis of such a sexual identity. Moreover, to anyone familiar with the semiotics of such photographs, the portrait that emerges of the individual is highly detailed, conveying a rough idea of his age (probably early to mid-forties, since the majority of the photographs are from the 1970s, as the hairstyles, body types, and photographic techniques and conventions indicate), subclass within gay culture (leatherman), taste in men ("bears"), and even some indication of his sexual practices (light b and d). But the point is not simply that, by presenting the artifacts of their friend's interpellation, the creators of the memorial have produced a highly effective (even touching) re-creation of him. By re-presenting these images for re-consumption, they have opened the possibility that the viewer of the memorial might himself find them erotic, thus coming to occupy the very site of identity that is being memorialized. If a memorial is, by definition, always an attempt to give presence to what is absent, it is difficult to imagine a more effective memorial than this.

ELECTIVE ANTAGONISMS: ŽIŽEK AND THE ESSENCE OF THE "REAL"

The latter point should not only help to demonstrate that a consumer-created identity need not inevitably be understood as superficial. The possible substitution of the consumer of the tribute in the place of the individual memorialized should also indicate a final problem with Hennessy's conception of identity. Despite her presentation of consumption as individual choice, the insertion of individual consumption into a larger structure of social meanings suggests that the significant pattern at work here is finally not the creation of a self-fashioned individual but the formation of collective identities, of classes and subclasses of persons. This recognition brings us to the third of the difficulties in Hennessy's essay, her conception of the social contradictions at work in the consumption of queer identity. If consumption is not merely a process of individual stylization but the consumption of identity categories defined through their difference from other identities, then we need to rethink the ways in which such a system functions and reconceptualize how social contradictions are negotiated in such a system. Hennessy's analysis implicitly posits class conflict as the core of social antagonism, with gender conflict standing in some unspecified ancillary relation to it. Moreover, as we have seen, Hennessy assumes that such conflicts are worked out through a process of mystification, with consumption masking the exploitations of the system of production. If we take Baudrillard seriously, however, we need to construct an interpretive apparatus that does not privilege any particular group or groups as the primary analytic category and that acknowledges that the modalities for negotiating social contradiction differ in different historical and cultural situations.

In "The Spectre of Ideology," an attempt to establish the "pre-discursive kernel" upon which ideology is based, Slavoj Žižek is concerned with precisely this problem of reconceptualizing social relations. Žižek argues that this kernel, the "real," cannot ever be articulated, since it is precisely what has to be repressed or excluded from cultural constructions of "reality" in order to insure that ideology, the assumptions that form the basis for the reproduction of existing social relations, will function. Nonetheless, Žižek argues, such symbolizations are always incomplete and continually allow glimpses of "the real." The essence of "the real," of the preideological, Žižek argues, is class conflict, although he redefines the term here more broadly as "antagonism" or social contradiction, which must be repressed for the system to function. The primary difference between such an analysis and Hennessy's is the way that Žižek opens up the possibility for a broader understanding of the workings of such contradiction.

First of all, we can note that the social groups that stand in an antagonistic relation are not fixed (i.e., the proletariat and the bourgeoisie, women and men). Rather, once class struggle is redefined as antagonism, the two "poles" become structural positions, the content of which is flexible. In and of itself, this seems far more useful than trying to specify particular analytic categories (class, gender), which then become transcendental, mystifying the fact that our understandings of these terms are historically and culturally limited. Moreover, as Žižek makes clear, the relation of the categories is not, in fact, polar, the reduction of antagonism to two opposed entities being itself an ideological operation, according to Žižek, because it implicitly assumes the existence of a "neutral medium within which the two poles exist."[17] A more radical reading, Žižek argues, would recognize that there is no neutral ground shared by the two antagonistic positions. Rather, the two positions represent two interpretations of the same entity, antagonism arising from a battle over which interpretation will become hegemonic. Žižek goes on to posit a reconceptualization of the relation between the two terms. They are best conceived, he argues, as two versions of the same notion, the first representing the term understood in its ideological universality, the second representing the concrete, material existence of the idea. Here Žižek's argument intersects with a good deal of recent thinking in feminist theory as well as in the theorizing of race and sexual orientation. His example of what he means should therefore sound familiar: "Ideology compels us to assume 'humanity' as the neutral medium within which 'man' and 'woman' are posited as two complementary poles—against this ideological evidence, one could maintain that 'woman' stands for the aspect of concrete existence and 'man' for the empty-ambiguous universality. The paradox (of a profoundly Hegelian nature) is that 'woman'—that is, the moment of specific difference—functions as the encompassing ground that accounts for the emergence of the universality of man" (24–25). In effect, then, Žižek is summarizing all the arguments in identity theorizing that have noted how "man" or "white" or "heterosexual" or "bourgeois" are themselves constructed by the constitution of a category of "difference" ("woman," "black," and so on) that then allows them to posit themselves as both universal and invisible.

Yet the very familiarity of this point should give us pause. Having moved beyond specific analytic categories to identify "antagonism" as the preideological "real," Žižek's argument itself falls back into the trap of ideology. Thus, the examples that Žižek uses to illustrate the absence of a middle ground are "science" (bourgeois or Marxist) and "discourse" (male or female) to discuss class and gender conflicts, respectively, and his analysis then concludes that there is only one science and one discourse.

The difficulty here is that Žižek has retreated from the radical implications of his own argument by assuming the preexistence not only of particular conflicts (class, gender) but of particular entities ("science" and "discourse"). Yet, Žižek's essay itself allows us to think beyond these limits. Using an example from Levi-Strauss of the ways in which two subgroups of South American villagers draw the spatial ground plan of their village, Žižek realizes that the exact content of both of the two plans or of the specific social antagonism they represent is, finally, not the issue. The splitting into two spatial perceptions cannot be seen as simple cultural relativism, in which perception depends on one's (classed or gendered) position in the society. Rather, this perceptual splitting has reference instead to a constant. Significantly, Žižek does not identify this constant as a specific social division (gender, class) or as the literal arrangement of the village. Rather, the constant ground here is antagonism, the real that cannot be symbolized directly: "an imbalance in social relations that prevented the community from stabilizing itself into a harmonious whole" (26). As such, "the two perceptions of the ground-plan are simply two mutually exclusive endeavors to cope with this traumatic antagonism, to heal its wound via the imposition of a balanced symbolic structure" (26).

When Žižek's point is displaced onto and articulated through another society, then, the argument ceases to posit class or gender as preideological and illustrates his central point: that antagonism itself is the real. As such, the brilliance of his argument becomes fully apparent precisely because it does not then lead to a very familiar conception of gender or racial or class conflict or even to the assumption that "the genders" or "the races" are transcendental, ahistorical entities in the first place. If the trauma around which social reality is constructed is the trauma of antagonism or difference itself, then not only will the definitions and relations of the categories involved in social conflict change over time, but both the form of social contradiction and the means for resolving it should also vary in differing historical and cultural circumstances. By reconceptualizing social antagonism in this way, we can thus move beyond Hennessy's rather restricted notion of the functioning of social contradiction and examine the effect that an economy of consumption has on the ways in which the social difference between contemporary identity categories is resolved. Perhaps the best way to explore this issue, to understand how social antagonism is managed in a society of consumption, is to return, finally, to the question of the significance of the development of identity-based academic disciplines in the academy.

BACK TO SCHOOL: "DIFFERENCE" AND THE LOGIC OF CONSUMPTION

Just as postindustrial capitalism has transformed our conceptualization of identity, we can now see the introduction of identity-based courses into the academy as part of a history of responses by the university to shifting economic forces. Making the distinction between older academic disciplines and newer identity-based areas of study defined on a "consumer model," Judith Roof herself implicitly defines the former group as based on (industrial-capitalist) economic factors, a "convergence of industry need and tradition."[18] As such, rather than seeing identity courses as an unusual intrusion of economic concerns into an arena previously free of such influences, they might better be understood as an example of the academy's adaptation to changes in the economic system. Thus, to supplement Roof's distinction, one way to read this shift in the definition of academic disciplines is as a reflection of changing constructions of the role of the university in the reproduction of the bourgeois subject: from a university primarily designed to provide the managerial labor and technical expertise for an economy of production to a university whose function is also to ensure the reproduction of a variety of intersecting identity parameters (class plus gender plus race plus sexual orientation plus age plus . . .) that provide the categories of consumption in a postindustrial economy.

One explanation for the development of Lesbian and Gay Studies classes, then, is that lesbigay students often take such courses in order to confirm their identities (in part simply by signing up for the class in the first place), and it is not surprising that some students use such courses as part of the coming out process (since it allows them to compare, as it were, the "product characteristics" of lesbigay identity as defined in the class with their sense of themselves). Yet the point is not simply that Gay and Lesbian "identity" classes are yet one more commodity that can be consumed by queer students in the process of postindustrial identity formation, if only because such an explanation cannot account for the fact that a significant percentage of the students in Lesbian and Gay Studies courses are, in fact, self-identified as straight. The current understandings of this phenomenon, which would see such students as either imperialistically colonizing the (academic) space of the Other or as involved in a sort of "identity tourism," in which queerness is implicitly conceived as an exotic spectacle, seem inadequate.[19] While we cannot discard the notion, implicit in such understandings, that the constitution of any minority as an "other" serves to consolidate hegemonic power structures, we must extend this analysis to account for the ways in which postindustrial capitalism reworks the relations between identity categories and rewrites the meaning of "difference" itself.

As we have seen, the consumption of identity is based on difference, on the drive to construct the self through the differentiated signifiers of the objects of consumption. Moreover, identity categories themselves are defined by their differentiation from other identities. As such, what would seem to be happening when straight students, for example, take Gay Studies courses is that they are not really insisting on their (hegemonic) right to a Foucauldian surveillance of the abjected Other that forms the course's object of study. Rather, their presence in such classes might be better understood as an exploration of their own identities through the examination of another identity category. This is suggested by the responses that students typically give to an informal questionnaire that I hand out when I teach the class, which asks students to articulate what impact the course has had on them. While the lesbigay students invariably note that "I learned a lot about myself" (the course is, after all, about them), students who self-identify as straight generally assert that the class dispelled their stereotypes, made them more open minded, and helped them "to learn and understand about people." As one student succinctly put it, "Though some lifestyles may be much different from my own, I now feel that I can appreciate and respect them open-mindedly." What is crucial to note here is the way in which the "different lifestyles" that provide the basis of the course are understood, if only implicitly, through a comparison with this student's "own [lifestyle]." By exposing straight students to alternative identity categories, the course thus not only teaches them "about [certain] people" but also allows the straight students to "consume themselves" by letting them examine identity categories that define their own by their differentiation from it. In other words, then, straight students in Lesbian and Gay Studies courses could be said to be "comparison shopping," inspecting another identity/product that clarifies the nature of their own "purchase" and assures them of its validity (for them).

Yet identity-based academic disciplines reflect the shift to an economy of consumption in even more subtle and far-reaching ways, providing an indication of how a postindustrial economy reworks the means for negotiating social contradictions. Unlike the system of production, in which the underlying (class) differences are mystified by the commodity fetish to conceal the relations of exploitation, an economy of consumption does not deny difference but rather foregrounds it so that the traumatic kernel of differentiation that preexists any social system is taken up here as the explicit logic of the system itself. As a result, the antagonism of social difference is mystified under postindustrial capitalism not by concealing social difference but, far more subtly, through a revaluation and celebration of "difference," whether "difference" is conceived in a literal sense as "consumer choice" or represented in the intellectual and political realms in a modified form as the value of pluralism or multiculturalism or "diversity" (of a multiplicity of possible identity categories). I should hasten to add that I fully support the latter values. If the goods are going to get together, then everyone should be in the marketplace. Yet belief in such values should not prevent, in fact it would seem to insist on, a thorough examination of the underlying ideologies at work. If postindustrial consumption is, finally, not simply the consumption of an identity but the consumption of a particular conception of difference itself, then we need to look closely at the implications that conception has for our understanding of the development of identity disciplines in the academy in general and of Lesbian and Gay Studies courses and Queer Theory as an academic discourse in particular.

Thus, the straight students' comments also reflect a subtle but important shift in contemporary thinking about the relations of different identity categories. While it is certainly possible to interpret their responses to the questionnaire as subtly oppressive, as the reflection of a condescending "tolerance" by the heterosexual majority, it might be more accurate to argue that the impartiality expressed here is genuine and that it derives from a particular ideological position. Rather than reading the relations of "straight" and "gay" through a(n industrial-capitalist) narrative that stresses the exploitation of the minority group, the implicit philosophy of such remarks assumes the equal validity of all identity positions. "Such lifestyles are much different than my own," the student notes, and the assumption is that *everyone* has a "lifestyle" and that everyone must learn to appreciate and respect (human) differences. At first glance, such a perspective may seem merely sentimental, yet this philoso-

phy can more accurately be understood as a necessary corollary of an
ideology of consumption. For an economy of consumption to work, either
literally or conceptually, all the possible options, defined in relation to
each other by their differences, must be seen as equally valid "choices"
(whether the options in question are consumer goods or identity categories), and "difference" itself, as the structural logic of the system, must be
taken as a positive value.

This ideology becomes particularly clear when we look back at the
problematic narrative of Chrissie's change in sexual identity, the story
with which we began. The reason that Chrissie's movement from bisexual
to straight seems incomprehensible, I would argue, is that our current
notion of the coming-out narrative implicitly assumes the logic of an
economy of production in which the system is understood to mystify
relations of exploitation. Applied to sexual identity, this logic posits a
heteronormative regime that "represses" lesbigay sexuality (both in the
culture at large and in the individual psyche) so that coming out is a
process of demystification, of discovery of the "real" self. As such, the
model is unable to explain movement from a minority ("exploited") position to a majority ("normative") one except as false consciousness. If I am
right about the underlying ideology of an economy of consumption,
however, Chrissie's story can be seen as a reflection of an entirely different
logic. Here, following an ideology of difference, the individual's narrative
is the story of finding the right category or niche, and, because all identity
categories are understood as equally valid (since they are defined in
relation to each other), corrections of mistakes in self-identification can
move in any direction ("I thought I was ———, but then I realized I
was ———"; the blanks can be filled by any sexual identity categories.)
Put another way, the logic of consumption replaces a "political" teleology
(of "liberation") with a structural one (of finding "one's place").[20]

As such, what is happening in Lesbian and Gay Studies classes is more
than the consumption of an identity category (for those students who fit
it) or an investigation of an alternative that confirms the (different) identity category (of those students who don't fit it). As both Chrissie's
narrative and the students' comments about such courses suggest, what is
ultimately being consumed here is a particular notion of "difference"
itself, the mystification through which social antagonism is managed in an
economy of consumption. In other words, such courses both derive from
and promote an ideology that produces a number of illusions. First of
all, by presenting (sexual) identities as a variety of culturally equivalent

"positions," this ideology conceals the continued existence of social hierarchies. In other words, by implying that all identities are, as it were, electives that can count for three credits, the system glosses over the fact that, in reality, these "options" are not socially or culturally interchangeable, that it is not the same thing to be a lesbian in this culture as it is to be a straight woman. Even more significantly, however, this ideology manages to conceal the antagonism inherent in the very production of social differences. Rather than being seen as based on exploitation or oppression, the relations of different identity categories are implicitly presented as nonantagonistic, as interactions that are no more serious than, say, the rivalry between Ford and Chevy owners. In effect, then, the postindustrial ideology inherent in such courses resolves social contradiction through a process of denial that masquerades as honesty. By not only admitting but celebrating the existence of social differences, the ideology of consumption works to mystify the antagonism that Žižek identifies as inherent in the construction of social categories in the first place.

The same ideological process operates in a more subtle way within the academic writings that constitute contemporary Queer Theory, specifically in relation to changing understandings of the meaning of "difference" itself. Reading through the contributions to *Professions of Desire*, the collection of essays about Lesbian and Gay Studies published by the Modern Language Association of America, one becomes immediately aware that the word "difference" recurs with an almost obsessive frequency and refers to an entire spectrum of concepts. Generally, however, the term is used here to indicate two particular notions. The first is perhaps best represented by George Haggerty's essay on pedagogy, in which "difference" becomes synonymous with "minority," as in the assertion that exposing the students to multicultural literature(s) can lead them to "acknowledge difference" or in the argument that the "gay white male professor" can be sexist or racist only at a cost to himself since "his future lies with difference" (i.e., "similarly marginalized members of the academy").[21] If "difference" here means something like "deviation from the (straight white male) norm," a more complicated and more recent definition of the term is evident in Yvonne Yarbro-Bejarano's discussion of the need to expand the multicultural and multiracial awareness of Lesbian and Gay Studies. Yarbro-Bejarano argues for an analysis of how various identity categories (race, gender, class, sexual orientation) intersect both in individual instances and on the larger level of the cultural imaginary. The ideal, then, is an awareness of the multiplicity of identity, which includes an avoidance of discrete categories and of the ranking of oppressions while at the same time acknowledging the specificity of, for example, homophobic oppression.[22] Explicitly rejecting an idea of "difference" as "difference from" an implied norm ("the same"), Yarbro-Bejarano instead implicitly articulates "difference" as "different than" (other subject positions).[23]

If Haggerty's idea of "difference," with its assumption of predetermined majority/minority positions, can be seen to follow an industrial-capitalist logic that assumes a relation of exploitation between different social groups, Yarbro-Bejarano's definition of "difference" must be understood as a highly sophisticated version of the idea of "difference" that we have already seen operating among students in the Lesbian and Gay Studies classroom, a definition that replicates the ideology of an economy of consumption. Thus, like the meaning of objects in the marketplace, individual identity is seen by Yarbro-Bejarano as the effect of a (continual, mobile) process of differentiation from all other possible intersections of identity parameters. One can hardly fault the political impulses that promote a concept of "difference" that rejects the assumption that lesbi-gays are always already minoritized. Yet, once again, the problem with this concept is precisely that, by stressing the structural equivalence of all possible identity positions (since the analysis rejects a hierarchical ranking of oppressions), the argument inadvertently glosses over one of its own basic assumptions: the fact that social reality is not itself nonhierarchical, that all the possible identity positions are not equal in terms of social meaning or power. Moreover, by revaluing difference as the necessary exploration of the plural or the multiple, Yarbro-Bejarano substitutes a (positive) fetishization of "difference" for an understanding of "difference" as the product and sign of social antagonism. Implicitly suggesting that such antagonism can be dealt with by properly conceptualizing "difference," this analysis thus echoes, on an abstract level, the undergraduate (consumerist) sense that social contradictions derive not from the very existence of social categories but from a failure to acknowledge difference *enough:* whether by adequately pluralizing the concept on the theoretical level, or by being sufficiently tolerant of human variation on a personal level, or by providing enough "identity options" in the course schedule or at the mall or in "life itself." As such, Yarbro-Bejarano's "difference" inadvertently conceals, far more effectively than Haggerty's, the problems of thinking of identity in terms of difference to begin with.

A SAN FRANCISCO OF THE MIND: IDEOLOGICAL FAULTLINES
AND UTOPIAN SPACES

Ultimately, then, any assessment of the introduction of Lesbian and Gay Studies into the university must take into account how such a discipline both derives from and reinforces the ways in which a postindustrial ideology attempts to resolve the social conflicts produced by the construction of categories of sexual identity in the first place. We need to be aware of the complex process of mystification involved in the very logic of diversity or pluralism or "difference" that is so often used to justify this area of study, not simply the way that a postindustrial emphasis on the structural equivalence of identity options can conceal the continuity of economic and social inequalities (including, as Hennessy makes clear, an unequal access to consumption itself) but also the way that a valorization of difference masks the conflicts inherent in the very production of social difference. Yet, the situation is even more complex than this. As the coexistence within the same recently published volume of Haggerty's and Yarbro-Bejarano's radically different conceptions of "difference" suggests, the field of Lesbian and Gay Studies itself, like the academy and the culture in which it exists, finally reflects the persistence of the economic structures, cultural formations, and ideological premises of an economy of production within the emerging economic, cultural, and ideological parameters of an economy of consumption.

Thus, just as the university can be said to be divided between the continuing requirement that it produce a class of subjects whose labor capacity is adapted to industrial (and postindustrial) need and its newer role in reinforcing identity categories organized in relation to consumption, and just as postindustrial identity formation retains categories and social hierarchies derived from industrial capitalism, Lesbian and Gay Studies is also mapped across the fault line of the ideologies of production and consumption. If, for example, the discipline continues, on the one hand, to stress a narrative of oppression and liberation derived from the logic of production, it has also, on the other hand, increasingly embraced the (positive) fetishization of difference that characterizes the logic of consumption. A recognition of this ideological schizophrenia can be useful, if only because it suggests possible explanations for some of the incoherences within Queer Theory and the Lesbian and Gay Studies classroom that I noted at the outset. It would seem to give some clue, for example, to the tendency in theoretical work to pluralize, almost infinitely,

the contents of identity categories (since the development of postindustrial consumption thrives on the continual proliferation of new market
segments presented as "identities"), while at the same time such analyses
often argue that we need to retain, for the purpose of political liberation,
the (falsely) totalizing rubrics being critiqued ("lesbian," "bisexual," "gay,"
and even "queer"—as industrial-capitalist "classes" of oppressed individuals). By the same token, an awareness of the competing pressures of the
ideologies of industrial and postindustrial capitalism (specifically, essentialized notions of the bourgeois subject as opposed to identity formation
through consumption) might explain why students so vehemently insist
that (sexual) identity is involuntary or innate (due to "nature" or "nurture"
or some combination of the two) at the same time that they, far less
consciously, implicitly understand sexual self-identification as something
very much like (consumer) choice (since it is, as an expression of "who
one is," understood to be both mutable and reversible).

Thus, if the preceding analysis has suggested the importance of analyzing the emerging discipline of Lesbian and Gay Studies in light of the
ideology of postindustrial capitalism, we must also pay attention to the
persistence of industrial-capitalist beliefs, conceptual categories, and
modes of social organization if we are to gain a clear picture of precisely
what such a discipline does and what our goals are or should be. It would
seem to be both intellectually and politically necessary, for example, to
submit the various concepts of "difference" noted earlier to the same sort
of critique that "identity" has received. The goal of such an analysis would
be to move beyond the mystifications we have seen at work: to articulate
the interrelations of various identity groups in such a way that, on the one
hand, some groups are not automatically consigned to a minority position
(following an industrial-capitalist logic of exploitation) and that, on the
other hand, inequities and antagonisms are not glossed over (following a
postindustrial logic of "pure," depoliticized "difference"). In other words,
we cannot respond to the postindustrial denial of social contradiction
through a simple return to an industrial-capitalist narrative of oppression
and liberation that ignores changing modes of identity formation. Rather,
we need to find a new "symbolic structure," another way of conceptualizing, perhaps even of resolving, the social contradictions produced by the
very existence of identity categories. Moreover, precisely because the
development of Lesbian and Gay Studies as a discipline represents one of
the positive (side)effects of postindustrial capitalism, the emergence of
several previously ignored identity categories as (increasingly) viable op-

tions at the "identity mall," this does not mean that we should leave unexamined the deeper ideological implications of the logic of "difference" that enables this development. In fact, we need to look more closely at what Lesbian and Gay Studies courses really do. Do they, in fact, provide lesbigay students with a "liberated," even utopian, space of their own within the university and the culture? Or do they not rather (or also or *really*) serve, under the guise of a new rhetoric of pluralism and diversity, to suture queer subjects into their far less utopian, unequal place in the social system?

The last time I taught the introductory course in Lesbian and Gay Studies, what was striking was the way in which these questions were raised precisely by the literal topography of academic space itself. As anyone who has spent any amount of time in a college classroom knows, even without assigned seats, by the second or third day of the term most students have found a "place" where they invariably sit, usually a specific desk, less frequently a part of the room. This particular class was no exception—until the fourth week of the semester, when I walked into the classroom one day to discover that the class had unconsciously reorganized itself so that all the straight students were sitting on the left side of the room, the gay and lesbian students were sitting on the right, and the bisexuals were (where else, given the logic implicit here?) in the middle, an arrangement that persisted until the end of the semester. While this phenomenon was not lost on the students themselves (one woman even used it to come out to her mother: "So where do you sit, honey?"), I am not certain they grasped all its implications. If this realignment has obvious sociological and psychological explanations (the development of friendships and gossip circles, the play of sexual attractions and repulsions, the discovery of intellectual and political commonalities), it also seems symptomatic of the nature of the course itself, and not simply because the students had, in a sense, "chosen," yet again, to be who they were. Thus, despite many classroom hours of quite sincere rhetoric on the part of both the students and the professor about the need to value diversity and to respect human differences, the professor, at least, was left with some nagging doubts. Although this space sometimes seemed utopian, especially by comparison to universities twenty years ago in which there was little or no space for queers at all, I nonetheless have to wonder whether this celebration of difference didn't, after all, simply serve to gloss over the social antagonism inherent in difference, that unequal distribution of countless tiny moments of incomprehension or distrust or overt hatred that were not only waiting for everyone out in "the real world" but that were also there in the room with us, mutely but unmistakably inscribed in the territorial alignments of the desks.

NOTES

1. The germinal texts for this idea in relation to both sexual identity and gender are, of course, Judith Butler's *Gender Trouble: Feminism and the Subversion of Identity* (New York: Routledge, 1990), 134–41 and "Imitation and Gender Insubordination," *Inside/Out: Lesbian Theories, Gay Theories*, ed. Diana Fuss (New York: Routledge, 1991), 13–31.

2. It is important to note that the institutional status of Lesbian and Gay Studies is still highly tenuous. Despite the extensive proliferation of critical work on lesbigay subjects in recent years and the Modern Language Association's publication of a volume of essays on teaching courses in this field, most of the more than 50 colleges and universities that currently offer classes in this area do not have a Lesbian and Gay Studies program. Moreover, such courses are very often taught by less established members of the academy: graduate students, guest faculty, and junior professors. The situation is even bleaker, of course, when one moves beyond English and Cultural Studies departments to other parts of the university, such as medical schools, where Lesbian and Gay Studies has had little, if any, impact. Rather than deterring us from analyzing the ideological underpinnings of this discipline, however, the very insecurity of its place in the university would seem to make such an analysis even more necessary, as I suggest later. I would like to thank Jonathan Weinberg for his cogent observations on the precarious status of Lesbian and Gay Studies in the academy.

3. Largely for the sake of convenience, I use "Lesbian and Gay Studies" here as a comprehensive term to refer both to the development of college curricula devoted to the study of those identity categories (and, less frequently, bisexuals and transgendered individuals) and to the variety of academic discourses ("Queer Theory") that provide the theoretical and analytic base for such courses. It should be kept in mind that such labels tend to elide the differences among a number of philosophical and political positions, most notably between the concepts denoted by "lesbian" and "gay" and those understood in the term "queer," and to impart a misleading unity to the multiple and often contradictory discourses contained under the rubric of Queer Theory. For a succinct recent summary of these issues, see Lauren Berlant and Michael Warner, "What Does Queer Theory Teach Us About X?" *PMLA* 110 (1995): 343–49. See also Cheryl Kader and Thomas Piontek, "Not a Safe Space: Feminist Pedagogy and Queer Theory in the Class-room," *Concerns* 23 (1993): 25–36.

4. Michel Foucault, *The History of Sexuality*. Vol. 1: *An Introduction*, trans. Robert Hurley (New York: Pantheon, 1978), 42–44. For examples of articulations of the concept in recent Queer Theory, see, for example, Ed Cohen, *Talk on the Wilde Side* (New York: Routledge, 1993), 103–25; Eve Sedgwick, *Epistemology of*

the Closet (Berkeley: University of California Press, 1990), 44–48; and Jonathan Goldberg, *Sodometries: Renaissance Texts, Modern Sexualities* (Stanford: Stanford University Press, 1992), 1–26.

5. For a critique of Foucault's conception of power, see Slavoj Žižek, "The Spectre of Ideology," *Mapping Ideology*, ed. Slavoj Žižek (New York: Verso, 1994), 13.

6. Judith Roof, "Buckling Down or Knuckling Under: Discipline or Punish in Lesbian and Gay Studies," Conference Presentation, Midwest Modern Language Association, November 5, 1993.

7. Focusing on the categories of "gay" and "lesbian" themselves, most current analyses of the relation between late capitalism and lesbian, bisexual, and/or gay identity tend simply to discuss the commodification of these identity categories themselves. As a result, such studies do not adequately address the question of identity formation in postindustrial capitalism, simply assuming, instead, the existence of lesbigay identities that are somehow prior to processes of representation or commodification. One example is Danae Clark's "Commodity Lesbianism," *Out in Culture: Gay, Lesbian, and Queer Essays on Popular Culture*, ed. Corey K. Creekmur and Alexander Doty (Durham: Duke University Press, 1995), 484–500. Clark examines the growth of the concept of the "gay window" in advertising, the identification of lesbians and gay men as a target market. Such advertising, Clark argues, allows lesbian identification but serves, at the same time, to transform lesbianism into a "style of consumption" (494). Divorced from a "gay sensibility," such ads implicitly reject the notion of a distinct gay subject, suggesting that lesbians are not really different from heterosexual women (493). Although Clark is careful to avoid reifying "the lesbian" into a unitary, transcendental category by noting the heterogeneity of lesbian "reading strategies" and the ways in which advertising itself can modify or shape a lesbian consumer's self-conception, Clark's argument nonetheless rests on the assumption of a (politicized, "different") lesbian subject who is somehow prior to advertising (if not media representation in general). See also Sue-Ellen Case, "The Student and the Strap: Authority and Seduction in the Class(room)," *Professions of Desire*, ed. George E. Haggerty and Bonnie Zimmerman (New York: Modern Language Association of America, 1995), 40–42, and Frank Smigiel, "Shop-Talk: Exchanging Narrative, Sex, and Value," *Modern Fiction Studies* 41 (1995): 636–637. Compare Robyn Wiegman's more sophisticated discussion of lesbian commodification, in which Wiegman notes that sexual identity categories are always already commodified, "Introduction: Mapping the Lesbian Postmodern," *The Lesbian Postmodern*, ed. Laura Doan (New York: Columbia University Press, 1994), 1–5. For a discussion of the impact of industrial capitalism on the formation and development of gay and lesbian identity in the twentieth century, see John D'Emilio, "Capitalism and Gay Identity," *Powers of Desire: The Politics of Sexuality*, ed. Ann Snitow, Christine Stansell, and Sharon Thompson (New York: Monthly Review Press, 1983), 100–113 and Jonathan Katz, "The Invention of Heterosexuality," *Socialist Review* 20 (1990): 7–34.

8. This is particularly true of the way in which performative conceptions of identity, most notably the work of Judith Butler, are currently inflected. As *Bodies*

That Matter: On the Discursive Limits of "Sex" (New York: Routledge, 1993) suggests, Butler is careful to stress the ways in which the subject is interpellated into identity categories that, while modifiable by processes of resignification, preexist the individual and that determine conceptions of identity. What is striking, however, is that Butler's analysis of the sociocultural mechanisms operating to constitute the subject generally ignores the impact of the market on the constitution and deployment of identity categories. Rather, Butler's emphasis falls instead on The Law, which, whether invoked in its Lacanian or juridical forms, is endlessly cited as both an exemplum of, and the structure behind, the citationality that is identity. One need hardly add that a performative theory of identity need not exclude in this way a consideration of the subject's positioning in the economic field.

9. Rosemary Hennessy, "Queer Visibility in Commodity Culture," *Cultural Critique* 29 (1994–1995): 47–48. Subsequent references to this work are included parenthetically in the text.

10. Hennessy does, however, note that the construction of lesbigays as middle-class consumers conceals the existence of impoverished lesbians and gays (69).

11. Donna Haraway, *Simians, Cyborgs, and Women: The Reinvention of Nature* (New York: Routledge, 1991), 155–61.

12. Although, as Hennessy herself points out, "lifestyle" is a technical term in sociology (where it refers to status groups) and is frequently employed, in cultural analysis, to denote changing conceptions of identity in a postindustrial economy (57), Hennessy's almost exclusive application of the term to lesbigay consumers implicitly invokes a third, highly connotative use of the word to refer to "homosexuals." For a discussion of the history of the term and its current meanings, see Donald Lowe, *The Body in Late-Capitalist USA* (Durham: Duke University Press, 1995), 62–67.

13. For an extended explication (and defense) of Foucault, see David Halperin, *Saint Foucault: Towards a Gay Hagiography* (Oxford: Oxford University Press, 1995).

14. For an example of a far more pointed critique of Queer Theory from a traditional Marxist perspective, see Donald Morton, "Birth of the Cyberqueer," *PMLA* 110 (1995): 369–81.

15. Jean Baudrillard, *Selected Writings*, ed. Mark Poster (Stanford: Stanford University Press, 1988), 42. Subsequent references to this work are included parenthetically in the text. Although Baudrillard has also argued, in *Symbolic Exchange and Death* (London: Sage, 1993), that the sphere of production has now completely collapsed into the sphere of consumption (14), it seems more accurate to see postindustrial capitalism as a mutation in the system of production, a shift to an emphasis on consumption with a corresponding modification in production practices. For a detailed examination of this change, see Donald Lowe, *The Body in Late-Capitalist USA* (Durham: Duke University Press, 1995), 17–73. From the standpoint of cultural ideology, this economic transformation would have the effect of layering a variety of emergent beliefs and cultural practices onto the existing cultural formations of industrial capitalism, as I discuss later.

16. To provide a specific, if slightly reductive, example: in a society of con-

sumption, that Nine Inch Nails CD in the record store has not only a use value (being able to listen to it) and an exchange value (the price) but a semiotic value, which derives from its difference from the social meanings of all the other CDs in the store. To begin with, it signals one's taste for a particular genre of music ("alternative"), which itself has multiple meanings, suggesting, as "college music," a certain demographic (educated, middle class, age 18–34) and, as "complaint rock," a certain sensibility ("sardonic," "alienated," "GenX"). Moreover, the semiotics of the Nine Inch Nails CD are compounded by its difference from other examples of alternative music (so that it is marked as "male"—as opposed to, say, Tori Amos—and, more subtly, as "straight"—as opposed to, say, Sugar). As a result, buying the CD or listening to it or professing a taste for it is, finally, a social action that signifies, both to others and to oneself, some part of who one is. In the case of any particular individual, of course, the overall process of identity construction is enormously complicated and sometimes contradictory, not only due to the persistence of the identity categories (such as class) and modes of identity formation (e.g., defining oneself by one's job) of industrial capitalism, but also because of the multiple meanings of the objects of consumption themselves, the variety of identity parameters being signified (e.g., gender, race, class, age), and the extreme complexity of the (continual) process of consumption.

17. Slavoj Žižek, "The Spectre of Ideology," *Mapping Ideology*, ed. Slavoj Žižek (New York: Verso, 1994), 23. All subsequent references to this work are given parenthetically in the text.

18. Judith Roof, "Buckling Down or Knuckling Under: Discipline or Punish in Lesbian and Gay Studies," Conference Presentation, Midwest Modern Language Association, November 5, 1993.

19. See, for example, Eve Sedgwick, *Tendencies* (Durham: Duke University Press, 1993), 4–5.

20. This implicitly consumerist logic is more muted in relation to dislocations of identity categories, such as race and gender, that are commonly thought (following an older, essentializing model) to derive less from individual psychology than from the "reality" of ("visible") corporeal or biological difference, as Robyn Wiegman has pointed out in "Queering the Academy" (Lecture, West Virginia University, March 23, 1996). In the latter cases, the temporal shift in categories ("I was . . . I am. . . . ") is reconceived spatially: as a disjunction of outward appearance and inner, "true" identity, with the result that the individual's simultaneous coexistence in two categories must be problematized in the popular imagination: as ontological "error" (e.g., gender dysphoria, the rhetoric of transgenderism) or as politicized "choice" (e.g., white-identified blacks, black-identified whites). In the academy, of course, such dislocations are increasingly understood as performative, with the problematization being read back onto the system of classification itself. Thus, performative disruption of categories of race and gender is taken as an exposure of the (arbitrary) nature of the categories, rather than as a "fault" or anomaly in the individual. As Hennessy implies, one way to see such performative theories themselves is to posit them as part of a larger ideological shift from theories of identity as the body (as the locus of labor power and of the re-production of the means of production, following an industrial-

capitalist logic) to identity as "the self" (as the site of semiotic differentiation, following the structural logic of an economy of consumption).

21. George Haggerty, " 'Promoting Homosexuality' in the Classroom," *Professions of Desire*, ed. George E. Haggerty and Bonnie Zimmerman (New York: Modern Language Association of America, 1995), 15–17.

22. Yvonne Yarbro-Bejarano, "Expanding the Categories of Race and Sexuality in Lesbian and Gay Studies," *Professions of Desire*, ed. George E. Haggerty and Bonnie Zimmerman (New York: Modern Language Association of America, 1995), 131.

23. For an application of the same definition of "difference" to pedagogical issues, see David Roman, "Teaching Differences: Theory and Practice in a Lesbian and Gay Studies Seminar," *Professions of Desire*, ed. George E. Haggerty and Bonnie Zimmerman (New York: Modern Language Association of America, 1995), 113–23.

THREE

"She's Right Behind You"
Gossip, Innuendo, and Rumor
in the (De)Formation of
Gay and Lesbian Studies

John Champagne and Elayne Tobin

We live as though we stand knocking at doors which are still closed to us.
—Karl Jaspers, "Vom Europaischen Geist"

Our present is emphatically, and not merely logically, the suspense between a no longer and a not yet.   —Hannah Arendt, "Karl Jaspers: A Laudatio"

Owing to its relative newness as a field of inquiry, the discipline of gay and lesbian studies currently demands a queer kind of self-reflection: speculations must often carry the weight of analysis; working propositions must sometimes be treated as truths. The jury is still out on whether too much talk about the discipline is circulating, or not enough, or not enough of the right kind, or too much of the wrong kind. There is even disagreement about the existence of the discipline itself, emblematized by the title of a recent plenary session of the North American Lesbian, Gay, and Bisexual Studies Conference: "Unified Field or Dysfunctional Family: The State of Queer Studies." Having offered this requisite précis, we assert that gay and lesbian studies does suffer from a certain neglect: we note a failure to theorize the relation between what we would schematically characterize as a wide field of local "events" (gossip, innuendo, and rumor) and the larger professional dynamics of the emerging discipline. This neglect threatens to produce serious consequences. Refusing to engage in a public analysis of this wide field, gay and lesbian theorists inadvertently encourage the continued subjugation of certain queer kinds of knowledge, putting forth to the rest of the academic world the public face of a supportive and cooperative solidarity. Ironically, this refusal replicates the dynamics of the closet: under the guise of maintaining "professional" behavior, certain kinds of knowledge remain "hidden from history"; there are few "public" forums in which to raise certain kinds of queer critiques.

In this essay, we examine how a particular kind of queer knowledge— a knowledge that circulates at the level of gossip, innuendo, and rumor— might be exploited with an eye toward assessing productively the emerging discipline of Gay and Lesbian Studies. While this essay is obviously not gossip in and of itself, it borrows from gossip a number of discursive strategies. For example, like gossip, it hopes to provoke a variety of responses—affective, cognitive, psychic—to proliferate and disperse its critique of the emerging discipline of gay and lesbian studies and to challenge normative forms of knowledge. It is deliberately polemical and unsubtle. Like gossip, our arguments circle around themselves, take off in unanticipated directions, and may at times be repetitious, mimicking the aesthetic contours of chatter. Along the way, however, we return repeatedly to at least three particular strategies or themes:

1. We identify and analyze a number of representative anecdotes that, were they allowed to enter, in a more formal manner, public discussions of the emerging disciplines, might significantly alter narratives of the descriptive framework of the field.

2. We suggest how an attentiveness to the shifting relationship between representation as portrait and representation as proxy as outlined by Gayatri Spivak in her widely read essay "Can the Subaltern Speak?" allows us to surface crucial questions about the emerging discipline. This leads us to explore such things as what Leo Bersani has described as the disappearance of the homo under the rubric of queerness and the tendency to speak *of* and *for* gays and lesbians without speaking *as* gay or lesbian.[1] Another way to frame this discussion might be to examine the difference between who is "queer" and who is "a" queer.

3. We will speculate concerning some of the relations between capitalism and queers in and out of the academy, touching on such questions as class relations among queers as academics, the commodification of queer studies, and the transforming of capitalist productions.

We hope that the fact that this essay is authored by a man who self-identifies as gay and a woman who self-identifies as straight will at least alert readers to the fact that we are not invested in resurrecting essentialist understandings of sexual identity. Rather, we are interested in elaborating several of the micropolitical stakes involved in the (self)representation (by proxy, by portrait) of the emerging discipline of Gay and Lesbian Studies and its practitioners and in suggesting how these representations may or may not coincide with larger political and economic questions.[2] A reader's report in response to an earlier draft of this essay asked if we had changed our names to preserve our anonymity; we have not. This same report wondered about our working papers, as it were. Consequently: we are both white and middle class; one of us is a graduate student at a state-affiliated university and one of us is a nontenured assistant professor at another; our incomes are $10,000 and $37,000, respectively. This said, we wonder about the usefulness of such declarations. This essay emerged out of our shared concerns about the field of Lesbian and Gay Studies, concerns that are both intellectually and politically oriented. Intellectually formed within different theoretical paradigms, we thought we could bring different inflections to the questions we pursue here. We are aware, however, that it is difficult to assess to what extent coauthoring an essay such as this one with someone of a different "orientation" and somewhat different lifestyle can serve to shield one from the charges of homophobia, self-interest, tourism, and misogyny. We try to be attentive to these possible risks, while recognizing that simple declarations of identifying characteristics do not eviscerate the dilemmas of interest and subjectivity altogether: like Christina Crosby, we insist that the specification of an identity is not to be confused with its historicization and that, too often, "the differences which seem to refract and undo a substantive identity actually reflect a multifaceted, modified but all-too-recognizable subject." This is a version of the critique we bring to bear on the term "queer" later in this essay.[3]

What good can come of gossip? What is it, and what are the political stakes in gossip, if there are any at all? We assert that gossip functions simultaneously at a level of intimacy and a level of distantiation. Like "official" modes of knowledge—for example, essays or lectures—which at the outset are used to consolidate affiliations from within or to distance one critic or school of thought from another, gossip simultaneously performs both functions. As Robert Post has suggested, "When . . . situated within a certain kind of normative conversation, gossip supports community."[4] That is, gossip can function to bind a group around particular moral values, ethics, and sites of affective intensity. Gossip binds even those whom it might seem to exclude, since some form of intimacy (not to say love) must be intact in order to make gossip valuable in the first place; we don't gossip about strangers or intimately relay anecdotes that have no ethical, moral, or aesthetic function. (This is not strictly true, of course—there are those department bores who will tell a fifteen-minute story about directions to their own house.) Those who gossip consolidate intimacy with each other while distancing the subject (that is, the object) of gossip from the "scene," a scene dependent, ironically, on the very invocation of this third party. Thus, gossip is always at least a menage à trois, and occasionally an orgy, for distance here does not necessarily imply a geographical or emotional space. There are, however, different levels of intimacy at stake in every gossip situation: intimacy between the exchangers of gossip and intimacy with the subject-object of gossip by proxy. There is also a kind of intimacy born of the foreknowledge that one member of a community will understand the significance and/or value of a given anecdote. In other words, gossip activates a shared literacy and a system of value.

There is a dialectical relationship here that we are trying to get at between community formation and "informal knowledge": gossip retains little value if it is not meant to consolidate or rearrange power relations among the teller, the tellee, and the told about. It also, however, allows for distantiation; gossip is often told from a moral, aesthetic, and political distance. In addition, gossip can maintain its secretive status even if it involves, especially if it involves, people whom one has never met. Finally, gossip is a clumsy term used to identify very different kinds of activity. Gossiping about one's best friend to one's lover is quite a different thing from gossiping to a conference acquaintance about, say, the contents of Jeff Nunokawa's New York apartment or Judith Butler's allegedly humorless response to the fanzine devoted to her.

Rumor is distinct from gossip in that it generally has no traceable origin. As Spivak has suggested in an analysis of the work of the Subaltern Studies group, rumor "evokes comradeship because it belongs to every 'reader' or 'transmitter.' No one is its origin or source. Thus rumor is not error but primordially (originarily) errant, always in circulation with no assignable source. This illegitimacy makes it accessible to insurgency."[5] As for innuendo, it combines elements of these two discursive modes. It repeats the accusation without claiming to be its author and distances itself from its own iteration by refusing to say what it means (and mean what it says).

Why is an analysis of gossip, rumor, and innuendo of such pertinence to the emerging discipline of Gay and Lesbian Studies in particular? Like what Richard Dyer calls a gay sensibility, these modes of discourse "[hold] together qualities that are thought elsewhere to be antithetical: theatricality and authenticity . . . intensity and irony."[6] That is, like camp, they signify multivalently, coding as trivial potentially "resistant" forms of knowledge and protecting the transmitter from public censure. Through such things as gossip and rumor, serious critique "passes" as the chatty banter of bitchy queens. Perhaps because historically gay subjects and women have occupied positions so far removed from the center of the "public sphere," more private methods of transmitting information and forming ethicopolitical boundaries within and across a community have been called for. That is, perhaps queers and women do gossip more than straight men, and maybe there are good reasons for this. Gossip, innuendo, and rumor, all of which are employed in this essay, are made possible by the strictures of heteronormative culture. Their very illegitimacy is suggestive of their potential to interrupt bourgeois propriety. Our efforts here are thus both considered and tentative, reflective and impromptu, "legitimate" and suppositious.

In the defensive race to make the story of every alternative identity follow the self-same narrative, someone mentioned to us that our stories about the field of queer studies are not *that* different from other disciplines in the academy; much of what we say could apply equally and similarly to other academic fields, where gossip, innuendo, and rumor also construct a kind of phantom discourse set against the public image. Yes, and " 'If Grandmother had a beard, she would be Grandfather.' "[7] The point is, she doesn't. As far as we know, the role of gossip and innuendo in the formation of other academic disciplines has been thoroughly neglected, and this is not merely a coincidence. It is our contention that there is something about Gay and Lesbian Studies that allows it to take the challenge of gossip seriously. Gay and Lesbian Studies is an antidiscipline in certain respects; it never had the pretensions of other disciplines in that the fear of disciplinary cooptation, mediated in part by the concept of queerness, has been built in to much of the work in the field at the outset. One hopes that the discipline will always exist in a contentious relation to the academy. Like Women's Studies, it produces, provokes, and maintains a tension between "activism" and scholarly activity, with a strong desire not to slip into a silly anti-intellectualism that imagines both in extremely meager terms.

It seems to be the case that imagining why other fields have not been interested in analyzing the workings of gossip within their own formation can be as effective as trying to imbue Gay and Lesbian Studies with an absolute unique status in this regard. For example, we have learned through informal conversations with friends that many of the things we have heard and witnessed within Gay/Lesbian Studies are also pertinent to a discussion of the history of Women's Studies. For political considerations, however, certain folkloric aspects of the founding of Women's Studies remain undisclosed, known only to those active in its emergence; many incidents and events are still not held up, either formally or as rumor, for public discussion. We believe that there are salient ways in which gossip can unveil the commodification process of a disciplinary field only if that field can take hold of and challenge the ways in which it is formed and reformulated. One could then speculate that it may be the political and cultural tenor of the period of Women's Studies' inception (the 1960s and 1970s), or the long-established (as opposed to nascent) relationship of "feminine identity" to capitalist marketing, or its well-criticized indebtedness to essentialist politics that accounts for Women's Studies' resistance to gossip as a topic of intellectual interest. Perhaps women were/are rightly frightened to make intellectual use of such a shopworn stereotype of themselves. Indeed, it may be the refusal of pettiness or bitchiness as an acceptable dialogic style among the "sisterhood" of white academic women—or maybe it is simply a question of timing—that explains certain silences around the aforementioned circumstances.

If we want to investigate the example of Gay and Lesbian Studies as a commodity form, we need to explore the specific forms the commodification of Gay and Lesbian Studies has taken and is taking. As Marxism has well taught us, commodities make invisible the traces of their own production. To refuse to discuss such things as gossip, innuendo, and other "productive" forces is to collude in the mystification of this commodification process. Tracking value in the commodity form is not, however, a delicate activity. Because value is not itself a concrete thing but an abstract concept referring to a system of creating equivalences, value establishes relations between things and between people *as* things. Understanding value in this way allows us to begin to think about macro- and microsocial relations under capitalism. Many academics (and particularly those interested in the study of culture) discuss commodification as if it is something encroaching, an impending inevitability, if you will. But to our minds and to paraphrase Stuart Hall, commodification is best and most realistically thought of as the first instance, the thing that we should assume is already and in varying degrees under way. To ask, "Will such-and-such a discourse or area of study be commodified, and if it is tending that way, can it be thoroughly and effectively prevented?" is to pose something so close to a false question as to be indistinguishable from one. It is with this pessimism in place that we still suggest that the kinds of commodification we become a part of and the ways in which commodification is lived in the everyday of professional academia still deserve attention.

Because gossip consolidates intimacy in the ways we have described, it also consolidates communities by its very reliance on them. As we suggest at various points throughout this essay, contemporary gay and lesbian identity is deeply indebted to relatively recent developments in capitalism, including the disintegration of historically collective structures. Along with attempts to indulge in a mythical market-driven community formation by purchasing "queer" objects, then, gossip may be seen as a particularly "gay" response to an ever-shrinking civil society. Like such things as rainbow flag bumper stickers, gossip expresses the desire for a reconstituted public space.

Finally, an analysis of such subjugated knowledges as those that circulate through gossip, rumor, and innuendo is particularly vital to understanding the emergence of Gay and Lesbian Studies for yet another reason: assuming a Foucauldian-inflected paradigm of analysis, we might expect that when the historically interdicted—in this instance, homoeroticism—(re)circulates via the rational and rationalizing project of an academic discipline such as Gay and Lesbian Studies, certain kinds of unauthorized discourses will necessarily proliferate. When the forbidden becomes the hyperinvested, what constitutes "professional" behavior is necessarily up for grabs and likely to provoke an explosion of scandalous (if covert) chatter.

THE TRAFFIC IN HOMOPHOBIA

Following an interchange on the state of the emerging discipline of gay and lesbian studies, one of the attendees of an academic conference confides privately to another that homophobia does in fact still operate in academia with some rigor, even in those institutions that have allegedly made a sustained commitment to work in gay and lesbian studies. Specifically, it is reported that a very bright, very visible young scholar in the field is concerned that he will not ultimately secure tenure at his well-respected and increasingly elite flagship campus of a prestigious state university system. This, despite the fact that another "out" member of the faculty is a highly regarded scholar in queer theory with a national reputation. In fact, the junior professor had apparently gone up for tenure recently and was initially denied it. This denial is attributed, if not necessarily by the scholar then at least by the teller of the tale, as an instance of lingering institutional homophobia.

It is later learned that this same scholar had actually gone up for *early* tenure at a school where such requests are routinely denied due to budgetary constraints. He was in fact not the only person denied early tenure that year, and, the following year, when he once again applied for tenure, the vote was in his favor.

It seems useful to linger over the question of what it means to invoke homophobia in such circumstances as these and to examine the fact that charges of homophobia may circulate differently in different institutional contexts. We would obviously not suggest that homophobia does not exist in the university, or that such homophobia does not routinely influence decisions in such matters as hiring, promotion, and tenure. Broad charges of institutional and institutionalized homophobia, however, obscure the fact that "the institution" is not monolithic and that, at a few universities, gay and lesbian studies *is* provided with support in a variety of forms such as hiring and tenure. Doing gay and lesbian studies at an Ivy League school, for example, is not the same as doing gay and lesbian studies at a community college, a state-funded school, or even a small, funky liberal arts college that welcomes admittedly tokenized marginals. Different also are the real disciplinary differentiations of support even within the same institution; while a university may encourage queer work in one discipline, it may discourage it in another. And these differences are not just superficial but are deeply structural, geographic, and economic. Extremely different kinds of employment situations and conditions affect the potential for labor. Hence, it makes little sense for us or anyone else to refer consistently to the academy as a functional referent. By doing this, we may risk homogenizing the very marginalized subjects who are railing against homogeneity. Not all doors are closed to "us."

Our point here is not simply that there are class differences among gays and lesbians as a group but that there may be power-inflected microdifferentiations among gay and lesbian academics as part of a middle class. Invocations of a generalized homophobia to which we are all equally subject obscures those differences, lending credence to the myth that gays and lesbians are all equally oppressed (as well as its conservative corollary—that all gays and lesbians are middle-class conspicuous consumers with plenty of disposable pink dollars) and obscuring the work that must be done to forge alliances among gays and lesbians and their supporters across differences of class. As Cindy Patton has argued in a very different context, it is possible to "[press] too hard on the homophobic core. . . ."[8]

The myth that "our" interests always already coincide by virtue of the fact that we are working in the same discipline has been disproved again and again. Yes, our subjectivity is formed through labor. But, as Matthew Tinkcom has argued, "the ability to labor . . . the potential work which capital anticipates, differs for various workers. . . . [C]apitalism is predicated upon difference that it can exploit."[9] While we would not want claims of "difference" to prevent us from seizing opportunities for collective action, we would want to factor into our efforts a knowledge that "gay and lesbian" or even "queer" does not automatically designate a group whose every interest coincides. This is obvious in the world "outside" the "academy," given the increasing political presence of such phenomena as the Log Cabin (Gay) Republicans, the conservative editor Andrew Sullivan, and Bruce "our place at the table" Bawer. Differences in geographic and institutional location may translate into differences in real income. Without resorting to a vulgar notion of class difference, we nonetheless want to note that, ubiquitous charges of "bourgeois intellectual" to the contrary, practitioners of Gay and Lesbian Studies may not all inhabit the same class position; the culturalist tendency to declare one's class position via affiliation rather than income is at the very least worthy of interrogation. In addition, the terms "intellectual" and "academic" do not function interchangeably across various cultural spheres. These two problems alone signal the difficulties of consolidating collective interests.

Working to produce a coinciding of interest is always a daunting task, particularly in a period of "down-" or "right-sizing" in American business activity. Job opportunities are fewer, and pieces of the research money pie get smaller and smaller. (Clearly, they are already nonexistent in certain places.) Given the fragile sociopolitical environments most of us inhabit, charges of homophobia need to be rendered with caution. While "homophobia" should not be the convenient shorthand for complicated economic processes, we should also not overlook the ways in which homophobia *is* intrinsically linked to the activity and effects of capitalism.

A footnote concerning the use to which secrecy in the university may be put: the secrecy of the tenure process itself makes it readily available for innuendo. It is not that gossip and rumor are tacked onto the narrative of the tenure process, for example, but that the secret nature of the process—the fact that candidates have no right to know the identities of those who vote for or against them—sets off a process of paranoid guesswork and creates strange alliances of rumor and reportage. Such gossip is not "parasitical" but rather is produced by the play of power and resistance immanent in this strategic situation. Gossip is sometimes treated as a "parasite" that allegedly attacks and feeds off a preexisting "legitimate" field of discourses. We might want to think of gossip as constitutive of fields of knowledge, not distinct from and outside them. Gossip is not viral in nature; clearly, the "feminization" and "homosexualization" of gossip by its critics is not irrelevant here.

"UNIFIED FIELD OR DYSFUNCTIONAL FAMILY?"

At the yearly meeting of a Marxist literary conference, a heated discussion occurs concerning the formation of Gay and Lesbian Studies as an academic discipline. Some conference participants argue that the current "success" of the discipline is more alleged than actual; while a handful of highly visible scholars have secured positions at elite institutions, there are still relatively few opportunities to work in Gay and Lesbian Studies, little support for research in the field, and almost no advertised jobs requesting such expertise. While the growing boom in gay and lesbian publishing and the accompanying plethora of conference panels and papers on queerness, queericity, and lesbian and gay concerns might appear to indicate a growing institutionalization of the field, these phenomena are simply symptoms of an emergent commodification.

Other participants in the discussion, particularly concerned about the limitations and perils of academic disciplinarity and its links to what Foucault has called the production of docile bodies, argue that the discipline has in fact regretfully arrived, evidenced by the handful of scholars whose work regularly and increasingly appears in anthologies and "special issues" and who appear on star panels on gay and lesbian studies and by the fact that Ph.D. students working in gay and lesbian studies, prior to completing their dissertations, are often being courted by publishers— occasionally, by several publishers simultaneously. While this success is in fact symptomatic of a nascent commodification of the field, this is no less characteristic of gay and lesbian studies than of any other emerging discipline. It is no secret that "late" capitalism has reinvigorated the gay and lesbian consumer market. Eric O. Clarke has recently insisted that we be attentive to "the by-now-well established tradition in the United States of propitiating disempowered and underrepresented groups' demands for greater access to, and fundamental changes in, the public sphere with inadequate substitutes. Too often the demand for a greater diffusion of power is displaced onto, and thus substituted by, a 'visibility' within dominant modes of representation: economic equity is substituted by economic representation (direct marketing for *and by* lesbians and gays). . . ." [10] Occupying a particular place within the circuit of capital, institutions like the university are obviously not immune to this process; whatever else they may be, new curricular developments in gay and lesbian studies are also a form of direct marketing for and by lesbians and gays.

Given the dismal employment prospects facing many new Ph.D.s in the humanities and the feelings of desperation that accompany this situation, the discussion gets particularly heated when someone brings up the example of a recently advertised job in gay and lesbian studies. Specifically: the English department of a prestigious and (many would argue) elitist university routinely advertises a string of positions in myriad different fields. While candidates often assume that these advertised positions represent a variety of real jobs to be filled, in fact, what the university is actually doing is creating a huge pool of candidates from which, following the feeding frenzy, it will choose its single favorite (or two). It just so happens that the lucky surviving candidate that year is someone working in gay and lesbian studies who happens to possess superb Ivy League credentials. This position is one of less than a handful in gay and lesbian studies advertised and filled that year. Participants in the discussion are left wondering whether or not this anecdote evidences a "success" for the discipline of gay and lesbian studies.

One of the most depressing signs of the institutionalization of both Gay and Lesbian Studies and queer theory is Peter Barry's *Beginning Theory: An Introduction to Literary and Cultural Theory*. This text provides a Cliff Notes version of gay and lesbian criticism. Following a brief summary of the field, including a section on queer theory, Barry provides a list of "what lesbian/gay critics do." These include:

1. "Identify and establish a canon of 'classic' lesbian/gay writers whose work constitutes a distinct tradition."
2. "Identify lesbian/gay episodes in mainstream work and discuss them as such." Barry offers the example of Jane and Helen in *Jane Eyre*.
3. "Set up an extended, metaphorical sense of 'lesbian/gay' so that it connotes a moment of crossing a boundary, or blurring a set of categories." Barry argues here that self-identification as lesbian or gay "is necessarily an act of conscious resistance to established norms and boundaries."
4. "Expose the 'homophobia' of mainstream literature and criticism."
5. "Foreground homosexual aspects of mainstream literature which have previously been glossed over."
6. "Foreground literary genres, previously neglected, which significantly influenced ideals of masculinity or femininity." [11]

Undergraduate textbooks are arguably one of the most active sites for the consolidation of a discipline. While Barry's narrative is hopelessly reductive, it nonetheless tells us much about how we are being "realized." If it is representative, it alerts us to the fact that "we" are being configured in ways that we cannot fully control, ways that would leave many theorists in despair.

The problem with Barry's prescription is at least twofold. First, it is based on the content of individual works. It asks queer studies to invest in a canon built upon the evidence of an author's homosexuality or a textual articulation of (homo)sexuality, homophobia, and so forth. Trying to locate "gay-friendly" texts and uncovering "homophobic textual moments" implies a static theory of literary artifacts as transparent and in and of itself provides little conceptual guidance in determining how one knows a gay text or author when confronted by one. This is related to a second concern—that while Barry does suggest a useful hermeneutics of suspicion toward previously canonized straight literature, this strategy seems unlikely to yield anything like a connection between sexuality and larger social processes. Barry's analysis resonates strongly with Foucault's description of disciplines in his essay "The Discourse on Language." [12]

That is, it wants us to construct in the most traditional manner an archive and attendant rules for that archive's use—practices that support the archive, rules that govern the texts within it, guidelines for those reading subjects who enter it. As Foucault suggests, "Disciplines constitute a system of control in the production of discourse, fixing its limits through the action of an identity taking the form of a permanent reactivation of the rules."[13]

Not insignificant are Barry's contradictory desires with regard to this archive. Designating queer identity as "blurry and boundary crossing" seems, if not to contradict, then at least to sit incongruously with "identifying gay writers who constitute a distinct tradition." In addition, Barry's approach makes several false promises. It promises to make readily available a very complex and contradictory set of identities and discursive practices. Were we able even to fulfill the role as writers, readers, and teachers that Barry prescribes, we would have to ask ourselves 1) if this would be a desirable thing in the first instance; 2) whether we want the tradition that may exist or may be in the processes of forming and reforming to be so clearly denoted and identifiable; 3) whether we want to be eaten by the categorizing machine or to advocate for a more murky and obtuse relation between the sexual identities of readers and the sex of the text. As practitioners of gay and lesbian studies, we cannot *not* desire the continued "success" of the discipline. We can, however, defer its emergence thorough a persistent critique of the limits of academic disciplinarity—limits made available for discussion through formulations such as Barry's.

DUST JACKET DIVAS

One: The dust jacket of D. A. Miller's *The Novel and the Police* features a provocative photograph of the author. Miller is dressed in a ribbed tank top. His arms folded across his chest, producing that instant cleavage look, Miller is mustached, defiant, squinting, his bulging biceps both a threat and a promise: "I like it rough." At one point in the book, Miller also refers to his weight-training routine, making clear that he's a "gym queen." This seems innocent enough at first glance, though one wonders, perhaps jealously, why D. A. Miller merits a dust jacket photo in the first place.[14] Distancing this representation from a discussion of the interests and desires of Miller the person, one might be tempted to ask what this photo says about the commodification or at least the promiscuity of the gym queen as a circulating and recognizable identity in gay male culture in general, and in Gay and Lesbian Studies in particular. While it is true that readers cathect libidinally to books, authors, and even ideas, one also wonders at the logic that makes it possible to use these particular kinds of cathexes for profitable ends. Why does a certain butch masculinity seem a marketable idea to a publisher of academic texts? What sort of lure does it offer to a potential buyer of such texts? Perhaps the masculine segment of the academic world allows for such gayness if it is sufficiently macho in its representation? A tough fag is, after all, still tough and, by extension, manly. And gay male gym queen identity signals a transgressive potentiality without the pending threat of overt feminization that comes associatively linked with, say, drag identity or opera queens. This particular image has it all: muscles and sensitivity, brawn and brains—a queerly familiar sort of appeal. Where have you gone, Marlon Brando? To the dust jacket of academic studies of the novel and the police, apparently.

Another possibility: perhaps it was assumed that we would read this photo as camp, a kind of nose thumbing at the academic world, and an attempt to "deconstruct" dominant codes of masculinity by deploying them on the surface of the queer body. This kind of argument has been circulating for some time now: gay macho queens are not really encouraging gynophobia but rather are making mischief with hegemonic gender codes; men seeking "straight-acting" men in the personal ads are not actually victims of internalized homophobia but are rather "consummate homoerotic ironist[s] contriving a sophisticated scene in which [they] may be able to ensnare a virgin about to experience his first ecstatic incarnation of paradoxical masculinity."[15] Miller's image may thus be read as a particular kind of postmodern icon: he's not really a cop, he's a member of the Village People.

The problem with these formulations is that they forget that parody invites multiple significations, some of them "nonparodic." In other words, as is suggested by Jennie Livingston's *Paris is Burning*, one queer's parody is another's "reality." Like camp, parody relies on multiple literacies that don't make inviolate the possibility of a "straight" reading. While the photo may be available to be read as parody, given the way that this image replicates the genre of the theatrical head shot, it is arguably more likely to be read as precisely that: a glossy designed to commodify and advertise the image of a beloved star.

Two: Rolling Stone Magazine calls her "the soft-spoken queen of gay studies." Simon Watney suggests that she is "deservedly recognized as the primum mobile of lesbian and gay studies." The dust jacket of Eve Sedgwick's *Tendencies* offers a number of attempts to define Sedgwick's position in the field and presumably to use this position as a marketing blurb.[16] Imagery here has even less to do with the "person" of Eve Sedgwick. Rather, it relates to the *significance* of Sedgwick as the female monarch of a community of eager gay and lesbian subjects and the prime mover of an academic discipline with an attendant coterie of disciples. Parodic? As was the case with the image of Miller, yes and no.

Given the claims made on this dust jacket, it is important to consider the constellation "Eve Sedgwick" as it relates to the question of identification and gay and lesbian studies. It is well known that Sedgwick began her rise to fame in queer studies via her deft and provocative analysis of homosocial relations between men in the late-nineteenth-century novel. Her book *Epistemology of the Closet* asserts homosociality as the central episteme of modernity in the West. When Sedgwick's work first appeared in this area, she took flack from various feminist and lesbian scholars for identifying with gay men at the expense of other identities: woman who loves women, feminist interested in lesbianism, and so forth. Those critics who informally or formally offered complaints of this kind were, somewhat justifiably, scolded by Sedgwick's defenders for embracing a flat and blunt identity politics blind to the complexities of identification. It is not who gets left out, however, but what kinds of identifications Sedgwick's work does make possible that we feel is worthy of a look here.

In terms of academia, we usually assume that identifications are enough to justify one's interest in certain types of scholarship. It is not requisite, however, that these identifications map directly onto the (sexual) practices of that scholarship's author. What emerges as problematic in terms of the Sedgwick image are salient points about representation, interest, and motivation and the shifting distinction between Sedgwick as proxy and Sedgwick as portrait. Spivak has taught us to be attentive to the instability between representation as the standing in for another, as in the case of political representation, and representation as the portrayal of another, as in the case of semiosis, for example. Since it is factual, or nearly factual, that the kind of fame most academic work these days achieves is negligible, what kind of "responsibility of identification" do queer intellectuals have? That is, how significant is it that Sedgwick is called the queen of Gay and Lesbian Studies when most people don't know there is a kingdom at all?

It would be both disingenuous and patently untrue to suggest that

Sedgwick has no experiential links to gay male identity. She has ties to many members of the gay community, and she herself has noted the ways in which her physical weight, her illness, and her temporary baldness help to facilitate these identifications. In addition, she serves as a role model, in the traditional sense of the term, for many younger gay and lesbian scholars. These qualifications establish Sedgwick as a critic with identifications both "real" and "imaginary." However, in academic discourse as of late, identity in its noun form and identification in its verb form have become confusingly hinged. That is why it becomes helpful not to decide once and for all between any two opposing paradigms of alliance formation in queer scholarship but to couple intellectual and academic coalition building with a skepticism about the risks that this coalition building necessarily contains. In a struggle for seamless solidarity, the ties that bind us can be the same ties that blind us; fetishizing Sedgwick's *identification* with gay male subjectivity risks encouraging a more promiscuous and pernicious version of the familiar fag-hag-gay male continuum. In the eyes of her many fans, this identification risks becoming a sacred bond. Like all things sacred, this bond resists profanity.

This story has at least two dimensions. Sedgwick first gained notice as an astute literary scholar of the nineteenth-century novel and as an important critic of Henry James. In present-day intellectual life, any hopes we might maintain for an "emancipatory" or progressive period-based literary pedagogy rest on at least one urgent task: teaching others how to read traditional texts in radical ways. This can take place in the classroom or in a scholarly book or article. But no matter how radical any given reading might be, literary analysis in the current political climate in the United States is still a limited venture with somewhat diminishing returns. Our point here is that there is today a general safety attached to literary analysis. There is also apparently little room for this particular "defamation" of the discipline; as soon as attacks on the literary are mounted, they are met with powerfully armed minions from the ranks of those loyal to the most basic tenets of literary study. Given the rocky road leading to the acceptance of gay and lesbian scholarship, it is understandable that many of the earliest and most important analyses done by such scholars took literature as its subject. The enduring commitment to literary studies, however, is ripe for the questioning, and yet those best positioned to critique literature's academic primacy are often met with charges of scurrilous anti-intellectualism from within.[17] The question however, remains: Why does queer studies seems so obstinantly fascinated with Sedgwick's "literary" habits, given a variety of recent and not so recent attacks on the notion of the literary that have serious and valid political concerns at their center? [18] How this question is answered says as much about her fans as it does about her star image itself.

The second part of the story is that, by no fault of her own, Sedgwick has walked into one of the most clichéd tableaus of gay male identity: the pieta of young gay male and caring queen *mater*. This tableau may be symptomatic of an important political desire to combat the confederation of misogyny and homophobia so central to straight masculinity. Since it is clear that masculine heteronormativity already imagines gay men and women in an unholy alliance intent on extinguishing white straight men and taking all their toys away for good, gay men and women (straight and gay) have a vested political interest in transforming this fear into a real coalition politics. Insofar as Sedgwick's intellectual work has been central to many gay male scholars in the field, it makes much sense that she embodies such hope. Yet manifold problems are presented by her relative stardom. For a variety of reasons, the Sedgwick image makes available a set of relatively safe affective investments: Sedgwick as "contained" femininity. Mother womb, desexualized, generally nonthreatening to gay male identity, she does not evoke the image of the vagina dentate.[19] The "soft-spoken" nature of Sedgwick's work adds to this calming and soothing identificatory circuit. But what kind of detour of desire is in place here? What type of affective and intellectual configuration is being formed?

In his "Outlaws: Gay Men in Feminism," Craig Owens argues that "the myth of homosexual gynophobia remains perhaps the most powerful obstacle to a political alliance of feminists and gay men."[20] For Owens, this myth obscures the link between misogyny and homophobia, preventing important political work from getting off the ground. We might recast the problem as follows: the link between misogyny and homophobia has often *required* that some gay men be gynophobic. In a phallocentric sexist and homophobic culture in which gay men are constructed as feminized and, as a result, vilified, gay men will necessarily have an ambivalent identification with the feminine, choosing men will sometimes involve rejecting women, and homoeroticism will sometimes be structured by gynophobia.

This is certainly not to suggest that gay men are any more gynophobic than straight men.[21] In a patriarchal, phallocentric culture, gay men have no monopoly on gynophobia.[22] But are gay male critics frequently shamed by the misogyny question? While gay male fans might invest in select female stars, these investments do not automatically extend to all women; it is perfectly possible to be a misogynist and still love Barbra Streisand. Similarly, one might think of gay male critics' investments in "mother" Sedgwick as a screen that keeps the true concerns and debates about gay male misogyny out of sight. In other words, there may be a level of displacement activated by the queen image (the metaphoric mother of a nation) that does little harm in and of itself but that invites serious scrutiny when opposed to the very real (gyno)fears and phobias it may mask.

A question remains: what is at stake in our continued allegiance to the idea that political alliances are necessarily formed through processes of identification? Is a persistent, if cautious, commitment to the terms of psychoanalysis a symptom or an effect of a lingering loyalty to identity politics?

AIN'T I (A) QUEER?

When offered a position in English at a major university, a candidate who locates his work in queer studies and indeed is presumed by the members of the search committee to be gay announces that he will not be able to accept the position unless a similar job is found for his female partner.

A job candidate offers a talk discussing homoeroticism in Hollywood Westerns. When the department members meet to discuss his candidacy, a straight faculty member argues that the candidate seemed to have little stake in his own intellectual work. A gay graduate student counters that perhaps the problem is that the straight academy has not yet developed a way of hearing the investments of gay intellectuals. The student bases his assumption that the candidate is gay not only on the candidate's work but on the fact that the candidate cochaired a gay and lesbian organization. Later, a lesbian colleague of the student informs him that she has just discovered that the candidate, for whom both of them had gone to bat, is straight.

Ignoring the work of its own graduate students in queer studies, a university instead invites its (at the time, married) visiting fellow to act as native informant to the rest of its faculty concerning Queer Nation.

In the scramble to claim marginality, a scholar floats self-generated ru-
mors about her own identity—she is at various times straight, lesbian,
bisexual, white, black, thin, fat, Jewish, Italian.

Clearly, these anecdotes do not mean to suggest that one must "be" gay
or lesbian in order to do work in Gay and Lesbian Studies, nor are they a
call for a re-essentialization of a gay or lesbian identity. But the question
of the equating of social identity and occupation is a curious one. A friend
recently pointed out to us that if someone self-identified as a romanticist,
no one would ever whisper, "Do you think he's *really* from the nineteenth
century?" But this kind of outing is commonplace when one speaks of
queer-related scholarship.

As Sedgwick so scrupulously argues, outing hinges on the concept of
the closet or, more generally, the secret. In an essay on Colin MacCabe's
battles with Cambridge University, David Simpson argues, "Academics
love secrecy; it allows them to perpetuate squalidly personal policies
under the guise of professional confidentiality."[23] This is perhaps too
simplistic a formulation, in that it suggests that academics willfully and
deliberately use secrecy as a tool in the pursuit of raw self-interest.[24]
Obviously, the things we consider worthy of public celebration are also
things that, in this day of confession and identity-oriented knowledge,
seem at the same time inviolate. We can imagine, for example, a situation
where the knowledge of someone's "private" sexual orientation creates
situationally specific demands; such knowledge must remain closeted in
one instance and acknowledged in another. For example, the "fact" that a
job candidate "is" "gay" might be used productively either to strengthen
or weaken his or her desirability. If candidates choose to withhold or
reveal their sexual orientation, is this an instance of active self-interest?
Perhaps, but Simpson's charge threatens to obscure many of the institutional factors that lead us, often against our will or at least without
sufficient reflection, to engage in behaviors that divide our interests from
those of others. It makes possible the return of the sovereign subject, this
time under the guise of the scheming academic who is capable of acting
in such a way that his or her desires seamlessly coincide with his or her
interests, when in fact "economic agency or *interest* is impersonal because
it is systematic and heterogeneous."[25] As a result, it is too facile to claim
that the individual subject of/in the institution perceives clearly his or her

own interests and uses secrecy to pursue these interests accordingly. Perhaps this illustrates one of the perils of the kinds of knowledge that circulate as gossip, innuendo, and rumor: because gossip always consists of stories about specific people, the exchange value of the gossip is linked to whether one "knows," personally, professionally, or simply from his or her work in the field the individual to whom the gossip refers. The telling of gossip thus threatens to reinscribe the intentional subject through the placing of individual blame or responsibility.

The problem of interests, alliances, and identities is further complicated in Gay and Lesbian Studies in particular through the introduction of the term "queer." Both within and outside the university, for certain of its advocates, the term "queer" refers, among other things, to a more expansive, fluid, and contingent sense of sexual identity than is provided by the terms "gay and lesbian" or "homosexual." As permeable as it may be, the term indicates an identity nonetheless. As Sedgwick has approvingly hypothesized, "there are important senses in which 'queer' can signify only *when attached to the first person*."[26] "Queer" is thus a means of self-identification that does not necessarily depend on the sexual orientation of the speaker. Alex Doty refers to so-called queer readings as the "adopting [of] reception positions that can be considered 'queer' in some ways, regardless of a person's declared sexual and gender allegiances."[27] In particular circumstances, then, "queer" might produce effects "of identity, enforcement, seduction, challenge"—the effects of so-called linguistic performativity—that have little to do with who is fucking whom.[28] Specifically, "queer" might provide a means of "passing" as gay or lesbian.[29]

Following the euphoria with which its initial (re)entrance into the lexicon was greeted, the term "queer" has been subject to a number of important interrogations by such scholars as Sedgwick, Clarke, Doty, Teresa de Lauretis, Sue Ellen Case, and Judith Butler. Those theorists who valorize the term often do so in an attempt to deploy its performative dimensions, to foreground what it makes possible, while simultaneously critiquing what it does not. For many, there is an insistent recognition of the need to keep homosex in queerness. For example, Sedgwick argues, "to displace [same-sex sexual expressions] from the term's definitional center, would be to dematerialize any possibility of queerness itself."[30] Yet she follows this with the proposal that queer might hinge on "performative acts of experimental self-perception and filiation"—which need not necessarily include, say, same-sex sexual expression.[31] She adds to this a possible corollary: "what it takes—all it takes—to make the description 'queer' a true one is the impulsion *to* use it in the first person." Suggesting that Sedgwick's work foregrounds "the promise *and* the difficulties" of the increasingly expansive term "queer," Clarke nevertheless concedes that this formulation "seems to echo the humanist predication of self-legislating, rationally self-fashioning individuals, able to 'transcend' their material conditions of subjectivation, conditions that at the same time would negate the very possibility of such transcendence."[32] It also fails to mention that many subjects can't afford the luxury of attaching "queer" to the first person, which threatens to produce serious consequences such as loss of job, alienation from one's family, and physical violence.

An interrogation of the various significations of the term "queer" might open up a discussion of sexual identity and capitalism. As capitalism pursues its "ultimate" goal—the commodification of everything—it necessarily increases and decreases the flow of capital, goods, and labor power. Theoretically, while the interests of capitalists as a class coincide, they are often divided by conflicting corporate (self-) interests; thus, it will be advantageous for some putative capitalists to "deregulate" this flow in their own interests and for others to use the possibility of regulation against their competitors. For example, as the crisis of capitalism accelerates, certain capitalists will find it in their interests to continue to restrict the entrance of woman into the labor force, guaranteeing her position in the household as producer of surplus value through the (re)production of the work force. Other capitalists' increasing need for cheap wage laborers will outweigh the benefit of maintaining semiproletarianized households, and they will therefore encourage women—historically paid lower wages than men—to enter the labor force. Thus, the identity of "woman" must ideally be "fluid"—she must increasingly be able to be produced as wage laborer or domestic laborer or a combination of the two. In other words, both "borderless" and fixed identities may be activated in the service of global capitalism. Fluidity of identity does not always correlate with liberation—at least not liberation from capitalism.

And where is gay and lesbian identity in this equation?[33] In his germinal essay "Capitalism and Gay Identity," John D'Emilio suggests that the emergence of gay and lesbian subjects "is associated with the relations of capitalism; it has been the historical development of capitalism—more specifically, its free-labor system—that has allowed large numbers of men and women in the late twentieth century to call themselves gay, to see themselves as part of a community of similar men and women, and to organize politically on the basis of that identity."[34] D'Emilio suggests that capitalism's continuing expansion has necessarily been accompanied by both an expansion of the system of free labor *and* a diminishing of the importance of the family as an economic unit; as the institution of wage labor has spread, some subjects have been capable of freeing themselves from economic dependency on the family and have been able to set up alternative kinds of households. Over time, the family has thus gradually lost its status as first an independent and then an interdependent unit of production. Given this reduction of the economic role of the family, theorists have suggested the use of the term "household" to designate the economic unit that has supplanted the family as the mechanism for reproducing and maintaining the labor force.[35]

This reduction of the economic importance of the family has in turn made it possible for sexuality to be freed from the obligations of procreation. Unlike the family, individual households do not necessarily feel the pressure to produce heirs—or at least not the same kinds of pressures that in the past influenced the family. This might also account for the escalating breakdown of kinship systems under contemporary capitalism; the optimal unit for survival need no longer consist of one man engaged in wage labor and one woman who maintains the household; kinship systems are no longer strictly necessary, since wealth no longer needs to remain within the family per se, for example.[36]

D'Emilio suggests that the increase in the institution of wage labor, accompanied as it is by a diminishing of the family's importance as an economic unit, has transformed the family into what is now primarily an affective unit providing sexual and emotional satisfaction and happiness to its members. It appears that the household has recently taken over this role from the family—or rather, individuals organized into a household rather than a family have been interpellated by the family's ideology and have thus sought to establish alternative institutions to recreate that ideology in the household. This is one way to account for such disparate phenomena as permanent homo and heterosexual monogamous pairings outside marriage, joint ownership of pets by the unmarried, and calls for gay and lesbian marriage and adoption.

In any case, D'Emilio concludes that "[i]n divesting the [family] household of its economic independence and fostering separation of sexuality from procreation, capitalism has created conditions that allow some men and women to organize a personal life around their erotic/emotional attraction to their own sex. It has made possible the formation of urban communities of lesbians and gay men and, more recently, of a politics based on sexual identity."[37] But what kinds of jobs were available to these newly formed free laborers? How did capitalism "manage" this new identity and secure it for continued capitalist expansion?

We might provisionally look to both gender and race as examples of how capitalism appropriates apparently "natural" physical characteristics allegedly rooted in biology and transforms them into signifiers of one's role in the (gendered, hierarchized) division of labor. Does capitalism make use of sexual identity, as it does race or gender, to assign subjects to particular positions in the division of labor, for example? Recall Matthew Tinkcom's formulation, cited earlier in this essay: "the ability to labor . . . the potential work which capital anticipates, differs for various workers. . . . [C]apitalism is predicated upon difference that it can exploit."[38] Given both the links between gender and sexuality and the continuing production of gays and lesbians as gender misfits, might this not be possible? This might account, for example, for the tolerance historically afforded to "out" employees in certain fields rather than others. In the past, being "out" has often meant exhibiting certain visible signs of a sexual identity coded as "effeminacy" in men and "masculinity" in women. Like race and gender, capitalism may have mobilized these outward signs of gay and lesbian identity in order to socialize some "inappropriately" gendered subjects into particular occupations—usually, though certainly not always, lower positions in the hierarchized division of labor. (Of obvious significance here are past and present attempts to treat sexual identity as a product of biology. It is advantageous to capitalism to make the argument, for example, that "effeminate men can't help it," as long as there are jobs that might more easily be filled by these "effeminate" men.)

The amorphousness of "queer," then, might in fact render it ideal for particular elements of capital development. Perhaps the emergence of the term "queer" in particular can be linked to the need for a more "fluid" sexual identity than that historically designated by "gay" or "lesbian." As we have already suggested, capitalism has historically needed to produce some gay and lesbian subjects (and only some) able to occupy positions in the lower echelon of the division of the labor hierarchy—hairdressers, waiters, convenience store workers, for example, workers whose "inappropriate" gender identifications have historically been "tolerated." "Gay" and "lesbian" might have historically designated these particular workforce allocations. Changes in capitalism's dynamic, however, have perhaps opened the door for gay and lesbian workers in more prestigious fields—

law, medicine, and higher education, for example.[39] Immanuel Wallerstein has argued that racism and gender discrimination under capitalism have always functioned alongside a system of meritocracy.[40] This system guarantees positions of prestige to token individuals so that the illusion of freedom to choose one's position in the division of labor might be maintained.[41] In recent history, capitalism has produced token privileged gay workers—interior decorators, for example. Perhaps the increasing presence of "out" gay and lesbians in these higher positions in the division of labor is a testament to capitalism's need to maintain, under increasing pressures, this illusion of a system of meritocracy. The expanded "visibility" of gay, lesbian, and queer subjects, combined with various fluctuations in the demand for wage laborers, increasingly requires capitalism to make a more "fluid" use of sexual identity as a means of assigning subjects to their proper positions within the division of labor. This might also help us to account for such things as the increasing "class" hostility directed to gay people; in a period of shrinking jobs, capitalism may mobilize the myth that all gay and lesbian people are middle class in an effort to produce a kind of class resentment against them from the economically underprivileged and thus to interrupt gays' and lesbians' attempts to secure a "proper" place at the table of the bourgeoisie. Conversely, the reconsolidation of the middle class's inclusivity imperative can be seen as part of larger and still active efforts at reinvigorating the notion of the "classless" America.[42]

Capitalism's movement toward the commodification of everything has clearly involved more than just an increase in the institution of wage labor, however. Obviously, along with this increase has come an explosion of commodities and an escalating need to produce consumers for these commodities. Capitalism thus requires consuming subjects able to be interpellated along a variety of axes, and queer seems particularly to fit the bill here. As Clarke has noted, there is an increasing danger that queer liberation might become a market rather than a movement. Or, it may be a market that understands its audience to be as likely to camp around Ab Fab as to read "straight talk" about the queer consumer. It is thus no coincidence that the April 1996 issue of *The Advocate*, which sports a cover photo of Jennifer Saunders and Joanna Lumley, also includes a feature article on advertising and gay self-imagery.[43] The article offers such titillating observations as David Witz's "We view the gay market the same way we view attorneys and investment bankers. . . .These are people who go to restaurants and clean out the wine cellars."[44]

So what is to be said concerning the relationship between queer commodification and the field of Gay and Lesbian Studies? It is difficult to conjure the image of a Women's Studies department so devoted to the concept of gender destabilization that it would not be particularly concerned to supply jobs to female scholars. The slipperiness of the term "queer," however, makes possible a situation in which people whose interests initiated the field itself find they have no secure place of employment in it. To return to more local considerations: given the realities of a tight job market, scholars, particularly those in permeable fields such as cultural studies, are encouraged to diversify their theoretical interests and teaching qualifications to respond to the university's version of corporate downsizing. Hence, at least in terms of marketability, and given that queer theory increasingly becomes something one can *do* (in addition to doing a little bit of everything else), there is more and more incentive to "pass" as queer. Conversely, there are imperatives for queer scholars to professionalize their inquiry along traditionally straight terms.[45] Of course, "passing" between gay and straight is not a quid pro quo relation—there are serious social inequities between gays and straights that make for an uneven playing field in this regard.

Work that consistently explores issues of sexuality and gender across a range of texts too erratic or too current to be periodized does not have the advantage of market malleability; it would be tough to land a job as an early modern scholar having published a single paper on Mel Gibson-as-macho-Hamlet, for example. The publishing of certain kinds of work means never having the opportunity to secure certain kinds of jobs.

Given the newness of the field, its stars are generally people trained and published in other areas. There are less than a handful of jobs advertised annually in queer theory, most of which go—as most jobs do—to graduates of prestigious programs whose sense of what it means to do work in gay and lesbian studies might be quite different from that of someone, say, working at a community college, with few resources for research, little intellectual community, no graduate students, and serious fiscal restraints.

Representatives who are and are not "our" re-presentatives may unwittingly obscure that which arguably makes queers most reprehensible to "outsiders": women eating other women's pussies, men fucking other men up the ass, and so forth. While doing does not necessarily produce knowledge, it does not precisely produce non-knowledge, either. Engaging in certain culturally vilified acts must necessarily alter one's subjectivity—if we understand subjectivity as "produced" and not inherent. To be a subject means to act and not act in certain ways. Perhaps one needs strategically to be a sort of crude nominalist: the real-ization of certain activities is what leads to the production of one's subjectivity as "queer" (or gay or lesbian). Unless one mandates that affiliations be based exclusively on identities, no violence has been done by this insistence that a queer is as a queer acts—and this includes how s/he acts in bed. If you really want to call yourself queer, why not engage in a little homosex? We're talking about a community in which "some of my best friends are gay" really means something.

This is not to suggest that (sexual) subjects are self-fashioning, simply free to produce themselves as gay or queer. The trendy rush to forget Foucault makes it increasingly possible to ignore his later work on technologies of the self, in which he argues, for example, that (gay) subjects must work at becoming gay.[46] Sexual subjectivity is not simply chosen or chosen simply. It is produced by a wide field of institutions, techniques, practices, and procedures that are beyond the knowledge and control of any individual instance of that which appears to operate as a subject. Nonetheless, one is not condemned to be a particular kind of subject. Culture proposes and imposes a variety of patterns of subjectivity, and within these patterns there are opportunities for resistance and transformation. Thus, the need to develop what Foucault terms an aesthetics of existence.[47] In any case, homosex might be thought of as an invention of the subject; it simultaneously invents a subject and is (re)invented by a subject. This process does not guarantee pleasure; engaging in homosex promises to be both pleasurable and hazardous, given the ways it might alter dominant modes of subjectivity. It is not necessarily a recipe for the discovery of a self or an invitation to become one's own special creation. At the very least, such "creation" is not *merely* the commodification of homosexuality. It is also a form of labor, with its attendant gratification and pain.

CONCLUSION

Throughout this essay, we have tried to demonstrate—"perform," if you will—how gossip, innuendo, and rumor might be deployed productively in an effort to examine some of the stakes involved in the increasing institutionalization of Gay and Lesbian Studies. We offer this analysis at least partially in an effort to prevent gay and lesbian studies from simply becoming a midwife to a newborn gay and lesbian consumer culture. Nicola Field has argued that what she terms "the increasing commercialisation of gay life" has played a part in the formation of a fictional gay community held together by a shared sexuality that cuts across differences of class and social position.[48] This shared sexuality "has developed into a cultural code for shared consumer taste, a predilection for certain forms of art, decor, clothing, food and drink." Fields suggests that the concept of a separate gay community has led both to the production of a clear-cut gay market ready for penetration by entrepreneurs, gay and straight, and the "reduction of the vision of gay liberation into a lukewarm set of meagre single-issue demands which reflect the very few common interests of a fictional cross-class 'community.' "

Gay and Lesbian Studies/Queer Theory enters the academy both as a result of and in critical response to these historical factors, made possible by and attempting to confront the myth of a separate gay community. Necessarily, this is a dialectical process, although not a dialect whose stages operate in absolute synchronicity. Hence, it is possible today to imagine two versions of Gay and Lesbian Studies, one that, say, offers courses in great gays of the past and contemporary lesbian chic aligned in impulse if not intent with the commercialization of gay identity (a queerer version of traditional art appreciation courses), the other attempting to work against notions of sexual identity as fixed and to retard the commodification that accompanies that fixity. There are, however, activists and theorists for whom the term "queer studies" intervenes to waylay and undermine a Gay and Lesbian Studies unself-critical of its relationship to consumer culture. However, as Clarke has insisted, "lest [queer studies] become complicitious with . . . a self-representation unproblematically integrated into capitalist expansion . . . the moment of queer must also, necessarily, be a self-critical one."[49]

Gossip, innuendo, and rumor circulate as a "community"-based form of self-criticism and thus may be mobilized for the moment of queer. Nonetheless, a number of legitimate factors—a fear of right-wing forces eager to discredit Gay and Lesbian Studies, concerns relating to conditions of employment and support for work, and a desire to maintain queer studies as a kind of safe space not subject to the typical machinations, backbiting, and bitchiness of the academy, for example—seem to prevent gay and lesbian academics from engaging in a sustained critique of the emerging discipline. This situation is further complicated by the emergency of HIV and AIDS within and outside the academy. Rendered all the more vulnerable by this emergency, gay and lesbian scholars attempting to protect the interests of their constituencies may be reluctant to introduce possibly divisive critiques. We have heard that a proposed book on the state of queer studies and the limitations of Gay Studies as an academic discipline was judged by some in the discipline to be too divisive and counterproductive; we have attended panels where a writer's HIV status was raised by a participant as a rationale for not criticizing that writer's work. Gossip, innuendo, and rumor all currently work to keep certain kinds of self-critique in circulation. They play a vigorous role in the (de)formation of queer studies. And it is particularly vital that we pursue a critique of the discipline now that we have arrived on the eve of its future—while we still have the ability to shape the specific ways it is being commodified. Neglecting gossip's already existing role in the field forces us to discard the richness of queer and queer-affiliated practices and to ignore the more nefarious elements that the activity of scandal can foster. If Gay and Lesbian Studies as an academic discipline hopes to alter the terrain of disciplinarity and to transform the heteronormative conditions for knowledge, confuse the relationship between the academy and its alleged "outside," make mischief with distinctions between the public and the private, it must be willing to take the risk of stonewalling what constitutes professionalism and professional discourse.

There are many ways in which, at various times, in different places (and depending on who is in the room) the issues we've brought up change as do our relations to them. There are also many people within the field who are offering up rigorous, scandalous, and inventive responses to the problems of disciplinarity and queer studies. Sadly, the best reads of the field often occur in fleeting and conjunctural moments: a quick word over drinks at MLA or a thinly veiled reference to a rival in an article. The stuff of history is likely to be small, minute in fact, and yet it opens onto large questions, questions that wonder over and over what we are up to, anyway. Stonewall, the AIDS emergency, lavender capital, the identity wars—we are suspended within a risky discipline whose emergence has signaled the no longer but whose current crises emphatically (and laudably) denote the not yet.

NOTES

We would like to thank the following for their insightful commentary on earlier drafts of this essay: Carol Stabile, Matthew Ruben, Amy Villarejo, Lisa Schwartz, and Roberta Salper.

1. Leo Bersani, *Homos* (Cambridge, Mass.: Harvard University Press, 1995).

2. For a discussion of these two meanings of the term "representation," see Spivak, "Can the Subaltern Speak?," *Marxism and the Interpretation of Culture*, ed. Cary Nelson and Lawrence Grossberg (Urbana: University of Illinois Press, 1988), 271–313, as well as "Practical Politics of the Open End," *The Post-Colonial Critic*, ed. Sarah Harasym (New York: Routledge, 1990), 108–9.

3. See Crosby, "Dealing with Differences," in *Feminists Theorize the Political*, ed. Judith Butler and Joan W. Scott (New York: Routledge, 1992), 137.

4. Robert Post, "The Legal Regulation of Gossip," in *Good Gossip*, ed. Robert F. Goodman and Aaron Ben-Ze'ev (Lawrence: University of Kansas Press, 1994), 71.

5. Gayatri Spivak, "Subaltern Studies: Deconstructing Historiography," in *In Other Worlds, Essays in Cultural Politics* (New York: Routledge, 1988), 213.

6. Richard Dyer, *Heavenly Bodies: Film Stars and Society* (New York: St. Martin's Press, 1986), 154.

7. Cited in Spivak, "The Politics of Interpretation," in *In Other Worlds*, 131. The source of this maxim is Spivak's father.

8. Cindy Patton, "Performativity and Spacial Distinction: The End of AIDS Epidemiology," in *Performativity and Performance*, ed. Andrew Parker and Eve Kosofsky Sedgwick (New York: Routledge, 1995), 179.

9. Matthew Tinkcom, "Working Like a Homosexual: Camp Visual Codes and the Labor of Gay Subjects in the MGM Freed Unit," *Cinema Journal* 35, no. 2 (winter 1996): 28.

10. Eric O. Clarke, "All about Eve," *GLQ* 3:111. See also Clarke and Matthew Henson, "Hot Damme! Reflections on Gay Publicity," in *Boys: Masculinities in Contemporary Culture*, ed. Paul Smith (Boulder, Colo.: Westview, 1996), 131–49.

11. Peter Barry, *Beginning Theory* (Manchester: Manchester University Press, 1995), 148–49.

12. Michel Foucault, "The Discourse on Language," in *Critical Theory Since 1965*, ed. Hazard Adams and Leroy Searle (Tallahassee: University Presses of Florida, 1986), 148–62.

13. Foucault, Michel, "The Discourse on Language," 155.

14. The increasing presence of authors' photos on the dust jackets of academic books is notable. Gayatri Spivak has a photo on the back of one recent book and a head shot close-up on the cover of the *Spivak Reader*. Add to this list of dust jacket divas Jonathan Dollimore, Jane Gallop (a crotch rather than a head shot), bell hooks, Frank Lentricchia, Andrew Ross, Drucilla Cornell, and Stuart Hall, among others.

15. Brian Pronger, *The Arena of Masculinity* (New York: St. Martin's Press,

1990), 149. One wonders if Pronger would offer the same analysis of a personal ad that required "white men only." A parody and eroticization of racism?

16. Eve Kosofsky Sedgwick, *Tendencies* (Durham: Duke University Press, 1993).

17. For a critique of the dominant role literary studies has played in the emerging discipline of gay and lesbian studies, see *Fear of a Queer Planet*, ed. Michael Warner (Minneapolis: University of Minnesota Press, 1993).

18. Critiques of the category of the literary and of literary scholarship include the complaint that literature is too often treated in isolation from real historical developments; that it is treated as transcending such historical developments; that the term "literature" acts to differentiate texts worthy of serious study from more allegedly transparent and insignificant texts; and that many literary analyses lack any theory of mediation.

19. Sedgwick has played off of this trope herself. A fruitful area of discussion for queer studies is the functioning of the maternal dynamic in lesbian and gay scholarship in general.

20. Craig Owens, "Outlaws: Gay Men in Feminism," in *Men in Feminism*, ed. Alice Jardine and Paul Smith (New York: Methuen, 1987), 219.

21. Freud's "symptomatic" confession that "[p]robably no male human being is spared the terrifying shock of threatened castration at the sight of the female genitals" (216) illustrates this. See Sigmund Freud, "Fetishism," in *Sexuality and the Psychology of Love*, ed. Phillip Rieff (New York: Macmillan, 1963), 214–19.

22. In fact, some theorists have recently argued that patriarchal phallocentric heterosexuality is predicated on a traumatic relationship to difference, heterosexual masculinity being necessarily "more" gynophobic than homosexuality. See Leo Bersani, *Homos* (Cambridge, Mass.: Harvard University Press, 1995).

23. David Simpson, "New Brooms at Fawlty Towers: Colin MacCabe and Cambridge English," in *Intellectuals: Aesthetics, Politics, Academics*, ed. Bruce Robbins (Minneapolis: University of Minnesota Press, 1990), 264. Now referred to as the Cambridge affair, this collision between the then emergent theories of poststructuralism and psychoanalysis and more traditional kinds of literary scholarship featured several players, among them Colin MacCabe, Raymond Williams, Frank Kermode, and Stephen Heath. It was considered by the British press to be, among other things, a fantastic case of intellectual patricide.

24. In addition, the oxymoronic nature of the phrase "personal policy" leads one to raise the question of where personal issues blend with policy concerns, especially in the case of the university.

25. Spivak, "Can the Subaltern Speak?," 276.

26. Sedgwick, *Tendencies*, 9.

27. Alexander Doty, *Making Things Perfectly Queer* (Minneapolis: University of Minnesota Press, 1994), xi.

28. Sedgwick, *Tendencies*, 11.

29. Of course, it is crucial to note that "passing" in the gay and lesbian context involves a radically different hermeneutics and politics than is the case in questions of racial passing.

30. Sedgwick, *Tendencies*, 8.

31. Ibid., 9.

32. Clarke, "All about Eve," 114.

33. It is only with much caution that we propose a tentative analogy: like wage labor, can queer function as an antidote to binary configurations such as fixed and fluid labor forces? Wage labor is the means by which capitalism forges an uneasy compromise between the need for a fixed labor force and the need for an unfixed labor force. Perhaps capitalism similarly needs both gays and lesbians and queers, "stable" and "fluid" identities. On this point we are of two minds: Elayne is nervous about abstracting from Marxist categories in this way, whereas John is more willing to risk abstraction for the sake of productive analogies.

34. John D'Emilio, "Capitalism and Gay Identity," *Making Trouble* (New York: Routledge, 1992), 5.

35. In this particular essay, however, D'Emilio does not use this distinction.

36. Clearly, these developments are uneven; we are still living through some of these transitions. One of the interesting consequences of the gay marriage debate has been the recent attempt by Congress to insist that a marriage must consist of one man and one woman. Such legislation rearticulates institutionalized sexism and woman's subordinate place in the household bound together by state-regulated marriages.

37. D'Emilio, "Capitalism," 7.

38. Tinkcom, "Working Like a Homosexual," 28.

39. These changes include increasing investment in the gay and lesbian consumer market, responses to liberal initiatives of inclusion and civil rights victories for gays and lesbians, as relatively rare as they may be, and the somewhat unchecked embourgeoisment of some segments of the gay and lesbian community, often pejoratively termed the gaygeoisie.

40. Immanuel Wallerstein, *Historical Capitalism* (London: Verso, 1983), and "The Ideological Tensions of Capitalism: Universalism versus Racism and Sexism," in *Race, Nation, Class: Ambiguous Identities*, ed. Etienne Balibar and Immanuel Wallerstein (London: Verso, 1991), 29–36.

41. According to Wallerstein, meritocracy also makes possible the creation of privileged marginals whose role it is to manage the (minoritized) work force.

42. Or, in the case of the United Kingdom, the hijacking of the concept of the working-class nation, as in Maggie Thatcher's famous dictum "We're all working class—we all work."

43. Steve Friess, "Target Practice," *The Advocate* 705 (April 16, 1996): 32–34.

44. Ibid., 34.

45. At Elayne's undergraduate university, for example, in one year, three out of four female graduate students who were thought to be lesbians upon admission to the graduate Literary and Cultural Theory program turned out to be variously political lesbians, bisexual but living with a man in a monogamous relationship, and straight—every configuration, it appears, except legible lesbianism itself.

46. Michel Foucault, "Sex, Power, and the Politics of Identity," *The Advocate*, no. 400 (August 7, 1984): 26–30, 58.

47. For an overview of Foucault's account of subjectivity and how it might inflect an understanding of gay and lesbian subjectivity in particular, see John

Champagne, *The Ethics of Marginality* (Minneapolis: University of Minnesota Press, 1995).

48. Nicola Field, *Over the Rainbow: Money, Class and Homophobia* (London: Pluto Press, 1995), 37.

49. Clarke, "All about Eve," 115.

FOUR

Straight with a Twist: Queer Theory and the Subject of Heterosexuality

Calvin Thomas

Indeed, it may be only by risking the *incoherence* of identity that connection is possible.   —Judith Butler, *Bodies That Matter*

The final chapter of Judith Butler's *Bodies That Matter: On the Discursive Limits of "Sex"* bears the conspicuous and rather provocative title "Critically Queer." At first glance, this title could seem to be offering only the less than startling suggestion that "queers"—with the word understood as referring to lesbians, gays, or bisexuals—are or can be "critical." More interesting, however, the title also suggests that, just as there is more than one way to be "critical," there may be many more ways than one (or two or three) to be "queer." This suggestion of multiple if not limitless forms of queerness corresponds to certain formulations in the work not only of Butler but of other lesbian and gay theorists engaged in the postmodern "labor of ambiguating categories of identity."[1] It also provokes no few questions.

To begin with, to what extent does *critical* queerness—as differentiated from some other form or forms of queerness—depend on a specific identification with the words "homosexual," "bisexual," "lesbian," or "gay," and the outlawed sexualities these terms conventionally represent? How might a lesbian, gay, or bisexual subject *fail* to be sufficiently *critically* queer?[2] Conversely, and more to the point of this discussion, to what extent could an otherwise "straight" subject elaborate a queer criticism? If, as Lauren Berlant and Michael Warner suggest, membership in "queer publics" is "more a matter of aspiration than it is the expression of an identity or a history" (344), what accounts for, or disallows, the decidedly ambiguous labor of straight queer aspiration? What problems and possibilities are opened up by questions of straight engagement with or participation in queer theory (or, as Berlant and Warner prefer to call it, "queer commentary")?[3] What does reading queer theory tell the straight reader about being queer, about being straight, about being, about becoming, what one putatively is, what one (supposedly thereby) isn't, the permeability of the boundaries between the two, the price of their maintenance? Of what, if anything, might "otherwise straight" "critical queerness" consist? What exactly would it, or should it, if anything, perform? Other than voyeurism, appropriation, theoretical trendiness, or the desire to be a "good" responsible heterosexual critic, what might the draw of queer theory for straights be? What can antihomophobic straights *do* to help "make the world queerer than ever?"[4]

As an "otherwise straight" subject—an academic man, a reader and professor of feminist, queer, and other theory, who has long been involved in a committed, monogamous, state-sanctioned, fully benefited, but nonetheless quite happy, childfree relationship with an artist and therapist who is a woman—I would like to explore some of these questions here. I will do so, eventually, by focusing on my own problematic but perhaps illustrative response to a particular passage in *Bodies That Matter* in which Butler specifically describes (albeit in passing) the possibility of a straight affiliation with the term "queer." I begin, however, by examining some recent formulations within queer theory which, by virtue of their anti-essentialist emphasis on queerness as "resistance to regimes of the normal" (Warner, *Fear* xxvi), would seem to invite, or at least not explicitly forbid, something like a "queer aspiration" on the part of subjects who do not identify themselves as homosexual, gay, lesbian, or bisexual—or who at least could not base such identification on particular sexual practices, corporeal stylings, or specific "bodies and pleasures." These are formulations of discursive, performative, or "dis-positional" queerness that, given the inherent instability of discourse itself, would seem to trouble the stable boundaries of sexual identity or identity politics.[5]

For example, L. A. Kauffman writes in the *Village Voice* of "a new kind of politics, a post-identity politics of sorts. Queerness, in this view, [is] more a posture of opposition than a simple statement about sexuality. It [is] about principles, not particularities. 'To me,' explained [Queer Nation/San Francisco activist Karl] Knapper, 'queerness is about acknowledging and celebrating difference, embracing what sets you apart. A straight person can't be gay, but a straight person can be queer.' "[6] In *Making Things Perfectly Queer*, Alexander Doty writes of "cases of straight queerness, and of other forms of queerness that might not be contained within existing categories or have reference to only one established category." Although he does not elaborate on what constitutes straight "cases," Doty does suggest "that new queer spaces open up (or are revealed) whenever someone moves away from using only one specific sexual identity category—gay, lesbian, bisexual, or straight—to understand and to describe mass culture, and recognizes that texts and people's responses to them are more sexually transmutable than any one category could signify—excepting, perhaps, that of 'queer.' "[7]

Michael Warner, in his introduction to *Fear of a Queer Planet*, writes the following about shifts in self-identification from "gay" or "lesbian" to "queer":

The preference for "queer" represents, among other things, an aggressive impulse of generalization; it rejects a minoritizing logic of toleration or simple political interest-representation in favor of a more thorough resistance to regimes of the normal. For academics, being interested in queer theory is a way to mess up the desexualized spaces of the academy, exude some rut, reimagine the public from and for which academic intellectuals write, dress, and perform. . . . For both academics and activists, "queer" gets a critical edge by defining itself against the normal rather than the heterosexual. . . . The insistence on "queer" . . . has the effect of pointing out a wide field of normalization, rather than simple intolerance, as the site of violence. (xxvi)

Unlike Knapper or Doty, Warner does not allude to straight queerness here. Like theirs, however, his formulation does leave open the possibility of straight "resistance to regimes of the normal," if only because Warner does not explicitly state what would constitute the impossibility of such a stance. For other than the (admittedly formidable) unlikelihood born of safety and privilege, what is to prevent straights from "protesting not just the normal behavior of the social but the *idea* of normal behavior" (xxvii), from engaging in such protest even if the straights in question themselves behave largely (if not exactly) according to the norm? What would it mean for straights really to understand (and not just theoretically toy with) the queer argument that the normative regimens they inhabit and embody are ideological fictions rather than natural inevitabilities, performatives rather than constatives? After such knowledge, what normalness?

Warner provides a way of producing such antinormative knowledge in his essay "Homo-Narcissism; or, Heterosexuality." There Warner points out that "the modern system of sex and gender would not be possible without a disposition to interpret the difference between genders as the difference between self and Other" (191). According to this disposition, Warner writes, difference is always an allegory of gender and "having a sexual object of the opposite gender is taken to be the normal and paradigmatic form of an interest in the Other or, more generally, in others."[8] Conversely, according to this heterosexist view—particularly as insistently articulated in Freudian and Lacanian psychoanalysis—if one's sexual object is of the same gender as oneself, then one has "failed" adequately to discern self and other, to erect the proper barricades between identification and desire; homosexuality thus becomes defined as a "regressive" or developmentally "arrested" function of autoeroticism or narcissism. Warner brilliantly demonstrates how in psychoanalysis this normative view is simply and bluntly asserted by fiat, how heterosexual romance is just as implicated in narcissism as any homosexualized ego ideal, and how heteronormativity occludes its own narcissistic investments by displacing them onto the queer.

What Warner's discussion leaves open, however, is the possibility—indeed, the desirability—of a generalized resistance to this normative interpretation of sexual difference as difference itself, a resistance in which straights could conceivably participate, not by surrendering or repressing their desire for sexual objects of the opposite gender, but by questioning the dominance of the assumption that such interest constitutes the natural paradigm of interest in the Other, or in others per se. In keeping with the terms set forth elsewhere in Warner's work, such a questioning could in and of itself qualify as queer. Indeed, as the preceding examples may suggest, straights, who would be definitionally barred from the terms "gay," "lesbian," or "bisexual," could not be excluded from the domain of the queer except by recourse to the very essentialist definitions that queer theory is often at pains to repudiate.[9]

This definitional tension manifests itself in Eve Sedgwick's "Queer and Now" introduction to her essay collection *Tendencies*. There Sedgwick writes that "queer" involves "the open mesh of possibilities, gaps, overlaps, dissonances and resonances, lapses and excesses of meaning [that occur] when the constituent element's of anyone's gender, of anyone's sexuality aren't made (or *can't be* made) to signify monolithically."[10] Sedgwick gathers a number of fish into this widely thrown net, including not only some of the usual suspects—"drags, clones, leatherfolk"—but also "fantasists," "feminist men," "masturbators" (talk about a universalizing move!), and "people able to relish, learn from, or identify with such" (8). She then goes on to praise "work around 'queer' [which] spins the term outward along dimensions that can't be subsumed under gender and sexuality at all" (8–9). But Sedgwick also concedes that queer must denote "almost simply, same-sex sexual object choice, lesbian or gay" and states that "given the historical and contemporary force of the prohibitions against *every* same-sex sexual expression, for anyone to disavow those meanings, or to displace them from the term's definitional center, would be to dematerialize any possibility of queerness itself" (8). Thus, even though queer commentary such as Sedgwick's relies on the now familiar tropes of poststructuralist decentering—gaps, dissonances, lapses, and excesses of meaning—it must also revert to a nominally essential "definitional center" without which queerness wouldn't be what it is. Though on one level queerness as elaborated by Sedgwick, Warner, and others is sufficiently complex, mobile, and open not to exclude some antinormative, sympathetic, fantasizing, or masturbating straights, on another level it must also not displace "almost simple" same-sex sexual object choice, lesbian or gay. This caution against same-sex displacement seems obvious and, I would imagine, is welcome enough. But the crucial question thus perhaps becomes, Does the very suggestion of the possibility of including straights in the queer mesh in and of itself constitute the disavowal of certain specifically sexual meanings, the displacement of "almost simple" lesbians and gays, and consequently the dematerialization of "any possibility of queerness itself"?

Such would seem to be the conclusion of several theorists for whom the overly general inclusiveness and despecificity of the term "queer" provide grounds for its repudiation. Teresa de Lauretis, for instance, dismisses "queer theory" as a marketing ploy that "has quickly become a conceptually vacuous creature of the publishing industry."[11] Moreover, in *The Practice of Love: Lesbian Sexuality and Perverse Desire*, de Lauretis questions certain feminist (rather than queer) desexualizations of lesbianism that work to afford heterosexual feminist women access to the term. De Lauretis respects but interrogates and finds wanting both Adrienne Rich's notion of the "lesbian continuum" and psychoanalytic feminism's "figuration of a female desiring subjectivity to which all women may accede by virtue of their 'homosexual' relation to the mother. . . ."[12]

Leo Bersani, in *Homos*, also warns against the dangers of despecifica-

tion and desexualization posed by the emergence of the term "queer."
Citing Warner's appeal to "resistance to regimes of the normal," Bersani
writes, "This generous definition puts all resisters in the same queer
bag—a universalizing move I appreciate but that fails to specify the sexual
distinctiveness of the resistance. I find this particularly unfortunate since
queer theorists protest, albeit ambiguously, against the exclusion of the
sexual from the political."[13] Bersani himself, however, has already suggested that "if homosexuality is a privileged vehicle for homo-ness, the
latter designates a mode of connectedness to the world that it would be
absurd to reduce to sexual preference" (10). Later in *Homos* Bersani
amplifies what he means by homo-ness as "connectedness to the world"
when he writes that it is what he calls "self-shattering [that] is intrinsic to
the homo-ness in homosexuality." Homo-ness, he goes on to say, "is an
anti-identitarian identity" (101).

Readers familiar with such examples of Bersani's work as *The Freudian
Body* and "Is the Rectum a Grave?" will recognize his insistence on the
intrinsic self-shattering of *jouissance*. But we may also wonder why he here
connects such anti-identificatory self-shattering with the *homo-ness* and
not the *sex* of homosexuality. Indeed, the problem Bersani faces in his
elaboration of homo-ness is that of maintaining sexual specificity while at
the same time avoiding an "absurd" reduction to sexual preference. That
problem is at least partially resolved by the fact that for Bersani sexuality
specifically *is* self-shattering—or rather, what Bersani values in sexuality,
and in art, is the capacity of both to shatter that "coherent self" which for
him is both the effect of and condition of possibility for institutionalized
heteronormativity and hence "a sanction for violence."[14] As Jonathan
Dollimore points out in *Sexual Dissidence*, Bersani "sees gay male sexuality
as enacting insights into sexuality *per se* which heterosexual culture has to
repress ruthlessly."[15] Ultimately, I submit, Bersani holds that gay men in
certain of their specific sexual practices have a greater, a more probable,
perhaps even a more profound access to an antiredemptive, antirelational
(but thereby politically salutary) self-shattering than do straight men or
women but that such access is not finally exclusive to gay male sexuality.
Otherwise, Bersani would indeed be reducing the anti-identitarian mode
of connectedness he advocates (in terms similar to Judith Butler's in the
epigraph to this essay) not only to sexual preference but to a quite specific
sexual practice, rimming. He is not making that reduction, however, and
when he alludes to "celebrating 'the homo' in all of us" (10), he means, I
think, radically enough, us all.

Moreover, Bersani's comments on what he considers the intrinsic self-shattering of "sexuality *per se*" reveal what is perhaps the most salient irony of the phrase "sexual identity": its two terms are mutually incompatible, so any attempt to use sexual specificity to ground the exclusions that constitute identity and provide its contours must come to grief, or comedy. If, as Bersani has it, sexuality is inimical to identity, then identity can scarcely be based on sexuality. But if nothing can be firmly based on the specifically sexual, "sexuality *per se*" can become the "privileged vehicle" for baselessness itself, for the antirelationality and anti-identitarian identity that Bersani calls homo-ness.

Still, the question of differences in access to "sexuality *per se*," of differences between gay and straight celebrations of " 'the homo' in all of us," remains vexed. In a sense, Bersani is letting gay male sexuality and/or "sexuality *per se*" serve as "vehicles" (which is to say, metaphors) for our all connecting to the world as something radically other than autonomous, sovereign, phallicized egos willing to kill to protect the seriousness of our statements and the sanctity of our identities: he advocates an exuberant discarding of the self through sex, particularly through "de-meaning" receptive male anal eroticism. And yet, if homo-ness as self-shattering world-connectedness cannot finally be reduced to sexual preference or be said to depend on specific sexual practices, then it, too, like "queer," risks becoming an utterly generalized or dematerializing signifier; Bersani might as well be calling for a celebration of "the Buddha-nature" in all of us.[16]

The danger, then, of the overly generalized deployment of such terms as "queer" or "homo-ness" is that the terms can allow the straights who are drawn to them to sidestep interrogations of their own sexual practices—or, more precisely, the mutually reinforcing relationship between their culturally sanctioned sexual practices and their privileged and valorized social identities. Although, as I will presently suggest, the problem may be less practices than privilege, less heterosexuality than heteronormativity, none of these can or should be neatly separated. The ease with which straights can assume this separation—an ease to which my own thinking in working through this essay has been susceptible—is a conspicuous marker of privilege itself: straights have had the political luxury of not having to think about their sexuality, in much the same way as men have not had to think of themselves as being gendered and whites have not had to think of themselves as raced. Straights drawn to formulations of queerness or homo-ness need to interrogate their own sexual practices and the exclusions and repressions that make them possible. At the very least, a straight male theorist who feels "able to relish, learn from, or identify with" the insights of a Bersani or a Sedgwick needs to make some attempt to understand and work through his relationship to the receptive anal eroticism that they celebrate and that the dominant culture represses and reviles.[17]

However, though heterosexuality and heteronormativity cannot be separated, Bersani's formulation of homo-ness as a self-shattering "sexuality *per se*" to which we all have putative access but that "heterosexual culture has to repress ruthlessly" (Dollimore 321) does allow an interesting, if problematic, distinction to be drawn between the heterosexual and the heternormative, a distinction that could bear directly on the question of straight queer aspiration: heterosexuals may have some access to homo-ness, whereas heteronormativity is perhaps constitutively antisexual. Again, I do not mean to suggest by this assertion that heterosexuality can be unproblematically pried loose from its heternormative moorings. Nor do I mean to posit some natural, pure, or unsullied form of sex between men and women that exists before or outside the heteronormative institutions that produce the very cultural intelligibility of sexual practices. I do mean to suggest that, in terms of the "labor of ambiguating categories of identity" (Berlant and Warner 345) and thus helping "make the world queerer than ever" (Warner, *Fear* xxvii), the problem, the obstacle, may be less straight sexual practices per se than the privileging of those practices. What queerly aspiring straights need to interrogate, challenge, and work toward changing is less their own sexual practices than their condition of possibility.[18]

I will be returning to this distinction. Here, however, I turn to Judith Butler, and to the way my own troubled response to her work can help exemplify the problems in straight interrogations of heteronormativity, the problems in straight queer aspirations or identifications. Butler herself is of course an insistently anti-identitarian thinker, perhaps queer theory's strongest advocate of committing political and discursive "disloyalty against identity"—a disloyalty, as she puts it, "that works the iterability of the signifier for what remains non-self-identical in any invocation of identity."[19] In *Bodies That Matter*, Butler addresses the way the signifier "queer" has been reappropriated and reworked by lesbian and gay activists—transformed, so to speak, from taunt to flaunt, from a hurtful slur into an emblem of positive identification. Butler writes that "queer" has become the discursive rallying point for younger lesbians and gay men and, in yet other contexts, for lesbian interventions and, in yet other contexts, for bisexuals and straights for whom the term expresses an affiliation with anti-homophobic politics. That it can become such a discursive site whose uses are not fully constrained in advance ought to be safeguarded not only for the purposes of continuing to democratize queer politics, but also to expose, affirm, and rework the specific historicity of the term. (230)

Allow me to report that, when I first read this passage, I underlined it heavily and then wrote in the margins, just alongside the phrase concerning "straights for whom the term expresses an affiliation," the words "at last!" I confess that this "at last!" marked a small outcry of what I can now call only pleasure on my part: the pleasure of being recognized, acknowledged, included, if only in this completely anonymous way. "At last," after several hundred pages, Judith Butler was finally calling me a name, interpellating or hailing me as a straight subject for whom the term "queer" does indeed express an affiliation with antihomophobic politics. Or so I wanted, and still want, to think, and to argue.

And yet, though I didn't quite go so far as to erase my little outburst—as if anyone were likely to be examining my marginalia anyway—I did almost immediately think better, or at least more hesitantly, of this fleeting moment of jubilation before the mirror of queer theory. I began to question this "at last!" with its rather obnoxiously impatient "it's-about-time-you-mentioned-*me*" tone of self-congratulation and self-insistence. After all, what business had I, het male, reading a lesbian's book and desiring recognition, expecting acknowledgment, demanding inclusion, like Mr. Ramsay demanding sympathy in Virginia Woolf's *To The Lighthouse?* What was the meaning of this desire to be mentioned, this impatience to be named, this insistence on visibility (though I wasn't *conscious* of being desirous, impatient, or insistent, my spontaneous response certainly seems to suggest that I was all three)? What was this unconscious anxiety, then, in the face of reading a few hundred pages that didn't seem closely to concern my particular subject-position? What does *that* discomfort amount to when compared with the thousands of pages of straight literature and theory, the countless reels of mainstream film and hours of compulsorily heterosexual television, that lesbians and gays have suffered through for years without finding any such specific *and positive* trace of recognition but only the dominant culture's silence, hatred, and derision? Where did I get off with this "at last!" when "my" subject position had already gotten, still gets much more attention than it ever deserved?[20]

Moreover, why exactly did I think I needed to jump at the straight bait when Butler's critically queer line already had me hooked? Why did I think that it was only now, at last, with this one positive reference to queerly affiliated straights, that Butler was finally counting me *in* when "I"—or perhaps the instability and incompletion of the subject-formation marked by that signifier—was actually "being addressed" all along? While on one level I was apparently searching *Bodies That Matter* for some indication that the book was "also" about me, on another, less apparent level "I" must have been satisfied that the book was *already* about me, about the constitutive exclusions that form and thereby include "me," that it was "really me" who was being hailed, that my relationship to Butler's discourse could not be one of complete exteriority.

I should say that my interest in *Bodies That Matter* was, on the one hand, professional and academic. Familiar with *Gender Trouble*, and just finishing my own book on the abjected "matters" of the male body and their potential to trouble gendered (masculine) identity, I wanted to see how Butler's latest arguments would complement or complicate my own, what fresh footnotes would need to be appended to which chapters, and so on (in other words, whether my book was or wasn't actually "finished").[21] On the other hand, my interest in her book *while I was caught up in reading it* was not "purely" academic but seemed rather to be affectively engaged on the unpredictable level of identification and desire; this engagement must have been evident to me well before the phrase in which "I" found myself "named." Otherwise, I doubt I would have read so thoroughly, so emphatically, so lovingly. Sure, lovingly: for though I would stop short of saying that I "simply loved" *Bodies That Matter* (not *enough* bodily matters, for my tastes), I would still submit that one rarely finds any sort of book compelling unless it somehow tugs on the bonds of love. As Jonathan Culler has recently pointed out, to read "with love" is not to read uncritically or disinterestedly, but rather to be caught up in or possessed by a variety of different and often contradictory psychic and libidinal investments, among which he lists "aggressivity, transference, sadomasochism, identification, or fetishization."[22]

It is the penultimate item on Culler's list that seems most pertinent here in relation to the questions opened up by my marginalia. Or rather, what seems to pertain here is the way "identification" as an active, ongoing, potentially endless *process* can be reified into "identity" as a putatively finished *product*, the way the process always threatens to subvert the product even as the latter works relentlessly to reconsolidate, or terminate, the former.

What my "at last!" seems to articulate is exactly this tension, simultaneously libidinal and semiotic, between *desire-identification* (in which the boundaries between the two are unpredictably permeable and mobile) and *desire/identity* (in which the boundaries are ostensibly stable and thus the two terms mutually exclusive): on the one hand, a desire to be engaged, to be possessed, to be *liked* in the affective sense; on the other, the desire to be named, to be acknowledged, recognized, made visible, counted in, to be *liked* in the mimetic sense of having one's "own" *likeness* reproduced.

The fact remains, however, that though I had for several hundred pages of reading been caught (up) in the act of queer discursivity and had been unselfconsciously identifying with many of Butler's performative reiterations, it wasn't until I "at last" saw "myself" *named* as a *straight* "for whom the term [queer] expresses an affiliation" that I imagined I had been, finally, *liked* (in both the affective and mimetic senses). Now, since in the Lacanian terms that Butler adopts and reworks it is the phallus that governs the dispensation of meanings and names, my pleasure in being named by Butler might indicate a sort of acknowledgment of her "lesbian phallus" within my "morphological imaginary." So far, perhaps, so good. But perhaps I also took Butler's strap-on all too like a man. For what my jubilation over "finally" being positively "recognized" as a "*straight* queer" may also indicate is that, in the name of *identity* and according to its exclusionary logic, my "at last!" had to some extent just consolidated the *refusal* of the very queer *identification* that had already been happening all along. Had I not, after all, just enacted what Butler would call a "refusal to recognize [an] identification that is, as it were, already made" (*Bodies* 113)? And doesn't the "refusal to identify with a given position [suggest] that on some level an identification has already taken place" (*Bodies* 113)? As Butler poses the question:

> What is the economic premise operating in the assumption that one identification is purchased at the expense of another? If heterosexual identification takes place *not* through the refusal to identify as homosexual but *through* an identification with an abject homosexuality that must, as it were, never show, then can we extrapolate that normative subject-positions more generally depend on and are articulated through a region of abjected identifications? (*Bodies* 112)

Following Butler's questions, I submit that my allowing her to like me only as a *straight* (for whom the term queer expresses . . .) could in itself have expressed my "own" *dislike*, my "own" heteronormative disidentification with or abjection of the very term I had, in fact, been liking. In other words, my jubilant recognition of myself in Butler's mirror-ph(r)ase concerning "straights for whom the term [queer] expresses an affiliation with anti-homophobic politics" could itself have been an expression of antihomophobic politics, of straight queer aspiration, *and of homophobia at the same time*. My "at last!" could mark a politically salutary move toward a disidentificatory practice, "a disloyalty against identity" (*Bodies* 220), a desire to reiterate heterosexuality differently, to be straight *otherwise* (which is of course what I want it to signify), and, at the same time, an all too familiar erasure of *otherness*, a most unwelcome reassertion of and insistence on "*my*" *straight* subjectivity's normative centrality (which is what I don't want it to signify but which it may despite my best intention).

There are, then, it seems, valid political reasons for both my desire to identify with the phrase concerning "straights for whom the term [queer] expresses..." and my growing suspicion of that desire. I dare say that many gays and lesbians will with justification be considerably more suspicious of my desire than I have managed to be in this essay thus far. On the other hand, I would like to imagine that there are no few straights who, like me, have begun to see the need for a critical interrogation of their "own" relationship to, and problematic identification/disidentification with, the queer theory I presume and hope they've been reading. For whatever the level of "our" straight aspirations toward or negotiations with queer theory may be, it needs, I think, to be accounted for, to be theorized. It should neither be simply proclaimed (for, as I hope to have just demonstrated, there would hardly seem to be any *simple* way to proclaim it) nor cursorily dismissed as "appropriation," as what James J. Sosnoski describes as "the assimilation of concepts into a governing framework .... [the] arrogation, confiscation, [or] seizure of concepts."[23]

But if there are valid political reasons for straight negotiations with queer theory to proceed (and equally valid reasons for proceeding with caution), such proceedings themselves raise questions about the institutional delimitations of such theoretical, political, and pedagogical projects. For example, it should be noted that just as the 1980s saw what some consider a egregiously depoliticizing move in the academy from "feminism" or "women's studies" to "gender studies"—a move that by some strange coincidence seemed to work largely to accommodate men like me[24]—so the decade of the 1990s has seen what could be considered a similarly depoliticizing shift from specifically "gay and lesbian studies" to the more general "queer theory"—a move that potentially opens the doors to straights, again like me.[25] In that thin volume the October 1994 *MLA Job Information List*, for example, Cornell University's English

Department invited applications for twentieth-century specialists working "in Queer Theory or Gay and Lesbian Studies." I doubt I'm the only one who noticed that "or" and pondered its implications.

I submit, however, that these terminological shifts within the profession—from feminism to gender studies, from gay and lesbian studies to queer theory—are, while potentially dangerous, not necessarily normativizing breaks with or betrayals of the political projects inscribed in the more specific nominations. They need to be read dialectically, in Fredric Jameson's sense of containing both reactionary and utopian potential. On the more obviously reactionary hand, what these transformations could be said to underscore is the deadly gravity that threatens to pull subversive or transgressive movements back toward the mainstream, thus emptying them of their subversive, transgressive content. Like my "at last!" dissected earlier, these shifts could be said to reveal just how intolerable it is for "my" subject-position and the structures that produce and maintain it to be denied the privileged place of absolute centrality: men *must* be accommodated; straights *must* be allowed in the door.

On the more tenuously utopian hand, however, the possibility might be left open that gender studies, queer theory, even my "at last!," are not altogether or necessarily signs of business as usual. After all, "gender studies" can do something more and other than waste faculty positions on " 'bright boys' "[26] or allow men "into" feminism (an allowance that for some erases or deradicalizes the feminist agenda); it can also designate the critical process by which (some) men learn *from* feminism in order to make subversive interventions into the reproduction of normative masculinity itself.[27] From a certain feminist perspective, such interventions into masculinity—by feminist women and men—are necessary because, as Kaja Silverman puts it, "masculinity impinges with such force upon femininity [that] to effect a large-scale reconfiguration of male identification and desire would, at the very least, permit female subjectivity to be lived differently than it is at present."[28] I submit, however, that a such a *large-scale* reconfiguration is unlikely without the participation of feminist-informed men who are or have been themselves the putative subjects of heteromasculine paradigms of identification and desire.[29]

Similar points can be made about queer theory, which may do more than squander rare queer faculty positions on straights (if such has ever happened) or in some other way allow straights "into" gay and lesbian studies (again, an allowance that for some would dematerialize the very possibility of queerness itself); rather, it might designate the critical process by which straights can learn from gay and lesbian theory to make interventions into the reproduction of heteronormativity or compulsory heterosexuality. To use Silverman's language, such interventions are necessary because heteronormativity impinges with such force on homosexuality that to effect a large-scale reconfiguration of heterosexual identification and desire would, at the very least, permit queer subjectivity to be lived differently than it is at present. Again, however, I submit that any large-scale reconfiguration is unlikely without the participation of those women and men who are themselves the putative subjects of heteronormative paradigms of identification and desire but who for whatever reason are "able to relish, learn from, or identify with" queers and queer theory.

Perhaps, then, my own troublesome marginalia and the very fact of my writing this essay need not necessarily be read as heralds of what Butler calls the "institutional domestication of queer thinking," that "normalizing [of] the queer [that] would be . . . its sad finish."[30] After all, despite the way I glommed on to the word "straight" in Butler's phrase (in a desire for acknowledgement perhaps politically inappropriate but nonetheless difficult to eradicate), and despite the desire for a safe identity that continued to subtend the risk of identity's incoherence (so that identification was abjected and identity itself perhaps never really put at risk)—despite all of that, I still maintain that there is something, well, queer about wanting to be recognized as a straight for whom the term "queer" expresses an affiliation with antihomophobic politics (as problematic as that desire for recognition itself might be). Though lesbians and gays may be justifiably suspicious of me as an ally, those who are our (if I can risk that possessive pronoun) most conspicuous enemies—the Christian Coalition and their Republican cohorts—would hardly mistake me for a friend.

Because I do teach their children.[31] And I do hope to participate in what bell hooks calls "teaching to transgress," in "education as the practice of freedom."[32] I believe not only that it is important for "us" to make antihomophobic politics a structural component of "our" teaching practice (along with feminism and antiracism) but that it is important, indeed crucial, for me *as a straight white man* to do so. For one political irony I've noted, and have asked students to note, in the six years or so that I've been professing feminism as an academic man is that I often have some modest success in making feminist interventions—i.e., in getting nonfeminist-identified male and female students to recognize the social and political realities of male domination and women's oppression—precisely because I am a man, because the students are all too well trained by patriarchy to associate my male voice with that of disinterested and objective authority and truth and so, sadly enough, to accept feminism from me more readily than they would from a feminist woman. My being a man at least prevents students from dismissing, with the all too familiar blather about male bashing, axe grinding, or merely "personal" grievance, the feminist analysis I present to them (while feminist students, when I'm lucky enough to have them in my classrooms, can help me see the blind spots in my own presentations).

That this irony obtains is, of course, as I also point out to students, a clear sign of how much feminist work remains to be done. In the feminist work that I try to do, I exploit my privileged position as much as I can in a way that, arguably, only someone in such a position is able. Or so I like to think. But of course the phrase "as much as I can" is troublesome. How can I know to what extent I "exploit" my position, to what extent I "subvert" it—the old saw about "subverting from within"—and to what extent I merely preserve my straight white male privilege and resist any real threat to it? For I, after all, can always retreat to that position of safety that I may, in fact, have never left; I can always reclaim that identity whose incoherence I may never really have risked. My body is never "really" put on the line. I have the *luxury* of a political unconscious.

Moreover, there is a certain tenuousness in the analogy I've been leading up to here between professing feminism as a man and in some way "doing" queer theory as a straight. On the one hand, there is some basis for the analogy in the strong connections between misogyny and homophobia that prevail within the dominant culture. Despite the complexities of these connections, the fact remains that one of the reasons for the dominant culture's hatred of gay men is that, in liking to be fucked by other men, they are perceived as behaving sexually "like women." As Catherine Waldby writes:

Homophobic violence . . . and homophobia in general might also be ways of adjudicating the anxiety aroused in heterosexual men by their own penetrability. If a potential for passive anal pleasure is denied, its denial can be acted out as violence against or contempt for, those who are interpreted as wishing to either experience such pleasure themselves, or to 'impose' it on another. In this sense the repression or elision of anal eroticism in heterosexual men can be seen to work not only along the lines of the masculine/feminine divide, but also along the homosexual/heterosexual divide.[33]

Heterosexual male derogation of "penetrable" women, then, helps consolidate and exacerbate straight hatred of, anxieties about, and violence against gay men. Conversely, the celebration of women in *all* human capacities—including the capacity to enjoy being fucked—can work to defuel and dissipate the hatred of men who may enjoy the same thing.[34] Not that straight male anxieties about penetrability totally account for misogyny and homophobia; not that varieties of homophobia among feminists and misogyny among gay men don't flourish; not that feminist and queer politics are automatically or necessarily the same thing: but there are compelling reasons for projecting the two as being in structural solidarity. So there would seem to be a political logic in suggesting that the project of being/teaching as a male feminist leads necessarily to that of being/teaching as a straight for whom the term queer expresses.

And yet, on the other hand, I can teach and profess feminism until the cows come home without ever feeling myself "in danger" of being "mistaken" for or, more to the point, "treated as" a woman. In fact, given the number of films in the last ten years or more that feature men "getting in touch with their 'feminine' side"—from *Tootsie,* with Dustin Hoffman in drag, to the more recent *Junior,* which offers the spectacle of a pregnant Schwarznegger—I imagine that discourses of androgyny or imputations of male "femininity" are no longer particularly troublesome for many straight men—provided, of course, that "femininity" or even "maternity" imply absolutely nothing sexual. In other words, it's quite all right for straight men to "get in touch with 'the feminine side,' " to acknowledge the "woman within," provided that "she" neither "values powerlessness"—to use Bersani's words[35]—nor enjoys being fucked.

But the comfort level plunges—and conventional, exclusionary logic reels—at the more radical suggestion that the straight man might "get in touch with his queer side." After all, there is little "danger" in an untransgendered man's being literally mistaken for a woman; the mistake rarely happens and can be easily "rectified." But there can be nothing more terrifying to what Monique Wittig calls "the straight mind"[36] than being "mistaken" for a "queer." This power of horror dominates the straight mind, particularly the straight male mind, not simply because the dominant culture's most repetitive message to men is that it is infinitely preferable for them to compete with each other viciously, to batter each other violently, even to murder each other brutally, than it is for them to fuck each other passionately. This terror of being mistaken for a queer dominates the straight mind, again, not simply because, since bad things do happen to "real" queers, bad things could also happen to the straight "mistakenly" or (worse) "unjustly" taken for a "queer" ("unjustly," as if, according to the same logic for which there are "innocent" victims of AIDS, the real queers who get bashed, or murdered, or AIDS, are simply getting their just deserts).

The terror of being mistaken for a queer dominates the straight mind because this terror *constitutes* the straight mind; it is precisely that culturally produced and reinforced horror of/fascination with abjected homosexuality that produces and maintains "the straight mind" as such, governing not so much specific sexual practices between men and women (after all, these things happen) as the *institution* (arguably antisexual) of heteronormativity itself. For according to some queer theorists, heteronormativity, "straightness as such," is less a function of other-sexual desire than of the disavowal or abjection of that imagined same-sex desire on which straightness never ceases to depend. To quote D. A. Miller, the "only necessary content" of male heterosexuality is "not a desire for women, but the negation of the desire for men" (128). As Miller continues, this necessary negation is such that "straight men unabashedly *need* gay men, whom they forcibly recruit (as the object of their blows or, in better circles, their jokes) to enter into a polarization that exorcises the 'woman' in man through assigning it to a class of man who may be considered to be no 'man' at all."[37]

Homophobia, then, is on one level the fear of homosexual women and men. On another level, it is the disavowal of this dependence on homosexuals, of the structurating necessity of this negation. On another level still, homophobia entails not only the fear of those who are abjectly identified (and depended on) but also the fear of being abjectly identifiable oneself—the fear, as the word most literally means, of being "the same as." This latter fear is arguably a much stronger component of homophobia than of, say, sexism or racism (despite the mechanisms of projection and abjection doubtless at work in those forms of hatred), because the sexist male or the racist white is in much less "danger" of being "mistaken" for a woman or a nonwhite than the straight is of being "mistaken" for a queer. For that reason, despite the structural, constitutive roles that "femininity" and "blackness" play in constructions of "masculinity" and "whiteness," the role played by "queerness" in the construction of "straightness" is even more structural and constitutive; racism and sexism, that is, certainly help to "keep one" white and male but not in the same way or to the same extent that homophobia works to "keep one" straight.[38]

Several consequences arise from this positing of homophobia as the fear of being out of one's own keeping, an aspect of the fear of nonself-identity as such and perhaps, at least at this particular historical juncture, the dominant culture's most prominent figure for that fear. First of all, despite postmodern theory's destabilizations of such "biological" matters as sexual difference or skin pigmentation as self-evident empirical indices of gendered or racialized identity, the dominant culture itself blithely continues to behave as if such matters could be taken "for granted" as compelling or reassuring evidence of identity-formation. But the dominant culture is more suspicious, more self-suspicious, and hence more self-policing, when it comes to "proving" heterosexuality. For it is possible, after all, to "fake" the "realest" possible "evidence" of heterosexuality; man or woman, one can participate in heterosexual marriage and even help produce a brood of spawn and still "turn out" to have been "living a lie," to have been "really" gay or lesbian all along. Precisely because there is no final "proof" of heterosexuality, heterosexuality must constantly set about trying to prove itself, assert itself, insist on itself. Indeed, as Butler argues, heterosexuality as hegemonic institution is finally nothing more than its own repetitive self-insistence, nothing other than "a constant and repeated effort to imitate its own idealizations" (*Bodies* 125). Or, as Janet E. Halley puts it in regard to legalistic constructions of heterosexuality, normative heterosexuality "is a highly unstable, default characterization for people who have not marked themselves or been marked by others as homosexual." As Halley continues, "The resulting class of heterosexuals is a default class, home to those who have not fallen out of it."[39] Heteronormativity, then, has something—itself—to prove, but it has no other proof of itself than its own repeated efforts at self-demonstration. The structurating persistence of homophobia within heteronormativity seems the strongest evidence not only that its best efforts have proven insufficient but that such insufficiency—and, hence, the relentless need for "proof"—is integral to heteronormativity's very mechanisms of self-production.

A second point arising from the notion of homophobia as fear of nonself-identity per se is that such fears can be conflated only in response to specific historical pressures that work to constrain and maintain identity-formation as such. If we follow Foucault's well-known argument in

The History of Sexuality that it wasn't until the nineteenth century that a network of medical and juridical discourses produced the equation between sexual practices and the "truth" of personal identity—that it wasn't until the nineteenth century that the homosexual "became a personage"[40]—then we recognize that it is only after the nineteenth century that homophobia as fear of being identified as homosexual could subtend in any extensive way the fear of nonself-identity per se. In other social and historical contexts, other fears, involving class, nationality, race, or religious affiliation, could have a more dominant role in the maintenance of coherent identity boundaries or ego-syntony. However, in this particular context—by which I mean the contemporary United States—I argue that homophobia is so dominant among the fears of nonself-identity that are currently culturally deployed to produce identity as such that the fear of being marked "different" as such is thoroughly intricated with, if not overdetermined by, the fear of being queered.

My point here is that the fear of being queered, of being out of one's own keeping, can work to "constrain in advance" the otherwise straight's queer aspiration, his or her desire to affiliate with a term that expresses antihomophobic politics, in ways the aspirant may not immediately recognize. As Bersani puts it in *Homos*, "Given the pressures and privileges intrinsic to the position one occupies on the great homo-heterosexual divide in our society, we can . . . appreciate the anxiety, on the part of those straights most openly sympathetic with gay causes, not to be themselves mistaken for one of those whose rights they commendably defend" (1). *I* must admit, then, that this anxiety may subtend whatever risks I may think I take as a straight professor who "does" queer theory (for I could hardly profess straightness and at the same time claim not to participate in that which I've just argued constitutes it). Certainly this anxiety is inscribed in my "at last!," in my effort to reclaim identity in the midst of a (potentially) radically disidentificatory gesture (for what is identity, after all, but the effect of having controlled, having reeled in, one's errant identifications?). With that "at last," in other words, I seem to say that I'm quite pleased and satisfied to have identified with queer discourse and even to identify with the signifier "queer"—so long as it's understood that I'm "really" straight.

I also must confess that I confront my own fear of being queered when I encounter, in Lauren Berlant's and Elizabeth Freeman's essay "Queer Nationality," the following advice from a treatise called "I Hate Straights": " 'Go tell [straights to] go away until they have spent a month walking hand in hand in public with someone of the same sex. After they survive that, then you'll hear what they have to say about queer anger. Otherwise, tell them to shut up and listen.' "[41] Although this passage is directed not at "straights for whom the term queer expresses..." but rather toward "straights [who] ask the gay community to self-censor, because anger is not 'productive' "—a request I've never made—the passage nonetheless leads me to face my own hesitancy to conduct the month-long experiment it describes.[42] It suggests that, while identity may be discursively constructed, to risk identity only at the level of discourse is to risk very little indeed. It compels me to admit that "I" must, after all, be deeply afraid of being taken for a queer.

However, one important point that arises from Butler's argument is that on a certain level the straight is, to use a tired phrase, always already taken for a queer, self-mis-taken for a queer, and that there is, therefore, in a sense, really no mistake at all. For as Butler might put it, to profess straightness is to claim identity within an economy that assumes that one identification can be purchased only at the expense of another. But what this expensive assumption lays bare is the fact that other identifications are available for purchase but have been refused. As Butler suggests, however, the refusal of an identification indicates that on some level it has already taken place. If straightness, therefore, depends structurally less on other-sex desire than on abjected queer identification, then to profess straightness is always to acknowledge that, on some level, *one must have already taken oneself for a queer.*[43]

One possible goal, then, of a straight negotiation with queer theory is to let this acknowledgment proceed. The point would be neither to appropriate the signifier queer nor to arrogate or confiscate queer theory but rather to proliferate the *findings* of queer theory in unexpected ways, or at least from unexpected points of enunciation, in the hope, however feeble, of reiterating heterosexuality otherwise. Such a reiteration begins with, and perhaps can be nothing more than, the recognition and acknowledgement that straightness, like all identity-formation, is an effect of constitutive exclusion and thus never ceases to depend on the excluded, the *part maudit*, the abjected itself—the recognition and acknowledgement that all along one has needed "the queer" that one really is(n't) to be "the straight" that (no) one (ever) really is. Such a recognition would constitute a challenge—a limited challenge, granted, but a challenge nonetheless—to an institutional heterosexuality that imagines itself safely ensconced within its own "natural" self-sufficiency, that reiterates itself as solely and transparently a function of other-sex desire, that presents itself as what Diana Fuss calls "a practice governed by some internal necessity" rather than by constitutive exclusion. For if, as Fuss writes, compulsory heterosexuality "secures its self-identity and shores up its ontological boundaries by protecting itself from what it sees as the continual predatory encroachment of its contaminated other,"[44] then radical heterosexuality or self-conscious straightness—which is to say, other-conscious straightness, straightness that recognizes and somehow acknowledges its dependence on the queerness in which it does(n't) participate—would not protect but rather *open* itself to the possibility of its own structural dependence *on* its constitutively excluded other. It would, in other words, own up to the exclusions by which it proceeds, as well as to the ultimate unownability of its own idealizations. For if heteronormativity or institutional heterosexuality is nothing more than the effort to live up to its own relentlessly reiterated ideals, "a constant and repeated effort to imitate its own idealizations" (*Bodies* 125), then self(-as-other)-conscious straightness—straightness, that is, with a twist[45]—is not and can never exactly be the "ideal" (institutional, compulsory) way for heterosexuality to reiterate or imitate itself. Straightness with a twist would, rather, work to mitigate, or militate against, those institutional, compulsory ideals, those compulsory performances. As Butler puts it:

Insofar as heterosexual gender norms produce inapproximable ideals, heterosexuality can be said to operate through the regulated production of hyperbolic versions of "man" and "woman." These are for the most part compulsory performances, ones which none us choose, but which each of is forced to negotiate. I write "forced to negotiate" because the compulsory character of these norms does not always make them efficacious. Such norms are continually haunted by their own inefficacy; hence the anxiously repeated effort to install and augment their jurisdiction. The resignification of norms is thus a function of their inefficacy, and so the question of subversion, of *working the weakness in the norm*, becomes a matter in inhabiting the practices of its rearticulation. (*Bodies* 237)

Of course, like any other form of postmodern "subversion," the political value of "working the weakness in the norm" is open to question. But if there is any political value in straight queer aspiration, in straight disloyalty to straight identity, it may be only this: to assist in working the weakness in the heterosexual norm, to *inhabit* the practice of heterosexuality's rearticulation and *inhibit* its hegemonic dominance. If heterosexual norms are, as Butler puts it, "continually haunted by their own inefficacy," then perhaps the work of the straight theorist with queer aspirations is somehow to be the inefficacious ghost in the house of heteronormativity.

As I hope to have suggested here, however, such work, such haunting, can be conducted only from critical positions that are themselves constrained by culturally produced anxieties that may be acknowledged after the fact but cannot always be known and mastered in advance. As Butler would argue, however, it is exactly this lack of mastery, this *productive failure* to master the terms of identity, anxiety, and desire, that needs to be safeguarded and promoted in the interest of proliferating critical queerness, of risking (if only in critical discourse) identity's incoherence. What and how much straights can do to proliferate queerness, to make the world queerer than ever, remains to be seen, and I hope here to have opened a question rather than to have offered any final words. But I submit that whatever any of us do, however we perform (and whomever we perform with), the extent to which our actions and performances are "critically queer" may be the extent to which we promote connections—erotic and political, with others and with the world—that indeed seem possible only if identity and identity politics are allowed to be put at risk.

CODA

Butler writes: " 'Queer' derives its force precisely through the repeated invocation by which it has become linked to accusation, pathologizaton, insult. This is an invocation by which a social bond among homophobic communities is formed through time. The interpellation echoes past interpellations, and binds the speakers, as if they spoke in unison across time. In this sense, it is always an imaginary chorus that taunts 'queer' " (*Bodies* 226).

As a straight, I know that I have most likely in some way (though I can't recall specific instances) lent my voice to this chorus. But I have also heard it singing and thought that it was singing to me. Two choral incidents, or echoes of past interpellations, both well before the possibility of my considering any "straight" affiliation with the signifier "queer": I am sixteen or so, standing with a group of men in the grocery store where, working for my father, I spent no small part of my childhood and adolescence. I have managed to "establish" my heterosexuality, letting the fact of my being "sexually active" with my "girlfriend" be known, participating in the heteromasculinist rituals of ogling and "rating" women shoppers, and so on. And yet, when a woman passes by pushing a shopping cart laden with screaming kids and I casually remark that I don't really like children very much, one of the men (he worked in the meat market) turns to me. Eyes narrowed to slits, he says: "What are you, some kinda queer?"

He did have a point. That is, he spoke the logic of heteronormativity with a relentless precision. For the imperative behind the norm is not simply to enjoy having sex with women but (since we're using the Althusserian language of interpellation here) to reproduce the conditions of production. Heteronormative sex is teleologically narrativized sex—sex with a goal, a purpose, and a product. The ends—children—justify the means, which are otherwise unjustifiable. The child, then, is not simply the outcome of but the justification for having engaged in sex. For as Bersani puts it, "There is a big secret about sex: most people don't like it" ("Rectum" 197). That is, most "people" don't like sex because, again, as Bersani has it, sex is inimical to personhood, incompatible with the self as a structured (heteronormatively structured) ego. So perhaps, as I suggest in passing in the body of this essay, heteronormativity is antisexual in that it tolerates sex only as a means toward the reproduction of "the person"— in terms of both "the child" and the ego. Perhaps heteronormativity, then, is abrogated whenever people actually like sex. And perhaps people who do like sex (the childfree het couple, for example) are, in a sense, "queer" (the man in the grocery store certainly thought as much). Correspondingly, perhaps people who fuck in the name of identity, who make an identity out of whom they fuck, who fuck to reproduce "the person," are fucking heteronormatively—are, in a sense, "breeders"—even if "the person" or "identity" thereby reproduced is "homosexual."

Second incident/interpellation: It is ten years or so later, and I am walking in daylight through my neighborhood in Atlanta: Midtown, an area so well known to have a large gay male population that goon squads from the suburbs and hinterlands often drive through looking for gays to taunt and bash. So it is no surprise when a car pulls up from behind and slows down, and the chorus sings: "Hey *queer!*"

I turned. Perhaps not in the full "one-hundred-and-eighty-degree physical conversion" described by Althusser in his example of interpellation as turning in response to being hailed by the cop who says "Hey, you there!"[46] but I did turn. Had it been night, I might have had to turn and run, since I'm not sure what I might have done to "prove" that they had "the wrong man," had "mistaken" my "identity." After all, I had turned. I was walking in a "gay" neighborhood. I was wearing "gay" clothes: jeans and a shirt. And I don't think the postmodern argument that all identity is a mistake, a "necessary error" (*Bodies* 229), would have been much help even if I had even known anything about such notions at the time. Fortunately for me, the car sped on, with a great squealing of tires on the hot Georgia asphalt, and I was left only with the knowledge that I had turned—a vague knowledge, a recognition, with which I didn't exactly know what to do. Fifteen years and a whole lot of theory later, I don't know in the name of what I would say that it wasn't "really me" who was really "meant by the hailing," that it wasn't "me" who was "really" being addressed.

NOTES

1. Lauren Berlant and Michael Warner, "What Does Queer Theory Teach Us about *X?*" *PMLA* 110, no. 3 (May 1995): 345. Further references to this work will be included parenthetically in the text.

2. "Critical" in this usage obviously invokes political investment, as Andrew Parker's discussion in "Foucault's Tongues," *Mediations* 18, no. 2 (Fall 1994), would suggest: commenting on "the genealogy of queerness as a non-gender-specific rubric that defines itself diacritically not against heterosexuality but against the normative," Parker goes on to say that this distinction is "captured neatly in what I think is a pretty fair joke: 'What's the difference between gay and queer?' 'There are no queer Republicans' " (80).

3. In "What Does Queer Theory Teach Us about *X?*" Berlant and Warner write: "In our view, it is not useful to consider queer theory a thing, especially one dignified by capital letters. We wonder whether *queer commentary* might not more accurately describe the things linked by the rubric, most of which are not theory. The metadiscourse of 'queer theory' intends an academic object, but queer commentary has vital precedents and collaborations in aesthetic genres and journalism. It cannot be assimilated to a single discourse, let alone a propositional program" (343).

4. Michael Warner, "Introduction," *Fear of a Queer Planet: Queer Politics and Social Theory*, ed. Michael Warner (Minneapolis: University of Minnesota Press, 1993), xxvii. Further references to this work will be included parenthetically in the text.

5. I take the word "dis-positional" from Ed Cohen's essay "Are We (Not) What We Are Becoming? 'Gay' 'Identity,' 'Gay Studies,' and the Disciplining of Knowledge," *Engendering Men: The Question of Male Feminist Criticism*, ed. Joseph A. Boone and Michael Cadden (New York: Routledge, 1990), 160–75. There Cohen answers the question of identity politics with a hearty cry of " 'Fuck identity.' Or perhaps more accurately, let's not make an 'identity' out of whom we fuck" (174). Cohen goes on to counsel "abjuring our hard-won gay and lesbian 'identities' in favor of more relational, more mobile categories: 'gay dis-positions'

or 'lesbian attitudes,' for example" (174). See also Cohen's "Who are 'We'?: Gay 'Identity' as Political (E)motion (A Theoretical Rumination)," *Inside/Out: Lesbian Theories, Gay Theories*, ed. Diana Fuss (New York: Routledge, 1991), where he asks: "How can we affirm a relational and transformational politics of self that takes as its process and its goal the interruption of those practices of differentiation that (re)produce historically specific patterns of privilege and oppression?" (89).

6. L. A. Kauffman, "Radical Change: The Left Attacks Identity Politics," *The Village Voice* 37, no. 26 (June 30, 1992): 20.

7. Alexander Doty, *Making Things Perfectly Queer: Interpreting Mass Culture* (Minneapolis: University of Minnesota Press, 1993), xvii–xix.

8. Michael Warner, "Homo-Narcissism: or, Heterosexuality." *Engendering Men: The Question of Male Feminist Criticism*, ed. Joseph A. Boone and Michael Cadden (New York: Routledge, 1990), 191.

9. Although the question of exclusion seems prominent in my discussion thus far, I do not intend this essay as some inane lament that straights are being excluded from an interesting new theoretical project or that the contributions of straights to this project are not being adequately recognized. I do attempt to address the problematic of my own desire for inclusion, recognition, and visibility later in the essay, but here I stress that my purpose is not to whine about exclusion but to explore the productive definitional tensions opened up by new reworkings of the term "queer."

10. Eve Kosofsky Sedgwick, *Tendencies* (Durham: Duke University Press, 1993), 8. Further references to this work will be included parenthetically in the text.

11. Teresa de Lauretis, "Habit Changes," *Differences: A Journal of Feminist Cultural Studies* 6, no. 2&3 (1994): 297.

12. Teresa de Lauretis, *The Practice of Love: Lesbian Sexuality and Perverse Desire* (Bloomington: Indiana University Press, 1994), xvii. For negative or "critique-al" (*sic*) readings of queer theory that concern not its sexual overinclusiveness but its conspicuous failure to produce Marxist revolution, see Rosemary Hennessy's "Queer Visibility and Commodity Culture," *Cultural Critique* 29 (1994–95): 31–75, and Don Morton's "Birth of the Cyberqueer," *PMLA* 110, no. 3 (May 1995): 369–81. Hennessy's essay is for the most part a salutary reminder of the need to consider queer theory in terms of the relations between sexuality and capitalism; however, she seems overly eager to reduce all queer theory to an academic marketing ploy, to "capital's insidious and relentless expansion," to a "gay visibility aimed at producing new and potentially lucrative markets," and thus to strategies in which "money, not liberation, is the bottom line" (32). Morton similarly but less convincingly collapses all queer theory into a ludic postmodernism that he judges to be nothing but the latest ruse and symptom of late capitalism. See also his "The Politics of Queer Theory in the (Post)Modern Moment," *Genders* 17 (1993): 121–50.

13. Leo Bersani, *Homos* (Cambridge, Mass.: Harvard University Press, 1995), 71–72. Further references to this work will be included parenthetically in the text.

14. Leo Bersani, "Is the Rectum a Grave?" *October* 43 (winter 1987): 197–222. Further references to this work will be included parenthetically in the text.

15. Jonathan Dollimore, *Sexual Dissidence: Augustine to Wilde, Freud to Foucault* (Oxford: Oxford University Press, 1991), 321. Further references to this work will be included parenthetically in the text.

16. Actually, one could argue that in a strange way Bersani's arguments do resonate with certain Buddhist deconstructions of the self, but that would require another essay altogether. For discussion of "discarding the self" as the objective of Buddhist practice, see Mark Epstein, *Thoughts Without a Thinker: Psychotherapy from a Buddhist Perspective* (New York: Basic Books, 1995).

17. For an interesting extension of Bersani's points about anal eroticism to the specific question of straight male sexuality, see Catherine Waldby's excellent "Destruction: Boundary Erotics and the Refigurations of the Heterosexual Male Body," in *Sexy Bodies: The Strange Carnalities of Feminism*, ed. Elizabeth Grosz and Elspeth Probyn (New York: Routledge, 1995), 266–77. Waldby writes: "Anal eroticism carries disturbingly feminizing connotations. Part of the significance of intercourse understood in its ideological aspect is its assertion not just of the woman's penetrability but of the man's impenetrability, the exclusive designation of his body by its seamless, phallic mastery. . . . But the possibilities of anal erotics for the masculine body amount to an abandonment of this phallic claim. The ass is soft and sensitive, and associated with pollution and shame, like the vagina. It is non-specific with regard to genital difference in that everybody has one. It allows access into the body, when after all only women are supposed to have a vulnerable interior space. All this makes anal eroticism a suasive point for the displacement of purely phallic boundaries" (272). Given Waldby's comments, it may seem a tremendous evasion on my part to say that exploring the relationship between *my* straight male identity and *my* anal eroticism (digital, relatively shallow, and largely solitary) is beyond the scope of this essay. I do, however, rather extensively consider the question of the anus as a site of significant leakage for masculine subjectivity in *Male Matters: Masculinity, Anxiety, and the Male Body on the Line* (Urbana: University of Illinois Press, 1996), though even there, because I focus more on "productive" than receptive anal eroticism, I remain open to the charge of keeping my ass covered.

18. I find problematic anyway the notion that subjects can voluntaristically "change" their sexual practices. Certainly change is possible, but such voluntarism plays all too well into the right-wing religious rhetoric of homosexuality as a perverse but alterable "lifestyle choice" and pseudotherapeutic efforts to convert gays and lesbians to "healthy" heterosexuality. Moreover, though I agree with Bersani that there are salutary political *possibilities* inscribed in anti-identitarian sexuality per se, it isn't clear to me, or to him, that any specific sexual practice has an *intrinsic* political value in itself, or, correspondingly, that any change in sexual practice has intrinsic political value.

19. Judith Butler, *Bodies That Matter: On the Discursive Limits of "Sex"* (New York: Routledge, 1993), 220. Further references to this work will be included parenthetically in the text.

20. Judith Roof makes some comments in her review essay "Hypothalamic

Criticism: Gay Male Studies and Male Feminist Criticism," *American Literary History* 4, no. 2 (Summer 1992): 355–64, that are pertinent here. Referring to Boone and Cadden's *Engendering Men: The Question of Male Feminist Criticism* (New York: Routledge, 1990), Roof writes: "this anthology's biggest anxieties (and most annoying tics) are linked to problems of recognition: . . . to the proper acknowledgement of male feminist efforts, to the continual reminder of the presence of 'right-thinking,' well-meaning men. This is not to say that anxieties about visibility are necessarily harmful or appropriative; it is to question how the specific stake in visibility shapes the interrelation among connected but diverse critical practices" (356–57). My aim here is to interrogate my own anxiety, not to insist on visibility or to engage in what Roof calls "the struggle for the right kind of visibility [that] continues among men in a battle that seems to shift the stake of identity politics from authenticity and a 'right' to speak to the crucial importance of being seen speaking" (357). The unavoidable irony, of course, is that I am here visibly offering my self-interrogation up for recognition (or at least for reading).

21. See my *Male Matters: Masculinity, Anxiety, and the Male Body on the Line* (Urbana: University of Illinois Press, 1996).

22. Jonathan Culler, "Lace, Lance, and Pair," *Profession 94* (1994): 5.

23. James J. Sosnoski, "A Mindless Man-Driven Theory Machine: Intellectuality, Sexuality, and the Institution of Criticism," *Feminisms: An Anthology of Literary Theory and Criticism*, ed. Robyn Warhol and Diane L. Herndl (New Brunswick, N.J.: Rutgers University Press, 1993), 50. Concerning "appropriation," while I fully understand the sentiment that straight affiliations with queer theory can pose the threat of "appropriation" in the sense of an arrogant confiscation that negates difference and works to erase signs of the real social presence of lesbians and gays, it seems problematic to me that in some discursive contexts merely to *charge* appropriation—without having demonstrated where and how the appropriation takes place (a demonstration that would necessarily depend on some attention to specific existing articulations)—is to *prove* appropriation. This is politically understandable, perhaps even strategically desirable, and certainly the burden of proof should be placed largely on the subject supposed to appropriate. But the charge of appropriation can function as an expedient way of not actually having to consider or contest the legitimacy or validity of a specific interpretation or argument. As for myself, I admire the distinction Gloria Anzaldúa makes, in her introduction to *Making Face, Making Soul/Hacienda Caras: Creative and Critical Perspectives by Feminist of Color* (San Francisco: Aunt Lute, 1990), between "appropriation" and "proliferation." I would like, but do not expect, this essay to be received as an example of the latter.

24. In a recent interview, "Feminism By Any Other Name," *Differences: A Journal of Feminist Cultural Studies* 6, no. 2&3 (1994): 27–61, Rosi Braidotti characterizes gender studies as "the take-over of the feminist agenda by studies on masculinity, which results in transferring funding from feminist faculty positions to other kinds of positions. There have been cases . . . of positions advertised as 'gender studies' being given away to [i.e., wasted upon] the 'bright boys.' Some of the competitive take-over has to do with gay studies. Of special significance in this discussion is the role of the mainstream publisher Routledge who, in our

opinion, is responsible for promoting gender as a way of deradicalizing the feminist agenda, re-marketing masculinity and gay male identity instead" (44–45). Although she has valuable things to say in other portions of this interview, here Braidotti seems to see not just queer theory but all gay studies only as a marketing ploy with no other purpose than the erasure of feminism. This view is problematic in that it occludes the fact that, as Joseph Allen Boone points out, "many of the men in the academy who are feminism's most supportive 'allies' *are* gay"; see "Of Me(n) and Feminism," *Engendering Men: The Question of Male Feminist Criticism*, ed. Joseph A. Boone and Michael Cadden (New York: Routledge, 1990), 23. See also Craig Owens, "Outlaws: Gay Men in Feminism," *Men in Feminism*, ed. Alice Jardine and Paul Smith (New York: Methuen, 1987), 219–32. Braidotti also ignores the fact that some "studies of masculinity" have been conducted by feminists, for example, Kaja Silverman's *Male Subjectivity at the Margins* (New York: Routledge, 1992). Finally, Braidotti's formulation is also a bit disingenuous in that it pretends that feminism and the careers of certain feminist theorists have not been helped by the marketing strategies of "mainstream" publishers such as Routledge.

25. Does a straight male's engagement with feminism *necessarily* lead to a negotiation with queer theory? That is, can the gender system be investigated by anyone *without* a consideration of the hetero/homo divide, or, as Eve Sedgwick contends in *Epistemology of the Closet* (Berkeley: University of California Press, 1990), would anyone's investigation of any aspect of modernity be "not merely incomplete, but damaged in its central substance to the degree that it does not incorporate a critical analysis of modern homo-heterosexual definition" (1)? Conversely, as some feminists have charged, might a move toward queer theory, with its emphasis on sexualities, provide a convenient means of neglecting feminism's insistent focus on sexual difference and gender asymmetry? For discussions of the problematic relationship between feminism and queer theory, see the "More Gender Trouble: Feminism Meets Queer Theory" issue of *Differences* 6, no. 2&3 (1994), particularly Butler's "Against Proper Objects," 1–26, and her interview with Rosi Braidotti, "Feminism By Any Other Name," 27–61. For a discussion of the way queer theory's emphasis on sexualities can work to efface or ignore gender, see Biddy Martin, "Sexualities Without Genders and Other Queer Utopias," *diacritics* 24, no. 2–3 (summer/fall 1994): 104–21. As for the question of a necessary connection between male feminism and queer theory, I should say that my own work, as exemplified in *Male Matters*, began as a more or less self-consciously "male feminist" project but was pushed toward the question of queer theory not by my own desire to be theoretically trendy but by readers of the manuscript who suggested that the absence of attention to gay male criticism was its major blindspot. I have to confess that, for this straight male feminist, the push toward queer theory—a push against my own initial resistance and indifference—was a function more of the relatively autonomous velocity of an intellectual project than of my own conscious desire.

26. See Bradotti's comments in note 24.

27. Along with Joseph Allen Boone in his "Of Me(n) and Feminism" essay, I still consider Alice Jardine's essay "Men in Feminism: Odor di Uomo or Compag-

nons de Route?" *Men in Feminism*, ed. Alice Jardine and Paul Smith (New York: Methuen, 1987), 54–61, to contain the best practical advice for such men.

28. Kaja Silverman's *Male Subjectivity at the Margins* (New York: Routledge, 1992), 2–3.

29. And yet this "male feminist" participation is unlikely to reconfigure anything at all if it "redefin[es] feminist method as a politics of visibility . . . which then applies to males as *equal* victims of an oppressive, obscuring gender system" (Roof 356, emphasis added) or if "the turn to gender obfuscates or denies the asymmetrical relation of sexual difference" (Judith Butler, "Against Proper Objects," *Differences: A Journal of Feminist Cultural Studies* 6, no. 2&3 [1994]: 49). To say that the gender system is oppressive and to suggest that within that system "masculinity" is no less of a gendered position, no less of a "social category imposed upon a sexed body" (Joan Scott, "Gender: A Useful Category of Historical Analysis," *Gender and the Politics of History* [New York: Columbia University Press, 1988], 32), than is "femininity," is *not* to say that the two positions are symmetrical or that the system oppresses both genders equally, as some critics of the "turn to gender" suggest that the turn itself implies. Braidotti, for example, in "Feminism by Any Other Name," writes that "the focus on gender rather than sexual difference presumes that men and women are constituted in symmetrical ways. But this misses the feminist point about masculine dominance. In such a system, the masculine and the feminine are in a structurally dissymmetrical position: men, as the empirical referent of the masculine, cannot be said to have a gender; rather they are expected to carry the Phallus—which is something different. They are expected to exemplify abstract virility, which is hardly an easy task" (38). Though I would certainly grant Braidotti's last point, I fail to understand how the exemplification of abstract virility that is expected of masculinity is not gender, particularly if gender is understood in de Lauretis's terms as "the process of assuming, taking on, identifying with the positionalities and meaning effects specified by a particular society's gender system" ("Habit Changes" 302). To insist, then, on masculinity as gender, and on the politically salutary contributions of men to gender studies, is, again, *not* to presume that "men and women are constituted in symmetrical ways." Therefore, I would disagree with Bradotti's point "that gender studies presumes and institutionalizes a false 'symmetry' between men and women" (38).

30. Judith Butler, "Against Proper Objects," *Differences: A Journal of Feminist Cultural Studies* 6, no. 2&3 (1994): 21.

31. I turn this particular phrase to allude to comments reportedly made recently by America's favorite demagogue (and, as Al Franken has recently called him with great accuracy, "big fat idiot"), Rush Limbaugh: "When lampooning an academic who had written about 'male lesbians,' [Limbaugh] sternly offered this warning: 'This woman is teaching your kids.' When a caller told him, 'I'm gonna be a conservative professor,' Limbaugh responded, 'We need every one of you that we can get.' " Jeff Klinzman, "Life With Dittohead or How I Learned to Stop Worrying About Right-Wingers and Just Dig the Beat," *Wapsipinicon Almanac*, no. 5: 47. Now, I'm not sure exactly which of us academics it was who had written about "male lesbians" (though a likely candidate would be Jacquelyn Zita, "Male

Lesbians and the Postmodern Body," *Hypatia* 7, no. 4 [1992]: 106–27). Nor do I know exactly what a male lesbian would be, other than a male-to-female transsexual who has sex with women. But there are, I think, reasons for the designation to be attractive, not as a marker of identity—and let me clearly state that, while I might include the term in a general rubric of straight queer aspiration, I do not claim to identify or "style" myself as a male lesbian—but rather as a signifier that might strategically assist in "the labor of ambiguating categories of identity" or in resisting "regimes of the normal." Not the least reason for the term to be compelling is its rhetorical power to appall, irritate, and mystify a Rush Limbaugh. On the other hand, the umbrage that the term might cause some lesbians themselves, who have certainly been irritated enough, is sufficient reason to let it drop. Ed Cohen, for example, mentions "male lesbians" in "Are We (Not) What We Are Becoming" (174), and Judith Roof is not amused, calling Cohen's phrase "a jest perhaps, but too close to the truth of habitual masculinist assumptions to be really funny" ("Hypothalamic" 362). Butler, however, in *Bodies That Matter,* apparently isn't joking when she asks, "And if [a] man desires another man, or a woman, is his desire homosexual, heterosexual, or even lesbian? And what is to restrict any given individual to a single identification?" (99). It is, of course, salutary to ask about the grounds for restriction. But one might also ask what, exactly, would constitute a man's sexual desire for a woman as "lesbian"? What, for that matter, constitutes lesbian desire as lesbian? In *The Practice of Love: Lesbian Sexuality and Perverse Desire,* Teresa de Lauretis writes about the problematic relationship between lesbian and certain feminist identifications. She writes that "the seductiveness of lesbianism for feminism lies in the former's figuration of a female desiring subjectivity to which all women may accede by virtue of their 'homosexual' relation to the mother. . . . Without denying for a moment that the relation to the mother has a fundamental influence on all forms of female subjectivity, I will argue that woman-identification and desire or object-choice do not form a continuum, as some feminist revisions of Freud would have it. The seduction of the homosexual-maternal metaphor derives from the erotic charge of *a desire for women which, unlike masculine desire, affirms and enhances the female-sexed subject and represents her possibility of access to a sexuality autonomous from the male.* But in the great majority of feminist psychoanalytic writings (Rose, Doane, Silverman, Sprengnether, Gallop, Jacobus, etc.), such access is paradoxically secured by erasing the actual sexual difference between lesbians and heterosexual women" (xvii, emphasis added). I do not want to address the larger terms of de Lauretis's argument here. Even less do I want to erase the actual sexual difference between lesbians and heterosexual *men* by suggesting that the two groups "have something in common"—i.e., women as objects of desire. What I do want to suggest is that, since there is nothing natural or inevitable about "masculine desire," there is no reason why heterosexual men could not adopt or aspire to the emphasized description just given as a sort of an ethics (provided, of course, that the word "autonomous" is read in terms of subjective sexual agency rather in the exclusive sense of separation). What I am suggesting, in other words, is the possibility of obversing the "masculinization of the lesbian" that obtains in classical, normative psychoanalysis and working toward what might be called a "lesbianization" of masculine desire—or rather, working toward a version of masculine desire, call it whatever, that, unlike the one de Lauretis names, affirms and enhances female-sexed subjectivity.

32. bell hooks, *Teaching to Transgress: Education as the Practice of Freedom* (New York: Routledge, 1995).

33. Catherine Waldby, "Destruction: Boundary Erotics and the Refigurations of the Heterosexual Male Body," *Sexy Bodies: The Strange Carnalities of Feminism*, ed. Elizabeth Grosz and Elspeth Probyn (New York: Routledge, 1995), 272–73.

34. On cultural assumptions about the incompatibility between penetrability and power—both male power/authority and female or feminist empowerment—see Bersani's "Is the Rectum a Grave?" Commenting on the notions of "moral incompatibility between sexual passivity and civic authority" that Foucault detected in ancient Greek thought, Bersani comments that "the moral taboo on 'passive' anal sex in ancient Athens is primarily formulated as a kind of hygenics of social power. *To be penetrated is to abdicate power.* I find it interesting that an almost identical argument—from, to be sure, a wholly different moral perspective—is being made today by certain feminists" (212). The feminists Bersani goes on to name are, of course, Catherine MacKinnon and Andrea Dworkin. In her critique of MacKinnon in *Beyond Accommodation: Ethical Feminism, Deconstruction, and the Law* (New York: Routledge, 1991), Drucilla Cornell also examines the putative incompatibility between having power and being fucked: "[I]n order to challenge MacKinnon's apparatus of gender identification, we also need to challenge the two kinds of selves, rigidly designated as male and female, that are produced by it. Under MacKinnon's view of the individual or the subject, the body inevitably figures as the barrier in which the self hides and guards itself as the illusionary weapon—the phallus—in which 'it' asserts itself against others. But why figure the body in this way? Why not figure the body as threshold or as position of receptivity. As receptivity, the body gives access. To welcome accessibility is to affirm *openness* to the Other. To shut oneself off, on the other hand, is *loss* of sensual pleasure. If one figures the body as receptivity, then 'to be fucked' is not the end of the world. The endless erection of a barrier against 'being fucked' is seen for what it 'is,' a defence mechanism that creates a fort for the self at the expense of *jouissance*. . . . My suggestion is . . . that it is only if one accepts a masculine view of the self, of the body and of carnality, that 'being fucked' *appears* so terrifying" (154). Cornell's formulation tying the terror of being fucked to a masculine view of the self, a view that necessarily masculinizes or phallicizes power, resonates with Bersani's definition of phallocentrism: "the temptation to deny the . . . strong appeal of powerlessness, of the loss of control. Phallocentrism is exactly that: not primarily the denial of power to women (although it has obviously also led to that, everywhere and at all times), but above all the denial of the *value* of powerlessness in both men and women" (217). I reproduce at such great length these comments from Bersani and Cornell not to suggest that straight men need necessarily to rush out and get fucked in order to prove their antimisogynist/antihomophobic mettle. What I submit is that straight men need to recognize the way their fears of being fucked, their anxieties about anal eroticism, and their participation in the devaluation of powerlessness all help constitute

heteromasculine subjectivity. Such recognition could perhaps help reconfigure that subjectivity, or at least help prevent the projections and disavowals that fuel misogynist and homophobic violence.

35. See note 34.

36. Monique Wittig, *The Straight Mind* (Boston: Beacon Press, 1992).

37. D. A. Miller, "Anal *Rope*," *Inside/Out: Lesbian Theories, Gay Theories*, ed. Diana Fuss (New York: Routledge, 1991), 128, 135.

38. In *Homos*, Bersani writes: "Unlike racism, homophobia is entirely a response to an internal possibility. Though racism and homophobia both include powerful projective energies, the projections are quite different. A white racist projects onto blacks some lurid sexual fantasies of his own, but essentially his version of 'the nature of blacks' . . . is a response to what he sees as an external threat, a threat to personal safety, economic security, and the achievements of white civilization. Blacks are a dangerous and inferior race, and they may destroy us. But not even racists could ever fear that blacks will seduce them into becoming black. Homophobia, on the other hand, is precisely that: to let gays be open about their gayness, to give them equal rights, to allow them to say who they are and what they want, is to risk being recruited" (27).

39. Janet E. Halley, "The Construction of Heterosexuality," *Fear of a Queer Planet: Queer Politics and Social Theory*, ed. Michael Warner (Minneapolis: University of Minnesota Press, 1993), 83, 85.

40. Michel Foucault, *The History of Sexuality: An Introduction*, trans. Robert Hurley (New York: Vintage, 1990), 43.

41. Lauren Berlant and Elizabeth Freeman, "Queer Nationality," *Fear of a Queer Planet: Queer Politics and Social Theory*, ed. Michael Warner (Minneapolis: University of Minnesota Press, 1993), 201.

42. I should stress that my hesitation isn't about holding a man's hand but about doing so in public, and for a month, particularly in the exceedingly small and backward Iowa town (it isn't even the relatively queer-friendly Iowa City) where I presently find myself. One doesn't have to be gay to be afraid, and justifiably so, of homophobic violence. In any case, the point of the "I Hate Straights" treatise is less to compel straights to prove their commitment by putting themselves in harm's way but rather to demand that straights recognize their own privilege, their ability to take for granted their own safety in public displays of physical affection or desire.

43. I like the auto/homoeroticism implied in the expression "to take oneself." I sometimes tell students that anyone who has ever masturbated—which is to say, everyone—is "queer" in the sense of having participated in what is necessarily a form of same-sex activity, whatever the heteroerotics of one's reveries or visual aids. A silly enough point, perhaps, but you'd be surprised how uncomfortable it makes the frat boys, who are, typically, the last ones to deny masturbation but also the ones most at pains to reiterate themselves as hets. And perhaps the homo-ness of masturbation as a universal form of self-shattering self-relation is partly what Bersani has in mind when he writes of " 'the homo' in us all" (*Homos*, 10). For, as he asks: "Who are you when you masturbate?" (103). Cf. again Sedgwick's inclusion of "masturbators" on her queer list in *Tendencies* (8).

44. Diana Fuss, "Inside/Out," *Inside/Out: Lesbian Theories, Gay Theories,* ed. Diana Fuss (New York: Routledge, 1991), 2.

45. In *The Self and Its Pleasures: Bataille, Lacan, and the History of the Decentred Subject* (Ithaca: Cornell University Press, 1992), Carolyn J. Dean writes that "Bataille remains, to be sure, a man, but a different sort of man; he remains heterosexual, but he is a straight man with a twist" (240). It has been suggested to me that I might provide some alternate term besides "queer" or "homo-ness" to designate the queer aspirations of self-critical straights. The phrase "straight with a twist" conveniently lends itself to acronym: SWAT Theory, anyone?

46. Louis Althusser, *Lenin and Philosophy and Other Essays,* trans. Ben Brewster (New York: Monthly Review Press, 1971), 174.

PART TWO

Interdisciplinary Readings

FIVE

Lifting the Veil
Robert Rauschenberg's *Thirty-Four Drawings for Dante's Inferno* and the Commercial Homoerotic Imagery of 1950s America

Laura Auricchio

The coded visual vocabulary of Robert Rauschenberg's *Thirty-Four Drawings for Dante's Inferno* (1959–1960) features mass-cultural, literary, and classical references that simultaneously create and conceal a subtext of male homosexual desire. Images of young male Olympic athletes and towel-clad men in locker rooms recur time and again in this suite of illustrations, suggesting that Rauschenberg's iconography may have been influenced by the contemporary "physique" magazines that offered male bodies for male delectation (figs. 1–6).[1] Although previous commentators have stressed that the modern imagery of the *Inferno* drawings translates Dante's literary classic into terms accessible to a twentieth-century mass audience, the present essay seeks to reevaluate the series in terms of its possible homoerotic connotations. This study argues, first, that Rauschenberg's *Inferno* employs veiled homoerotic imagery intelligible only to a small group of informed viewers and, second, that Rauschenberg did not merely update the journey taken by Dante's wayfarer but reimagined it as an excursion through a hidden terrain of same-sex love. Here, as elsewhere in Rauschenberg's oeuvre, indices of homosexuality hide in plain sight, introducing a camouflaged expression of homosexual longing into the predominantly heterosexual mores of the mid-century American avant-garde.

FIG 1 Robert Rauschenberg. *Canto XIV: Circle Seven, Round 3, The Violent Against God, Nature, and Art* from the series *Thirty-Four Drawings for Dante's Inferno.* 1959–60. Transfer drawing, watercolor, wash, pencil and red chalk on paper. 14⅜ x 11½ in. (36.7 x 29.1 cm) (slightly irregular). The Museum of Modern Art, New York. Given anonymously. Photograph © 1995 The Museum of Modern Art, New York.

120

FIG 2 Robert Rauschenberg. *Canto XVI: Circle Seven, Round 3, The Violent Against Nature and Art* from the series *Thirty-Four Drawings for Dante's Inferno.* 1959–60. Transfer drawing, watercolor, wash, colored pencil, and gouache on paper. 14⅜ x 11½ in. (36.7 x 29.2 cm) (slightly irregular). The Museum of Modern Art, New York. Given anonymously. Photograph © 1996 The Museum of Modern Art, New York.

FIG 3 Robert Rauschenberg. *Canto XXIV: Circle Eight, Bolgia 7, The Thieves* from the series *Thirty-Four Drawings for Dante's Inferno.* 1959–60. Transfer drawing, gouache, watercolor and pencil on paper. 14⅜ x 11½ in. (36.7 x 29.2 cm) (slightly irregular). The Museum of Modern Art, New York. Given anonymously. Photograph © 1995 The Museum of Modern Art, New York.

FIG 4 Robert Rauschenberg. *Canto XXVIII: Circle Eight, Bolgia 9, The Sowers of Discord: The Sowers of Religious and Political Discord between Kinsmen* from the series *Thirty-Four Drawings for Dante's Inferno.* 1959–60. Transfer drawing, pencil, gouache, watercolor and colored pencil on paper. 14½ x 11½ in. (36.8 x 29.3 cm) (slightly irregular). The Museum of Modern Art, New York. Given anonymously. Photograph © 1995 The Museum of Modern Art, New York.

123

FIG 5 Robert Rauschenberg. *Canto XXXI: The Central Pit of Maleboge, The Giants* from the series *Thirty-Four Drawings for Dante's Inferno*. 1959–60. Transfer drawing, pencil, gouache and colored pencil on paper. 14½ x 11½ in. (36.9 x 29.3 cm) (slightly irregular). The Museum of Modern Art, New York. Given anonymously. Photograph © 1995 The Museum of Modern Art, New York.

FIG 6 Robert Rauschenberg. *Canto XXXIII: Circle Nine, Cocytus, Compound Fraud: Round 2, Antenora, Treacherous to Country; Round 3, Ptolomea, Treacherous to Guests and Hosts* from the series *Thirty-Four Drawings for Dante's Inferno.* 1959–60. Transfer drawing, watercolor and pencil on paper. 14½ x 11½ in. (36.8 x 29.2 cm). The Museum of Modern Art, New York. Given anonymously. Photograph © 1995 The Museum of Modern Art, New York.

Beneath the colored washes and pencil hatchings that blanket the surface of the *Inferno* drawings, scores of whole and fragmented photographic images hover on the threshold of visibility. Though some are difficult to decipher, the majority of the photographs depict men in various stages of dress and undress—athletes, soldiers, policemen, astronauts, famous politicians, men in suits, men in tuxedos, men in riot gear, men in locker rooms, and men in bathing suits, among others. Also present, though in smaller numbers, are representations of birds, animals, sculptures, race cars, musical instruments, and industrial cranes. The diminished clarity of these photographs results from Rauschenberg's solvent transfer technique. Rauschenberg transferred each image to his drawing paper by brushing the magazine photo with lighter fluid or other chemical solvent, laying the image face down on paper, then rubbing the reverse side with an empty ballpoint pen.[2] Where the pressure of the pen was applied, the paper absorbed the printing ink, yielding a mirror image of the original photograph with blurry striations tracing the pen's path across the back of the magazine clipping.[3]

Although Rauschenberg clipped his photographs from magazines intended for the general public, his particular selection, grouping, and handling of images of male bodies may have carried specific, private meanings for a second, more limited set of viewers. The preponderance of familiar iconography derived from *Life, Sports Illustrated,* and other popular printed sources has led most critics to see Rauschenberg's men as typically modern, American cognates for the well-known Florentines described in Dante's text.[4] Yet a closer look at the dress, pose, and surroundings of these men suggests that many of the images could have functioned on two levels at once, pointing both to twentieth-century American popular culture and to conventional visual representations of male homoerotic desire. Trevor Fairbrother's observations on the legibility of homosexual references in the early works of Andy Warhol apply equally well to Rauschenberg's *Inferno.* Fairbrother writes that "the degree to which one could see, understand, and enjoy this aspect depended on the specific examples and on the awareness and openness of the viewer to the insider's world of gay subculture."[5] Like Warhol's imagery, the *Inferno* prevents most audiences from perceiving its homosexual implications, while it creates a community of viewers "in the know" to whom such connotations are transparent.[6]

The *Inferno*'s most frequently reproduced photograph, which appears at least once in each of fourteen cantos, features a man, naked except for a towel tied about his waist, standing in front of a tiled wall with his arms hanging at his sides (figs. 2, 3, 5, and 6). This figure originated in a series of advertisements for Pro Fit golf shafts published in numerous issues of *Sports Illustrated* in 1958 (fig. 7).[7] The ads include photographs of several towel-clad men and women, representing a variety of body types. The text promises "the 'sweetest feel' " by offering "the right PRO FIT shafts for *your* build, *your* height, *your* swing." Notably, the *Inferno* series reproduces several of the Pro Fit men but includes none of the women depicted in some ads. Though one hesitates to speculate, it is tempting to think that Rauschenberg, in choosing to employ the Pro Fit advertisements in his work, perceived the double entendre in the text, found himself amused by the seminude men seeking the "right shaft" for their "swing," and disregarded the female figures because they did not reinforce his alternative reading of the phrase.

Previous scholars have considered the *Inferno*'s towel-clad men as collective representations of a generic Everyman. Dore Ashton, whose canto-by-canto discussion of the *Inferno* drawings constitutes the most thorough account of the series to date, has identified the Pro Fit men as representations of Dante and Virgil. Yet she wonders at the "strange guise" of this "passive, near-naked man before what seems to be a medical measuring chart."[8] Elsewhere, Ashton puts aside any such musings as she asserts, "I take it that Rauschenberg had in mind the symbol for Everyman, a medieval prototype which certainly Dante had in *his* mind."[9] Indeed, Rauschenberg himself has denied that the figures harbor any more particular meaning; he once described the Pro Fit advertisement as simply "the most neutral popular image I could find on that scale."[10] To explain the men's seminudity, Rauschenberg stated, "[P]ictured in this way [the figures would] be removed from any specific time and place."

In their original locations on the pages of *Sports Illustrated*, the towel-clad men may well have functioned in such a "neutral" way. There, the images and texts of the Pro Fit advertisement worked together to invite the average, heterosexual sports enthusiast to see himself alongside the anonymous figures drying off in a locker room after eighteen holes of golf. In the *Inferno*, Rauschenberg has ripped these men from their mainstream context, separated them from their surrounding texts, isolated them from each other, and reproduced them in a set of intimate fine-art drawings. On the walls of a gallery or in the cabinet of a collector, the figures lose their identity as golf club spokesmen, along with any evident reason for their state of undress. The change in context also yields a

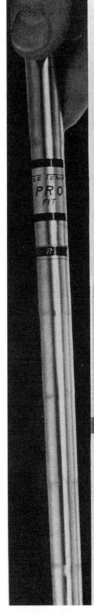

NEW PRO FIT GOLF SHAFTS
by *TRUE TEMPER.*

with the "sweetest feel" you've ever experienced

Try a club with a Pro Fit shaft and you'll "feel" what all the shouting's about. Made of a special CMB* steel, Pro Fit shafts give new control of flexibility, take all the *variation* out of golf shaft performance. They'll bring out the best game that's in you. Think not? Ask your pro for a demonstration.

chrome-manganese-boron alloy

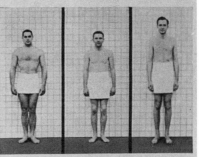

Because human bodies vary, your pro will "fit" you with the right Pro Fit shafts for your build, your height, your swing. Pro Fit shafts are being featured by the leading club makers . . . in a range of flexes, including one for women. Ask to see new clubs with Pro Fit shafts by True Temper. There has never been anything like them.

TRUE TEMPER.
CLEVELAND 15, OHIO

makers of Pro Fit, Rocket, Meteor, Century and Starmaker golf shafts

FIG 7 Advertisement for Pro Fit Golf Shafts by True Temper. *Sports Illustrated* (June 16, 1958): 71.

shift in reception. No longer can the seminude men be passed over as uninteresting fillers between articles, for they themselves have become the primary objects of careful scrutiny and visual pleasure.

If an audience of *Sports Illustrated* readers could understand the Pro Fit men as heterosexual athletes engaged in traditionally masculine sporting activities, a smaller audience of viewers familiar with homoerotic locker room imagery may have seen Rauschenberg's towel-clad figures in a different light. Scenes of men showering, drying themselves, or engaging in locker room camaraderie appeared regularly in the so-called physique magazines and low-budget movies that constituted much of the commercially available homoerotic male imagery of the 1950s and 1960s.[11] Locker room scenes provided plausible occasions for the display of the male body in a seemingly innocuous setting. Photographs and drawings of men in showers appeared so frequently in American magazines exported to England that they even colored the young art student David Hockney's first impressions of the United States. According to Hockney, a visit to California in 1964 confirmed his belief that "Americans take showers all the time—I knew that from experience and physique magazines."[12] A typical photograph of a young man drying himself with a towel appeared in the June 1959 issue of *Trim*, "Young America's Favorite Physique Publication" (fig. 8). The model, identified as the unusually mature "high school athlete Harry Raitano, 15," stands in a white-tiled shower stall with his face cast in shadow and a single drop of water glistening against his brightly lit torso. Although a well-placed towel hides "Harry" 's groin from view, it simultaneously calls attention to, and substitutes for, the region that it covers. The towel's dark stripes stand out sharply against a pale background of skin and wall, while its upward curve suggests a degree of sexual arousal.

In addition to providing alibis for open male nudity, bathing scenes resonate with references to homosexual bath house culture. George Chauncey, a historian of homosexual life in New York, describes baths as "the safest, most enduring, and one of the most affirmative of the settings in which gay men gathered in the first half of the twentieth century."[13] Personal accounts written by homosexual men throughout the twentieth century attest to the common use of public baths as meeting places for erotic encounters.[14] The memoirs of the scholar Martin Bauml Duberman highlight the significance of baths throughout the 1950s and early 1960s, when Duberman traveled from New Haven to Manhattan on numerous occasions to visit the Everard bath house on West 28th

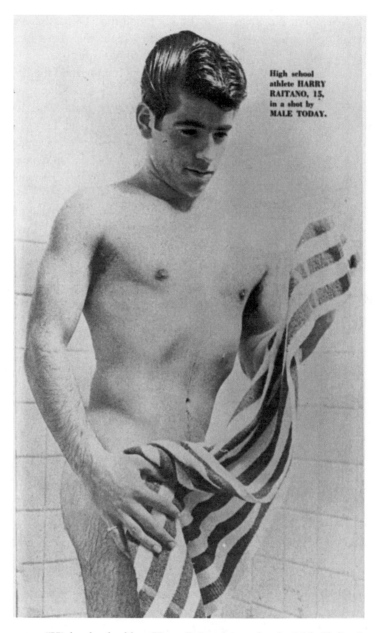

High school
athlete HARRY
RAITANO, 15,
in a shot by
MALE TODAY.

FIG 8 "High school athlete Harry Raitano, in a shot by Male Today."
Trim 12 (June 1959): 42.

Street.[15] The Everard retained its popularity among homosexual men for another twenty years, for although the original building burned down in 1977, a rebuilt Everard remained in operation until 1985, when the City of New York shut its doors as part of an attempt to curb the spread of AIDS.[16] Although the Inferno's toweled men do not appear in bath houses per se, they are surrounded by large numbers of partially clad, often athletic male bodies, just as they would have been in the Everard.

Previous scholars have commented on the innumerable athletes in Rauschenberg's *Inferno*, only to dismiss their presence as somehow natural. For example, Betite Vinklers asserts that Dante's text "almost demands this kind of visual interpretation."[17] Vinklers further explains that "Dante peopled his Hell with public figures of his time, and Rauschenberg's modern equivalent is the sportsman." Certainly, sports stars rank among the best known of American celebrities. However, Rauschenberg has decidedly not represented the recognizable faces of the great baseball and football heroes of 1950s America. Instead, he offers blurred images of anonymous athletes whose faces are sometimes obscured but whose muscular bodies often remain visible. Although Vinklers sees these athletes as reflections of "the physical, earthy atmosphere of Hell, where the emphasis is on physical endurance of punishment and on violence," the well-built figures may be linked more closely to physical pleasure than to bodily pain.

The homoerotic possibilities of Rauschenberg's brawny athletes often form a secondary narrative that can be read in tandem with Dante's epic. For instance, Dante's Canto XXIV describes the plight of thieves plagued by reptiles that "curl themselves about the sinners like living coils of rope, binding each sinner's hand behind his back, and knotting themselves through the loins."[18] Rauschenberg's corresponding drawing features three heavily muscled male torsos floating through a sea of snakes and fragmented bodies with their arms folded across their bare chests (fig. 3). Ashton, who identifies the headless torsos as wrestlers, provides a plausible, text-based interpretation of their iconography. She suggests that "the folded arms signify not only the knots one ties in one's own life and of oneself, but the symbolic retribution of thieves who made too free with their sticky-fingered hands."[19] Arms folded in this fashion form knots of a sort, but they also emphasize the impressive arm and chest muscles of the wrestlers. Indeed, as a relaxed version of a standard body-building pose, variations on this stance abound in physique magazines (fig. 9). In fact a large number of Rauschenberg's figures seem to represent weight

FIG 9 "Handsome, sun-tanned California body builder Clark Coffey can be right proud of his terrific arms, chest and deltoids." Photo by Douglas White. *Tomorrow's Man* (October 1956): 9.

lifters or body builders. Consider, for example, the shirtless man in tight briefs who flexes his arms above his head in the lower right corner of the illustration to Canto XXVIII (fig. 4). Like many of Rauschenberg's athletic images, this photograph might have originated in a general audience magazine and may illustrate Dante's poem, but it could also remind viewers "in the know" of homoerotic photographic conventions (fig. 10).

Rauschenberg's most striking weight lifters stand atop a winner's platform decorated with the Olympic rings at the bottom of Canto XXXI (fig. 5). Ashton sees these muscle-bound men as the titans who guard the innermost circle of Dante's hell and puts forth the reasonable argument that "their Olympian proportions are underlined by the insignia of the modern Olympic games at their feet."[20] However, John Ciardi's translation of the *Inferno*, which Rauschenberg read as he worked on the drawings, supports a more problematic, and more eroticized, reading of the titanic figures. In his synopsis of Canto XXXI, Ciardi describes Dante's giants as "the sons of the earth, embodiments of elemental forces unbalanced by love, desire without restraint and without acknowledgment of moral and theological law. They are symbols of the earth-trace that every devout man must clear from his soul, the unchecked passions of the beast" (*Inferno* 257). To a viewer familiar with Ciardi's translation, Rauschenberg's wrestlers may signify unnamed sexual urges that clash with social mores and must be kept in check.

While none of Rauschenberg's athletes engages in major American sports, almost all could be Olympic participants. In addition to weight lifters and wrestlers (Cantos XXVIII and XXXI), the *Inferno*'s Olympians include runners (Cantos XIV, XV and XXI), a skier (Canto XXXIII), swimmers (Cantos IV, XIV and XXXIII), a hockey player (Canto XXX), and boxers (Canto XXIII). Two additional images contain no information regarding the nature of their sport, as the men wear no visible clothing and are engaged in no specific activity. One, a team picture of men wearing no shirts, appears sideways at the lower right of Canto XIV (fig. 1). The other, a large yet barely visible photograph reproduced at the center of Canto XXIX, depicts a group of nearly naked men lined up in a shower or locker room.

The *Inferno*'s central concern with Olympic imagery may be understood as a broad reference to homosexuality hidden, once again, behind a seemingly innocent screen. Nineteen-sixty, the year that Rauschenberg completed the *Inferno* project, was in fact an Olympic year. On one level it is not surprising that Rauschenberg, who has consistently "let the world

BRUCE REED, 20,
construction worker,
athlete and promising
actor. Photo by
ZENITH.

FIG 10 "Bruce Reed, 20, construction worker, athlete and promising actor." Photo by Zenith. *Trim* 12 (June 1959)19.

in" to his art, would incorporate references to such a major media event.[21] Indeed, most viewers of Rauschenberg's *Inferno* in the early 1960s would most likely have understood its many Olympians as references to the recent games. Nonetheless, an audience versed in homoerotic visual conventions may have perceived additional connotations. Like locker room scenes, Olympic events held pride of place in contemporary physique photography and films. Certain Olympic sports, including wrestling, weight lifting, and swimming, lend themselves to the display of muscular male bodies, depicted alone or in pairs and dressed in tight-fitting garments. An advertisement for the Western Photography Guild published in the February 1959 issue of *Adonis* explains succinctly the sexual appeal of certain sports, as it offers pictures of "authentic wrestling action" featuring "virile masculinity photographed with impact." Most magazines forged more subtle links between Olympic sports and homoerotic pleasures in the manner of *Tomorrow's Man*, which employed a small silhouette of a discus thrower as its trademark icon.

In part, the ability of Olympic imagery to convey coded homoerotic meanings is predicated on a view of ancient Greece as a culture that openly embraced male homosexual activity. Speaking of his 1960 gold-colored transfer image of a bare-chested Andy Warhol, depicted in the folded-arm physique stance that we have already seen, Art Kane explained that "the golden-inspired period of Greek homosexuality turned over in my head and made me want to do a portrait of Andy in gold."[22] The golden age of homosexuality may also have "turned over" in readers' minds when they perused the references to antiquity that filled the pages of many homoerotic magazines. *Physique Pictorial* regularly carried an advertisement for "Athens Beautiful Classical Statuary," a California-based company that offered fifteen-inch statuettes of nude youths to be used for decoration or as lamp bases. Other magazines, including *Grecian Guild Pictorial, Adonis,* and *American Apollo,* bore titles that refer to the ancient world. According to its credo, the Grecian Guild dedicated itself "to those qualities first perceived and perfected by the people of ancient Greece."[23] Its magazine lists "the love of God, truth, honor, purity, friendship and native land" among the qualities associated with ancient Greece. Yet the provocative nude photographs that were published monthly in tandem with biographies of each featured "Grecian of the Month" suggest that the Guild also celebrated another variety of Greek love. Similarly, the 1959 "Olympic Issue" of *Art and Physique* praised "the glory that belonged to Ancient Greece."[24] Although the nature of Greek glory remains unnamed, the alluring poses of the seminude Olympians contained within suggest something more than athletic prowess.

If Rauschenberg's Olympians refer to ancient Greece, the prominence of Virgil in Dante's *Inferno* also points to ancient Rome. As a related classical culture, ancient Rome often served in physique magazines as another popular setting for images and narratives with partially concealed homoerotic connotations. "Marcus Sen in the Days of Rome," a comic strip that occasionally appeared in *Art and Physique*, featured drawings of muscular men in short togas couched in a "homosocial" narrative ostensibly concerned with heterosexual romance.[25] In other images, classicized trappings serve as justifications for male nudity. For instance, a 1956 issue of *Grecian Guild Pictorial* reproduced a painting of a Roman guard wearing only a plumed helmet and a loincloth. The same issue included an advertisement for mail-order posters of the *Baths of Ancient Rome* and *Spartan Soldiers Bathing* in surroundings that resemble a classical Everard's, with pairs of heavily muscled nude men featured prominently in each scene.

The use of classical references as coded signifiers of same-sex love has a long and distinguished history in the visual arts. Best known are the representations of the Ganymede myth that have served as more or less overt allusions to homosexual desire at various moments from the Renaissance to the present. Variations on the myth have been treated by artists including Michelangelo and Correggio in Italy and Charles Natoire and Carle VanLoo in France.[26] According to this tale, narrated by Ovid, Virgil, and others, Zeus was so smitten by the young mortal Ganymede that he adopted the form of an eagle, carried the boy to Mount Olympus, and kept him there as cup bearer to the gods. Like Rauschenberg's Olympians, Ganymede images could function on at least two levels, signifying either a spiritual apotheosis or a more erotically charged tale, with the choice of meaning depending on the artist, patron, viewer, and context. Rauschenberg's own oblique reference to the myth in *Canyon* (1959), which is almost exactly contemporaneous with the *Inferno* project, suggests a familiarity with this tradition.[27] Rauschenberg's combine includes both a collaged photograph of a young boy raising an arm toward the sky and a black stuffed eagle that protrudes almost menacingly from the support.

In addition to specific myths, generic citations of antiquity have also helped to create and conceal homoerotic subtexts in Western literary and visual traditions. In the history of art, no author has been more instrumental in conflating classical cultures with homosexual desire than the eighteenth-century German scholar Johann Jacob Winckelmann. In his *History of the Art of Antiquity*, Winckelmann lauds the Apollo Belvedere and other antique male nudes in terms laden with homoerotic appreciation.[28] For Winckelmann, the source of the sculptures' unsurpassed beauty lies not only in aesthetics but also in the very climate and culture of ancient Greece, which encouraged a physical masculine perfection that embodied an ideal state of freedom. In turn, the Victorian scholar Walter Pater employed Winckelmann in particular, and Greek ideals of homoerotic friendship in general, as vehicles for discussing same-sex desire in public contexts where the topic would normally be anathema.[29] In the same period, the writings of A. C. Swinburne and Matthew Arnold occasionally used a coded vocabulary of classical references to explore *erastes/eromenos* and other same-sex erotic relationships in a language that would evade the scrutiny of contemporary censors.[30]

The homoerotic photographs of Wilhelm von Gloeden, taken at the turn of the twentieth century, continue in this vein, as their classical allusions both excuse and enhance their sensual depictions of young men. These photographs feature adolescent boys, either nude or draped with togas, gathering on the cliffs of Sicily wearing floral wreaths in their hair. Some images render their antique referents still more explicit by depicting the youths posing next to Greek sculptures, leaning against marble columns, or fondling vases. Van Gloeden lends the pictures an air of classical erudition as he writes, "In Sicily the texts of Homer, the verses of Theocritus, spurred my fantasy. Cliffs and sea, mountains and valleys spoke to me of Arcadian shepherds and Polyphemus."[31]

Like these predecessors, Rauschenberg employs a homosocial narrative linked to antiquity as a frame that legitimizes an investigation of same-sex affection. Indeed, the *Inferno* may be understood as a tale that narrates Dante's companionate relationship with a wise and experienced classical guide, Virgil. Together, the two men embark on a voyage through the forbidden netherworld. This is no ordinary trip but a torment-ridden quest for divine truth and love. As Dante and Virgil journey together, their mutual affection manifests itself on several occasions. At the end of Canto XIX Dante reports that he has grown too weak to travel farther. At that point, he tells us that Virgil "gathered me against his breast,/remounted the rocky path of all the valley,/nor did he tire of holding me clasped to him . . ." (*Inferno* XIX.117–121). In his drawing for this canto, Rauschenberg has included a nude male figure reclining with his knees raised in a position that reveals the length of his body but conceals his genitals. In the context of Dante's narrative, the supine figure presumably represents the loving moment when Virgil "tenderly set down the heavy burden/he had been pleased to carry up that ledge . . ." (*Inferno* XIX.125–126). Yet it also recalls the photographs of men depicted in this provocative, but not indecent, pose that passed through the screen of contemporary censorship laws and therefore appeared occasionally in men's magazines.

In Dante's Cantos XIV, XV and XVI, the travelers experience the seventh circle of hell, where they encounter sodomites and others who have committed crimes "against nature" (*Inferno* 76). The art historian Jonathan Katz, who has written the only published discussion of the homosexual implications of Rauschenberg's *Inferno*, focuses on Rauschenberg's illustrations to Cantos XIV and XV.[32] Small, nude athletes and clothed runners dot the field of Canto XIV (fig. 1), and Canto XV features a prominent photograph of a lone runner. A first consideration of these drawings in light of Dante's text suggests that the runners simply represent the shades whose eternal punishment is to run naked over hot coals. Yet our analysis of Rauschenberg's athletes points to an additional, specifically homoerotic, meaning that is reinforced by the nature of the runners' crimes. Still more intriguing is Rauschenberg's inscription of his own presence into the circle of the sodomites by tracing the outline of his foot at the top of the illustration to Canto XIV. Katz argues that this unusually personal image may constitute a highly obscure revelation of the artist's own sexuality. Of course, only viewers familiar with both the *Inferno* and Rauschenberg's life would interpret the outline in this light. As Katz observes, the artist may have intended this and other hints of same-sex love to be evident only to the most select audiences, or even to no audience at all. In other words, "these images constitute a 'coming out' legible only to those who are 'in.' "

Literary historians have often singled out Dante's Canto XVI for its open discussion of, and apparent admiration for, prominent Florentine men whom it identifies as sodomites.[33] As we come upon these wraiths, Virgil informs us that "these are souls to whom respect is due," and Dante speaks of the departed with honor and compassion. It is interesting that Dante employs suggestive terms derived from classical games to describe the "violent against nature," who move "as naked and anointed champions do/in feeling out their grasp and their advantage/before they close in for the thrust or blow . . ." (*Inferno* XVI.22–24). Rauschenberg's drawing, one of the more sparsely illustrated works in the series, contains no explicitly athletic images (fig. 2). It does, however, feature the towel-clad man surrounded by a field of glowing orange wash. Other discernible images include group photographs of anonymous men, a series of small triangles, and a silhouette that vaguely suggests an embracing couple.

As with many of the *Inferno* drawings, Rauschenberg's illustration to Canto XVI provides so little iconographic information that a viewer seeking narrative content is compelled to turn to Dante's text for guidance. In this way, Rauschenberg effects a rhetorical denial of authorship. The freedom afforded by this denial may in fact have enabled the artist to produce a major series of drawings with extensive references to homosexual culture. For it is Dante who narrates the homosocial tale, while Rauschenberg could be, and has been, seen as merely supplying the necessary visual analogs. Jonathan Weinberg discusses the American artist Charles Demuth's incorporation of homosexual imagery into several works of illustration from the first half of the twentieth century in exactly this manner, as "a way to investigate safely parallels to his own sexuality: through illustration, moral responsibility seemed to shift to an absent author."[34]

Despite the work's own denials of originality, Rauschenberg has, of course, represented Dante's *Inferno* in an entirely new way. By illustrating the European classic with images selected from twentieth-century mass-market ephemera, Rauschenberg implies a degree of equivalence between two divergent cultural strata. Melding two spheres of culture was hardly new to avant-garde discourse in the middle of the twentieth century. Thomas Crow has observed that modernism has "repeatedly" made "subversive equations between high and low which dislocate the apparently fixed terms of that hierarchy into new and persuasive configurations, thus calling it into question from within."[35] What is new to the Dante drawings is the reconstruction of a cornerstone of Western literature on a foundation that is not only contemporary and ephemeral but also covertly homoerotic. In this sense, Rauschenberg's *Inferno* stands as an important attempt to translate a narrative selected from the dominant society into a vocabulary accessible only to viewers familiar with a homosexual subculture. As a result, the series blurs not only the bounds between high and low cultures but also those between gay and straight texts.

Carl Van Vechten, a novelist, photographer and critic associated with the Harlem Renaissance, compiled twenty homoerotic scrapbooks in the mid-1950s that constitute an illuminating precedent for Rauschenberg's manipulation of mass-market ephemera.[36] In this collection, Van Vechten combines his own photographs of nude men, many of whom are engaged in explicit sexual activities, with apparently innocuous images and phrases clipped from popular newspapers and magazines. Like Rauschenberg's, Van Vechten's selection of photos includes male wrestlers, tennis players, bicyclists, and runners. While these athletic figures might have carried latent homoerotic implications in their original, mainstream publications, Van Vechten renders manifest their homosexual connotations by recontextualizing them amid sexually suggestive quotations and overtly erotic photographs. Van Vechten plays with words in a similar fashion. For example, the phrase "tots atop queen" probably conveyed only the most innocent of meanings in the newspaper from which it was clipped. Yet, when placed below a photograph of three nude young men engaged in foreplay, its homoerotic implications rise to the surface. In Van Vechten's hands, texts and images intended for the general public become intensely private as they address a subculture all but forgotten by the mass market.[37]

To the extent that it, too, straddles cultural spheres, Rauschenberg's *Inferno* thrives on similar double meanings. In fact, Harold Beaver sees the "duplicitous" sign, which evasively adopts new meanings in new contexts, as typical of all homosexual semiotic systems. "For to be homosexual in Western society entails a state of mind in which all credentials, however petty, are under unceasing scrutiny."[38] Barred from producing his own code, the homosexual reproduces "counter-codes" by necessity and becomes "a prodigious consumer of signs—of hidden meanings, hidden systems, hidden potentiality. Exclusion from the common code impels the frenzied quest: in the momentary glimpse, the scrambled figure, the sporadic gesture, the chance encounter, the reverse image, the sudden slippage, the lowered guard ... in a flash meanings may be disclosed; mysteries wrenched out and betrayed."[39] In the *Inferno*, we see Rauschenberg as such a consumer, sifting through canonical literature and mass-market imagery to reveal potential homoerotic subtexts.

Bruce Boone's analysis of coded homosexual language in the poetry of Frank O'Hara, who was active in the same New York art community as Rauschenberg in the 1950s, sheds light on Rauschenberg's project.[40] Drawing an analogy between the relatively powerless positions of homosexuals and of colonized peoples, Boone sees both groups as blocked from speaking in their own languages. As a result, both are forced to filter their oppositional speech through the language of their oppressors, inevitably distorting both languages in the process. Homosexual codes take shape in the crucible where the dominant and subcultural worlds collide. Although codes give voice to homosexuality, they do so only in deforming, deceptive terms. Rauschenberg's *Inferno*, which employs images from general audience magazines to translate Dante's venerable text into a coded homoerotic narrative, effects such a distorting linguistic union.

Seen in the context of these semiotic analyses, the *Inferno*'s solvent transfer technique seems to give form to the distortion of codes. The blurring and striation characteristic of Rauschenberg's transfer process ensure that the identity of the transferred photographs remains at least partly hidden. In a general sense, these features call to mind the diminished legibility that is characteristic of much modernist painting. At the same time, the scrambling of figural images suggests that some crucial element of a given photograph must remain not quite visible and prompts inquiry into that elusive object. As Dore Ashton observes, "Rauschenberg has often drawn veils over his images, hungered for morsels of real life only to blur and reconstrue them."[41] Roberta Smith employs another metaphor for obstructed vision when she describes Rauschenberg's striations as "the graphic equivalent of a strobe light; they make the images flicker in and out of view...."[42] The conspicuous presence of these striations calls attention to their obscuring function and reinforces the sense that the *Inferno* drawings are coy documents that offer glimpses of signification but don't by any means tell all.

The social and political atmosphere of America in the 1950s and early 1960s may have compelled an especially strict adherence to obscured visual and linguistic codes. As Rauschenberg once noted, "the fifties were a particularly hostile, prudish time."[43] The contemporary press is, in fact, rife with evidence of antagonism towards homosexuals and homosexuality. A 1950 *New York Times* article reported that "[a] Senate investigation of alleged homosexuals in the Executive Branch was recommended unanimously today.... Perverts are described by intelligence officers as poor security risks because of their vulnerability to blackmail."[44] In 1955 Henry Hay, founder of the Mattachine Society, the first American organization devoted to homosexual rights, was brought before Senator Joseph McCarthy's House Un-American Activities Committee.[45] In 1963 another *New York Times* article bore the headline "Growth of Overt Homosexuality in City Provokes Wide Concern."[46] Moreover, in 1959–1960, the very years that Rauschenberg worked on the *Inferno* project, most of the gay bars in New York were closed due to antihomosexual propagandizing by an influential journalist.[47]

Even the men's magazines that we have been examining did not openly address their homosexual readership in this period. *The Mattachine Review*, *One*, and other primarily textual periodicals candidly concerned with social issues pertinent to homosexual audiences had begun publication in the early 1950s.[48] However, magazines devoted to homoerotic visual imagery were bound by strict censorship regulations and generally touted themselves as body-building magazines or journals for art lovers.[49] In 1957, *Grecian Guild Pictorial* prefaced its "art section" with a disclaimer that explained the ensuing nude and seminude photographs as "a ready reference for artists not employing live models. . . . This section also provides inspiration to body builders who seek to achieve an ideal physique."[50] Throughout the 1950s, several magazines featured photographs of unclothed men in "artistic" poses, such as leaning against classicized columns or hiding their groins behind classical busts. Others included photographs of classical and neoclassical sculptures that depict attractive male bodies. As David Hockney observed of the homoerotic "art" magazines: "In those days they weren't in any sense pornographic; they were just nudes. They were very unsexy, strangely unsexy; they were boys in sylvan glades, a bit artistic, old-fashioned artistic."[51]

If the open acknowledgment of homosexual interest was rare in the visual media, it was virtually unheard of in many professional realms. In the late 1950s, Martin Bauml Duberman feared losing his teaching position at Yale because "these were the years when a half dozen male faculty members were hounded from their jobs at Smith when discovered to be in possession of 'pornographic' gay materials."[52] Writing of Roland Barthes, who was also active in academia in this era, Maurice Berger observed that "it was not that he never revealed his homosexuality, but that, like most gay men of his generation, he did so elusively, with signals intended only for other queers."[53] Homosexuality also remained a well-guarded secret among many New York artists of the period. Although Robert Rauschenberg was romantically involved with Jasper Johns at the time of the Dante drawings, their relationship was not revealed to the general public for many years.[54] As Rauschenberg himself explained, "It was sort of new to the art world that the two most well-known, up-and-coming studs were affectionately involved."[55] Andy Warhol, one of the few major artists of the time to proclaim his homosexuality openly, reported being told that Rauschenberg and Johns disliked him because "you're too swish and that upsets them."[56] Emile de Antonio, the artist's agent who is cited as the source of this insight, further observed that although "the post-Abstract Expressionist sensibility is, of course, a homosexual one," Johns and Rauschenberg "wear three-button suits—they were in the army or something!"[57]

Given this homophobic context, it is not surprising that allusions to homosexual cultures should lie carefully buried in several of Rauschenberg's works from the same period. Once again, it is Jonathan Katz who has uncovered the bulk of these camouflaged details.[58] As early as 1954, Rauschenberg included a photograph of Judy Garland, whom Katz describes as "the high priestess of gay culture," in his *Bantam* combine. The art critic Robert Hughes perceives even more central references to homosexuality in Rauschenberg's *Monogram* (1955–1959).[59] The most memorable aspect of this combine is its inclusion of an entire stuffed angora goat that has been forced through a rubber tire. Hughes interprets the satyr-like goat as one of "the oldest metaphors of priapic energy" thrust into a tight-fitting sphincter. In this sense, the work constitutes "one of the few great icons of male homosexual love in modern culture" that helped to "expand the subject-matter available to American art in the 1950s."

Concealment itself, which permeated both Rauschenberg's daily life and the technique and iconography of the Dante drawings, becomes the primary subject of other works by the artist. Craig Owens has observed that "it remains impossible to read a Rauschenberg, if by reading it we mean the extraction from a text of a coherent, monological message. The fragmentary, piecemeal combination of images that initially impels reading is also what blocks it, erects an impenetrable barrier to its course."[60] Legibility and secrecy first emerge as interdependent themes in Rauschenberg's *Black Paintings* of 1951–1953. In this series, canvases covered with torn sheets of newspaper have been coated with uneven layers of black paint. Each painting features areas of thinly applied pigment where segments of newsprint are permitted to peek through. Although these glimpses of text raise the possibility of legibility, the viewer's wish for a full reading remains permanently thwarted, as the complete text will always be obscured.[61] In other pieces, Rauschenberg has signified concealment by experimenting with literal veils. In the combine painting *Rebus* (1955), a translucent veil partially covers a collage of photographs, newspaper clippings and other objects.[62] Andrew Forge sees this work as a "meditation on Rauschenberg's sense of identity," for its constituent parts resemble the personal memorabilia of a scrapbook.[63] However, the veil that obscures a reproduction of a self-portrait by the painter Albrecht Dürer stands as a reminder that the artist's identity is not completely available for public consumption.

Jasper Johns was equally engaged with issues of concealment.[64] His *Book* (1957) and *Newspaper* (1957) present actual reading materials that have been covered with thick layers of encaustic.[65] Although both the shapes and the titles of the works refer to printed texts, their encaustic coatings ensure that any attempt at reading will end in frustration.[66] In his more complex *Target* works, Johns weaves strands of concealment into a web of desire and bodily fragmentation. The well-known *Target with Four Faces* (1955) features a bull's-eye target surmounted by a horizontal wooden strip divided into four small compartments. The cubicles all contain fragmented faces that are said to represent the features of a woman. The target that dominates the composition heightens the sense of physical danger implied by the mutilated visages. At the same time, a target signifies a goal, something for which one strives. A target may also be defined as a desire. Jonathan Weinberg proposes that the structure of Johns's target may refer to a particular kind of sexualized desire, as its series of concentric rings surround a small, dark circle that suggests an anus.[67] Johns's similar *Target with Plaster Casts* (1955) combines the target/anus with sexually suggestive portions of male anatomy. The compartments surmounting this bull's-eye are equipped with hinged doors and contain casts of a disembodied penis, a male nipple, and other seemingly masculine body parts. Kenneth Silver has observed that the target, doors, and fragmented male genitalia bring an "association of danger" and closeting to the eroticized male body.[68] In this way, the work as a whole echoes the "besieged" status of the homosexual body, and may be seen as a nascent attempt at "mapping . . . gay desire" onto a work of avant-garde art.

An analogous network of bodily danger and homosexual desire laces through Rauschenberg's *Inferno*. The disembodied legs, feet, heads, chests, backs, and arms of innumerable nude or partially clothed men swirl about nearly all of the cantos. The better part of this disconnected anatomy bears no evident relationship to Dante's text and is consequently not discussed by the iconographers. As in Johns's *Targets*, these seemingly inexplicable body parts function within a broader context of desire. We have seen the ways in which many of Rauschenberg's male figures serve as objects of surreptitious sexual longings. In addition, Rauschenberg's solvent transfer technique reproduces a state of desire in the very structure of the drawings. The traces left by the nib of the ballpoint pen on the backs of the photographs suggest that the images have been abandoned in the process of becoming. Neither fully present nor wholly absent, the transferred photographs hover on the verge of completion and remain frozen in a perpetual search for fulfillment. Finally, the narrative of Dante's *Inferno* itself may be understood at its most basic level as the tale of a lover willing to risk the very horrors of hell in order to attain his divine beloved. Seen in the context of such a dangerous quest for love, Rauschenberg's ubiquitous dismembered male bodies seem to point to the perils that accompany certain types of desire.

If Rauschenberg's *Inferno* violently fragments physical bodies, so does it divide and multiply intangible identities. Most striking, Virgil and Dante appear in a panoply of guises throughout the course of the series. Dante is variously represented by several towel-clad men, a pair of eyes, a leg, a kicking foot, a pair of initials, and John F. Kennedy; Virgil is depicted as an arm, a hand, a towel-clad man, Adlai Stevenson, a runner, an astronaut, a baseball umpire, an antique statue, a scuba diver, and the letter V.[69] Moreover, the anonymous figures who spread across the drawings appear to be interchangeable, as they flicker in and out of view in a never-ending chain of substitutions. In Rauschenberg's *Inferno*, no self is ever stable or complete, and none is privileged over another. Instead, identity is figured in a state of constant flux and fragmentation.

The *Inferno's* series of ever multiplying identities stands in stark contrast to the unitary, masterful self that was said to emerge from the works of the Abstract Expressionist painters who dominated the American art of the period. Throughout the 1940s and 1950s the literature on Abstract Expressionism had celebrated the revelation of the singular, individual psyche through gestural painting. *Life* magazine's "Round Table on Modern Art" of 1948 declared "[t]he meaning of modern art is, that the artist of today is engaged in a tremendous individualistic struggle—a struggle to discover and to assert and to express himself."[70] Four years later Harold Rosenberg described the "American Action Painter" as one who "gesticulated upon the canvas and watched for what each novelty would declare him and his art to be."[71] Artists sometimes expressed similar views of their work. In a 1945 letter to the editor of the *New York Times*, Mark Rothko described the art of his generation as "a pictorial equivalent for man's new knowledge and consciousness of his more complex inner self."[72] Eleven years later Jackson Pollock asserted, "Painting is self-discovery. Every good artist paints what he is."[73]

Although the discourse of the self-expressive Abstract Expressionist gesture persisted throughout the 1950s, criticism of this rhetoric had begun to appear in American art in general, and in Rauschenberg's work in particular, several years before the *Inferno* drawings.[74] Rauschenberg had been engaged in a dialectical relationship with the Abstract Expressionist idiom since at least 1953, when he erased a pencil drawing by Willem De Kooning and exhibited the results as Robert Rauschenberg's *Erased De Kooning Drawing*. David Deitcher has observed that this anti-gestural gesture marked the beginning of Rauschenberg's long-standing interest in "unmasking the artist's 'presence' as an 'absence.' "[75] Most famously, two combine works of 1957, *Factum I* and *Factum II*, comment critically "on the nature of gesture and an artist's ability to fake spontaneity, improvisation, and action."[76] *Factum I* combines gestural brushstrokes, postage stamps, photographs, and other collage elements. *Factum II* is virtually identical to *Factum I* in every respect, as it includes the same stamps, the same photographs, and even the same gestural brushstrokes. When seen individually, each work appears to be a unique collection of highly personal markings. Yet seen as a pair, the combines reveal their compositions, and even their painterly brushstrokes, to be no more individual than the mass-produced postage stamps that they feature so prominently.[77]

Rauschenberg's *Inferno* drawings continue to critique the myth of the artist's individual, productive trace. Like the pseudospontaneous brushstrokes of *Factum I* and *Factum II*, the drawing marks that course through the *Inferno*'s transferred photographs both mimic and subvert the stereotypical Abstract Expressionist gesture. In the Dante photographs, the indices of the artist's touch seem to negate the possibility of self-expression, for they serve openly to reproduce appropriated images that were initially created mechanically. As Douglas Crimp has eloquently noted, "the fantasy of a creating subject gives way to the frank confiscation, quotation, excerptation, accumulation, and repetition of already existing images."[78] In light of this critical project, we may see the entire undertaking of Rauschenberg's *Inferno* as an elaborate effort to deny the notion that the artist's work reveals his or her identity.

The gestural markings of Rauschenberg's homoerotic *Inferno* also undermine the stereotypically masculine gendering of Abstract Expressionism. Rosenberg had likened the Abstract Expressionist painter to a virile athlete, as he wrote that modern art resides "in the tubes [of paint], in the painter's muscles, and in the cream-colored sea into which he dives."[79]

Later in the same essay, Rosenberg had compared the artist to the adventurous hero of *Moby Dick:* "The American vanguard painter took to the white expanse of the canvas as Melville's Ishmael took to the sea."[80] Contemporary photographs of the Abstract Expressionists enhanced this rugged aura. Rosalind Krauss notes that countless photographs of Jackson Pollock depicted him "in his James Dean dungarees and black tee-shirt," or "hunkered down on the running board of his old Ford," or engaged in "the athletic abandon of the painting gesture. . . . "[81] In addition, personal accounts by contemporary artists suggest that the male Abstract Expressionists adopted the macho role in their personal behavior. The sculptor George Segal observed of the Abstract Expressionists that "if you had an education, you had to hide it and sound like a New York cab driver."[82] Andy Warhol described the same phenomenon more colorfully: "The world of the Abstract Expressionists was very macho. The painters who used to hang around the Cedar bar on University Place were all hard-driving, two-fisted types who'd grab each other and say things like 'I'll knock your fucking teeth out,' and 'I'll steal your girl.' "[83]

The tough masculine persona of the Abstract Expressionists proved to be one more artificial construct that was ultimately doomed to collapse under its own weight. The most dramatic evidence that the macho myth could not be sustained comes from the biography of Jackson Pollock himself, whose alcohol-related death seems like more of a suicide than an accident.[84] The disintegration of the Abstract Expressionist myth of unbridled virility may have been hastened by a group of works, produced by the generation of artists emerging in the 1950s, that began to subvert the heterosexual rhetoric of the Action Painters. Moira Roth has discussed pieces by John Cage, Merce Cunningham, Jasper Johns, and Rauschenberg in these terms. Roth writes, "The *machismo* attitudes proudly displayed by the Abstract Expressionists were now countered by the homosexuality and bisexuality permissible and even common among the new aesthetic group."[85] Of Rauschenberg's colleagues, none rendered a more severe critique of Abstract Expressionist machismo than Jasper Johns in his *Painting with Two Balls* of 1960. At first glance the painting appears to be covered with spontaneous brushstrokes reminiscent of the Action Painters. Yet, as we have seen elsewhere, this spontaneity is clearly "a feint," for Johns has used the laborious encaustic technique to mimic a loose, gestural effect.[86] The most striking element of this work is, however, the two metal balls that have been inserted into a slit in the center of the canvas. As early as 1965 Rosalind Krauss understood the profoundly gendered implications of the balls, as she wrote, "The objects undoubtedly refer to the myth of masculinity surrounding the central figures of Abstract Expressionism . . . and the sexual potency read into their artistic act."[87]

The language of contemporary critics suggests that, although Rauschenberg's *Inferno* series was not widely seen as a critique of the myth of virile artistic masculinity, it was perceived in terms entirely foreign to the Abstract Expressionist project. A January 1961 review of the exhibition of the Dante series at the Leo Castelli Gallery in New York described the "delicate and painstaking detailing of these fragile illustrations."[88] Another observed that the solvent transfer process is "a trying and difficult technique involving considerable labor and much patience."[89] It would be hard to image terms such as "delicate," "fragile," and "patience" appearing amid the hypermasculine reviews of works by Jackson Pollock or Willem De Kooning.[90] If the homoerotic contents of Rauschenberg's iconography eluded most critics, the absence of traditional machismo in his technique clearly did not.

As Michel Foucault observes of sexual discourses, "there is no binary division to be made between what one says and what one does not say; we must try to determine the different ways of not saying such things."[91] This essay has attempted to determine the ways in which the technique and iconography of Robert Rauschenberg's *Thirty-Four Drawings for Dante's Inferno* both signify and refuse to signify homosexual desire in a coded, but potent, visual vocabulary. The *Inferno*'s male imagery echoes the visual vocabulary of an important homosexual subculture of 1950s America and allows viewers familiar with contemporary commercial homosexual representation to perceive a nascent homosexual iconography. At the same time, the use of a well-respected text that is not generally deemed homoerotic as the framework for this imagery permits all other viewers to discern only meanings that refer to Dante's *Inferno*. The solvent transfer technique as it is employed in this series must be understood as crucial to Rauschenberg's project, for it simultaneously signifies the obscurity that surrounds its homosexual references and brings the work into a critical relationship with the macho, heterosexual subjectivity that was widely attributed to the Abstract Expressionist gesture. Ultimately, the *Inferno* drawings belong to a group of works produced by Rauschenberg and several contemporaries in the 1950s that began to "read the culture against the grain in a way that made [homosexuals] more visible than they were supposed to be, and to turn 'straight' spaces into gay spaces."[92]

NOTES

This essay emerged from a seminar on histories and theories of photography offered by Benjamin Buchloh at Columbia University in 1994. I would like to thank Benjamin Buchloh, John Goodman, Jonathan Lopez, Carol Siegel, Jonathan Weinberg, and the anonymous reader from *Genders* for critiquing earlier versions of the paper and/or pointing me to crucial sources.

1. Robert Rauschenberg, *Thirty-Four Drawings for Dante's Inferno.* 1959–1960. 14 1/2 x 11 1/2 in. (slightly irregular). Transfer drawing, collage, watercolor, gouache, crayon, pencil, and colored pencil on single-ply Strathmore paper. The Museum of Modern Art, New York. Given anonymously. A selection of the drawings that feature male imagery are presented in Figures 1–6.

2. In an interview with Calvin Tomkins, Rauschenberg stated that he came upon the solvent transfer process during his 1952 stay in Cuba with Cy Twombly. Roni Feinstein, "Random Order: The First Fifteen Years of Robert Rauschenberg's Art, 1949–1990" (Ph.D. diss., NYU Institute of Fine Arts, 1990), 345. Images transferred, rather than collaged, from the popular press seem to have entered the vocabulary of American high art through Willem De Kooning's paintings of the 1940s. De Kooning would cover his partially dry paintings with newspapers whose print would adhere to the paint and appear in reverse after the paper was removed. Walter Hopps, *Robert Rauschenberg: The Early 1950s* (Houston: Houston Fine Art Press, 1991), 68.

3. Feinstein notes that it is possible to transfer images crisply and completely by applying equal pressure to all areas of the clipping, although Rauschenberg has elected not to do so. See Feinstein, "Random Order," 350.

4. Rauschenberg himself declares that each drawing corresponds in some way to one canto of Dante's poem, although the connections between the text and the image are often highly obscure. See, for example, Betite Vinklers, "Why Not Dante?" *Art International* 12, no. 6 (summer 1968): 100.

5. Trevor Fairbrother, "Tomorrow's Man," *The Early Art and Business of Andy Warhol* (New York: Grey Art Gallery and Study Center and The Carnegie Museum of Art, 1989), 50.

6. George Chauncey makes a similar observation regarding "gay argot," which hides meanings from unsympathetic ears while fostering a "sense of collective identity" among homosexual listeners. See his *Gay New York* (New York: Basic Books, 1994), 287.

7. Gotz Adriani, *Robert Rauschenberg: Zeichnungen, Gouachen, Collagen 1949 bis 1979* (Munich: Piper, 1979), 24.

8. Dore Ashton, *XXXIV Drawings for Dante's Inferno* (New York: Abrams, 1964), 5.

9. Dore Ashton, "The Collaboration Wheel: A Comment on Robert Rauschenberg's Comment on Dante," *Arts and Architecture* 80 (December 1963): 11.

10. Feinstein, "Random Order," 367.

11. In addition to professionally marketed homoerotic imagery, homemade photographs, slides, and videos also circulated among closed groups and may still be found in the storerooms of bookstores such as Gay Pleasures in New York's Greenwich Village.

12. David Hockney, *David Hockney* (New York: Abrams, 1984), 99.

13. Chauncey, *Gay New York*, 207.

14. Bath houses had also served as settings for homoerotic gatherings in American avant-garde painting since at least 1915, when Charles Demuth began his *Turkish Bath* watercolors. In the background of one of the more suggestive works in this series, a pair of men appears to be engaged in an act of fellatio, while two nude men touch each other's feet as they face the viewer in the foreground. In the midst of this open homoerotic activity stands a man draped from shoulder to calf in a large towel. As Jonathan Weinberg observes, the towel actually conceals very little, for full frontal nudity and explicit sexual acts are clearly visible in other parts of the painting. Nonetheless, the towel serves an important function as "a sign of covering up," reminding the viewer of the secrecy that surrounds even this relatively open homosexual meeting place. The towels on Rauschenberg's Pro Fit men may be seen as direct descendants of Demuth's earlier linens, for they play similar roles as signifiers of concealed pleasures. See Jonathan Weinberg, *Speaking for Vice: Homosexuality in the Art of Charles Demuth, Marsden Hartley, and the First American Avant-Garde* (New Haven: Yale University Press, 1993), 21–23, 97.

15. Martin Bauml Duberman, *About Time: Exploring the Gay Past* (New York: Gay Presses of New York, 1986), 364.

16. Chauncey, *Gay New York*, 216.

17. All quotations in this paragraph may be found in Vinklers, "Why Not Dante?" 104.

18. John Ciardi in Dante Alighieri, *The Inferno*, trans. John Ciardi (New York: New American Library, 1954), 205. Further references to this work will be included parenthetically in the text.

19. Ashton, "The Collaboration Wheel," 22.

20. Ibid., 29.

21. Leo Steinberg, *Other Criteria* (New York: Oxford University Press, 1972), 90.

22. Fairbrother, "Tomorrow's Man," 50.

23. "Creed of the Grecian Guild," *Grecian Guild Pictorial* 2, no. 2 (March 1957): 2.

24. *Art and Physique* series 8 (1959): 2.

25. On the term "homosocial" see Eve Kosofsky Sedgwick, *Between Men: English Literature and Male Homosocial Desire* (New York: Columbia University Press, 1985).

26. James M. Saslow thoroughly documents Italian Renaissance images of Ganymede, touching on the iconography in other cultures, in *Ganymede in the*

Renaissance: Homosexuality in Art and Society (New Haven: Yale University Press, 1986). Michael Preston Worley follows the theme into eighteenth- and nineteenth-century France in "The Image of Ganymede in France, 1730–1820: The Survival of a Homoerotic Myth," *Art Bulletin* 76, no. 4 (December 1994): 630–43.

27. Kenneth Bendiner has interpreted *Canyon* more specifically as a reworking of Rembrandt's *Rape of Ganymede* in "Robert Rauschenberg's *Canyon*," *Arts Magazine* 56, no. 10 (June 1982): 57–59. On *Canyon* as a homosexual text see Jonathan Katz, "The Art of Code: Jasper Johns and Robert Rauschenberg," in *Significant Others: Creativity and Intimate Partnership*, ed. Whitney Chadwick and Isabelle de Courtivron (London: Thames and Hudson, 1993), 193–208.

28. On homoeroticism in Winckelmann's art criticism see Alex Potts, *Flesh and the Ideal: Winckelmann and the Origins of Art History* (New Haven: Yale University Press, 1994).

29. On classical coding of same-sex desire in Victorian England see Richard Dellamora, *Masculine Desire: The Sexual Politics of Victorian Aestheticism* (Chapel Hill: University of North Carolina Press, 1990).

30. On *erastes/eromenos* relationships in ancient Greece, involving sexual encounters between older men and youths, see K. J. Dover, *Greek Homosexuality* (New York: Random House, 1978).

31. Peter Weiermair, *Wilhelm von Gloeden* (Cologne: Taschen, 1994), 18.

32. See Katz, "The Art of Code," 193–208, esp. 201–2.

33. For instance, James J. Wilhelm, the editor of *Gay and Lesbian Poetry: An Anthology from Sappho to Michelangelo* (New York: Garland Publishing, 1995) has included both Cantos XV and XVI in his selection. However, the traditional interpretation of this canto has been questioned by several scholars, who argue in part that the men mentioned by Dante are not documented as sodomites in any other texts and may have committed political, rather than sexual, crimes. See, for example, Sally Mussetter, " 'Ritornare a lo suo principio': Dante and the Sin of Brunetto Latini," *Philological Quarterly* 63 (Fall 1984): 431–38.

34. Weinberg, *Speaking for Vice*, 63.

35. Thomas Crow, "Modernism and Mass Culture in the Visual Arts," in *Pollock and After: The Critical Debate*, ed. Francis Frascina (New York: Harper and Row, 1985): 255.

36. The present discussion is based on Jonathan Weinberg's thorough consideration of the scrapbooks. See Jonathan Weinberg, " 'Boy Crazy': Carl Van Vechten's Queer Collection," *Yale Journal of Criticism* 7, no. 2 (Fall 1994): 25–49.

37. On the public/private binarism as a central structure of the closet see Eve Kosofsky Sedgwick, *Epistemology of the Closet* (Berkeley: University of California Press, 1990), 22, 70, 109–14.

38. See Harold Beaver, "Homosexual Signs (In Memory of Roland Barthes)," *Critical Inquiry* 8, no. 1 (autumn 1981): 104.

39. Ibid., 105.

40. Bruce Boone, "Gay Language as Political Praxis: The Poetry of Frank O'Hara," *Social Text* 1, no. 1 (winter 1979): 59–92. Boone's central thesis emerges from a rereading of Frantz Fanon, *The Wretched of the Earth*, trans. Constance Farrington (New York: Grove, 1968), esp. chapter 7, "Concerning Violence."

41. Ashton, *XXXIV Drawings*, 3. Vinklers also describes Rauschenberg's transferred photographs as "veiled images." Vinklers, "Why Not Dante?," 101.

42. Roberta Smith, "Art: Drawings by Robert Rauschenberg, 1958–1968," *New York Times* (October 31, 1986): C28.

43. Paul Taylor, "Robert Rauschenberg," *Interview* 20, no. 12 (December 1990): 147.

44. *New York Times* (May 20, 1950). Rpt. *Gay American History*, ed. Jonathan Katz (New York: Harper and Row, 1985), 95.

45. Cited in Katz, *Gay American History*, 105.

46. *New York Times* (December 17, 1963). Rpt. Duberman, 203–9.

47. George Chauncey, "A Gay World, Vibrant and Forgotten," *New York Times* (June 26 1994): E17.

48. The Mattachine Foundation was founded in 1950. *One*, the first continuously published gay magazine in the United States, was founded in October 1952. Michael Bronski, *Culture Clash: The Making of a Gay Sensibility* (Boston: South End Press, 1984), 80.

49. In an analogous fashion, production companies such as Apollo Studios and Athletic Model Guild specialized in beach, wrestling, or other film genres that offered opportunities to view well-built male bodies without explicitly acknowledging a homosexual audience or narrative. Several of these short films are available on videotape.

50. *Grecian Guild Pictorial* 2, no. 2 (March 1957): 15.

51. Hockney, *David Hockney*, 193.

52. Duberman, *About Time*, 362.

53. Maurice Berger, "A Clown's Coat," *Artforum* 32, no. 8 (April 1994): 82.

54. In bringing biographical information to bear on the present discussion, I hope to sketch the possible positions that the *Inferno* could have occupied in relation to the dominant sexual-political discourse. Moreover, as Weinberg argues, "biography is essential on a political level" in discussing the development of a homosexual iconography. "It is significant that certain artists took the risk of exposure to create records of homosexuality." Weinberg, *Speaking for Vice*, 42.

55. Taylor, "Robert Rauschenberg," 147.

56. Andy Warhol and Pat Hackett, *Popism: The Warhol '60s* (New York: Harper and Row, 1980), 10.

57. Ibid., 12.

58. Katz, "The Art of Code," 201.

59. Robert Hughes, *The Shock of the New* (New York: Knopf, 1991), 335.

60. Craig Owens, *Beyond Recognition: Representation, Power and Culture* (Berkeley: University of California Press, 1992), 76.

61. Helen Molesworth discusses these paintings in relation to anal desire in "Before Bed," *October* 63 (winter 1993): 68–81.

62. On veiling in *Rebus* see Vinklers, "Why Not Dante?" 101.

63. Andrew Forge, *Rauschenberg* (New York: Abrams, 1969), 18.

64. On "densely coded," "camouflaged," and "elusive" material in Johns, see Kenneth Silver, "Modes of Disclosure: The Construction of Gay Identity and the Rise of Pop Art," *Hand-Painted Pop*, ed. Ronald Ferguson (Los Angeles: Museum

of Contemporary Art, 1992), 181. See also Charles Harrison and Fred Orton, "Jasper Johns: 'Meaning What You See,' " *Art History* 7, no. 1 (March 1984): 76–101; and Jill Johnston, "Trafficking with X," *Art in America* 79, no. 3 (March 1991): 102–11, 164–65.

65. The following discussion is based on Roberta Bernstein, "Things the Mind Already Knows: Jasper Johns' Paintings and Sculptures, 1954–1974" (Ph.D. diss., Columbia University, 1975), 67–69.

66. Harrison and Orton, "Jasper Johns," 81.

67. Jonathan Weinberg, "It's in the Can: Jasper Johns and the Anal Society," *Genders* 1 (spring 1988): 43.

68. Silver, "Modes of Disclosure," 190.

69. William S. Lieberman, "Introductory Wall Label. Rauschenberg: *Thirty-Four Drawings for Dante's Inferno*" (Museum of Modern Art, December 21 1965–March 20, 1966).

70. "A Life Round Table on Modern Art," *Life* (October 11, 1948): 79.

71. Harold Rosenberg, "The American Action Painters," *Art News* 51, no. 8 (December 1952): 48.

72. See Michael Leja, *Reframing Abstract Expressionism* (New Haven: Yale University Press, 1993), 268.

73. Selden Rodman, *Conversations with Artists* (New York: Devin-Adair, 1957).

74. Deitcher argues that the Abstract Expressionist artists themselves maintained a dialectical relationship with mechanical reproduction throughout their history. He notes that Franz Kline and Willem De Kooning employed slide projectors to trace images onto their gestural canvases as they "internalized the mechanical, repetitive structures that dominated postwar American life in order all the more dramatically to stage their resistance to them." Moreover, for those Action Painters who employed no mechanical devices, "abstract imagery" itself "had become encoded" and "conventionalized." David Deitcher, "Unsentimental Education: The Professionalization of the American Artist," *Hand-Painted Pop*, 112. Similarly, Leo Steinberg argues that "Kline and de Kooning made their paintings with deliberation, worked and reworked them towards 'spontaneity.' " Steinberg, *Other Criteria*, 61.

75. Deitcher, "Unsentimental Education," 97. Moira Roth refers to this act as a "symbolic negation of Abstract Expressionism." Moira Roth, "The Aesthetic of Indifference," *Artforum* 16, no. 3 (November 1977): 50.

76. Paul Schimmel, "The Faked Gesture: Pop Art and the New York School," in *Hand-Painted Pop*, 27.

77. Lawrence Alloway in *Robert Rauschenberg* (Washington, D.C.: National Collection of Fine Arts, Smithsonian Institution, 1976), 8.

78. Douglas Crimp, "On the Museum's Ruins," *October* 13 (summer 1980): 56.

79. Rosenberg, "American Action Painters," 22.

80. Ibid., 48.

81. Rosalind E. Krauss, *The Optical Unconscious* (Cambridge, Mass.: MIT Press, 1993), 244. Michael Leja discusses two additional sets of photographs, one of Willem and Elaine De Kooning and one of Jackson Pollock and Lee Krasner,

which emphasize the painters' traditional gender roles. Each pair of pictures depicts the artist-couple in the man's studio, in front of the man's work, with the man standing while the woman sits passively. The women function here not as artists in their own rights but as "essential accessories" that "keep that image [of the male artist] within certain limits by confirming heterosexuality." Leja, *Reframing*, 254–55.

82. Roth, "Aesthetic of Indifference," 49.

83. Warhol and Hackett, *Popism*, 13.

84. On Pollock's suicidal demise see Krauss, *Optical Unconscious*, 1993.

85. Roth, "Aesthetic of Indifference," 49. Roth links the homosexuality that began to enter the new art to the influence of Marcel Duchamp, whose critique of the stereotypically masculine aura surrounding the avant-garde began just after World War I. American interest in Duchamp increased steadily during the 1950s and early 1960s, with the translation of Robert Lobel's catalogue raisonné in 1960. See Nan Rosenthal and Ruth E. Fine, *The Drawings of Jasper Johns* (Washington, D.C.: National Gallery of Art, 1990), 17. On Duchamp's subversions of stereotypical masculinity through masquerade and other critical strategies see Nancy Ring, *New York Dada and the Crisis of Masculinity: Man Ray, Francis Picabia, and Marcel Duchamp in the United States, 1913–1921* (Ann Arbor: University of Michigan Press, 1993). For the debate on the relationship of Rauschenberg's works to Dada aesthetics and politics see Laurie Monahan, "Cultural Cartography: American Designs at the 1964 Venice Biennale," in *Reconstructing Modernism: Art in New York, Paris and Montreal 1945–1964*, ed. Serge Guilbaut (Cambridge, Mass.: MIT Press, 1990), 369–416.

86. Silver, "Modes of Disclosure," 180.

87. Rosalind E. Krauss, "Jasper Johns," *Lugano Review* 1, no. 2 (1965): 2.

88. "Robert Rauschenberg," *Arts* 35, no. 4 (January 1961): 56.

89. "Robert Rauschenberg," *Art News* 59, no. 9 (January 1961): 14.

90. The drastic shift in vocabulary cannot be attributed simply to the time elapsed between Pollock's death, for example, and Rauschenberg's drawings. A review of works by Milton Avery in the same issue of *Art News* proclaimed, "He is a painter who feels the exaltation of freedom ... his paintings look daring." "Milton Avery," *Art News* 59, no. 9 (January 1961): 10.

91. Michel Foucault, *The History of Sexuality*. Vol. 1: *An Introduction*, trans. Robert Hurley (New York: Vintage Books, 1970), 27.

92. Chauncey, *Gay New York*, 288.

Brother/Outsider: In Search of a Black Gay Legacy in James Baldwin's *Giovanni's Room*

Myriam J. A. Chancy

Surely it is one kind of pain that a man reckons with when he *feels* and *knows* he is not welcome, wanted, or appreciated in his homeland. But the pain I find to be most tragic and critical is not the pain and invisibility he endures in his homeland, but the compounded pain and invisibility he endures in his own home, among family and friends. This occurs when he cannot honestly occupy the spaces of family and friendship because he has adopted—out of insecurity, defense, and fear—the mask of the invisible man.　　—Essex Hemphill, *Brother to Brother*

In going underground, I whipped it all except the mind, the *mind*. And the mind that has conceived a plan of living must never lose sight of the chaos against which that pattern was conceived. That goes for societies as well as for individuals. Thus, having tried to give pattern to the chaos which lives within the pattern of your certainties, I must come out, I must emerge.
　　—Ralph Ellison, *Invisible Man*

In his introduction to *In the Life*, "Leaving the Shadow Behind," the late Joseph Beam writes of the precarious social position he is forced to experience as a condition of living "out" his life as a Black gay male.[1] The instability Beam confronts results not only from the fact that he is forced to occupy a position of marginality induced by both his racial and sexual categorization in a world powerfully dominated by those who occupy what Audre Lorde has termed the "mythical norm" of white male heterosexuality,[2] a norm that few of us can encompass but against which we are all measured. It also results from the painful absence of representations in popular culture of Black gay life. As a writer himself, Beam seeks such representations in literature, or Black gay authors whom to emulate. He laments, in an adaptation of a Black feminist credo: "All the protagonists are blond; all the Blacks are criminal and negligible."[3] Undaunted, Beam continues to seek his likeness in the world about him as he also refuses to read those white gay writers who have rendered him invisible within the pages of their texts:

> More and more each day, as I looked around the well-stacked shelves of Gio-vanni's Room, Philadelphia's gay, lesbian, and feminist bookstore, where I worked, I wondered where was the world of Black gay men. I devoured *Blacklight* and *Habari-Daftari*; welcomed *Yemonja* . . . ; located and copied issues of the de-funct newspaper *Moja: Black and Gay*—but they simply weren't enough. How many times could I read Baldwin's *Just Above My Head?* . . .[4]

The irony of this passage resides in the double inscription of the work of the most notable Black gay American writer to date, James Baldwin, for literally just above Beam's head resides a marker of Black gay existence, the masthead of the bookstore itself. Though primarily stocking its shelf with white gay/lesbian literature, the Philly bookstore in which Beam works and searches for a compass to his marginalized life takes its name from Baldwin's oft belittled 224-page novel. Most peculiar, then, is the fact that the novel does not appear to belong in the Black gay archive. It would appear that in a space created to make visible gay lives, a space that takes its name from the only novel by Baldwin to deal *exclusively* with gay identity, Baldwin's *Black* gay contribution remains in the shadows, invisible within the larger context of gay existence, invisible to Beam within the walls of his workplace.

Baldwin's *Giovanni's Room* has nonetheless survived as a significant piece of gay literature, its name borrowed to christen gay bookstores and nightclubs in the United States and abroad, its author's race ultimately refashioned as universal and rendered invisible in the process. My pur-pose, then, in this essay, is to address just how and why this process of simultaneous exposure and erasure has taken place. My ultimate aim is to demonstrate that the novel is more transgressive than conventional liter-ary analyses have allowed, undermining the very process of racial and sexual identity it appears to posit along normative, psychoanalytically based tropes of colonial power structures so cogently articulated by Frantz Fanon in his seminal *Black Skins, White Masks*. For though the novel makes use of such tropes to examine the protagonist's struggle in coming to terms with his gay identity (its masking and unmasking), it reverses the identification process implicit in the colonial project. This is to say that readers are to find in Baldwin's novel a deliberate emphasis on undermining the process by which people of African descent (and other "nonwhite" groups) have been dehumanized at the service of colonial domination; by obscuring the ways in which racial identity is often conflated with, or defined by, sexual stereotypes affixed to racial groups in order to delimit "norms" and "deviants" at the service of colonial power structures of exploitation, Baldwin's novel appears to suggest not only that these categories are unstable but that, by intentionally rendering such categories seemingly fixed and then repositioning them as permeable or pliable, oppressive power structures are effectively undermined and personal, discrete identities put into question. Identity is understood as infinitely more complex and intrinsic to the individual than the social forces that seek to contain each of us. Further, he extends the scope of then current strategies of "racial" uplift in the African American literary tradition, that which Harryette Mullen has called "taking up the trope of the black body with a white soul in order to humanize the black, or the simple inversion of the trope" (also to humanize the black), which then became complicated by the "miscegenated texts" of mixed-raced writers such as Frederick Douglass and Harriet Jacobs.[5] He extends this tradition in *Giovanni's Room* not only by placing a "black" soul in a white body but by confounding the markers by which such a determination might be made by readers in the first place. This is to say that though as the novel progresses, as I make clear in the analysis to follow, it is possible to see in the protagonist's struggle with his sexual identity a parallel with identity struggles in the context of racial antagonisms in the 1950s in the United States, that parallelism erupts from Baldwin's imbrication of sexual identity with racial identity. This imbrication renders sexual identity and racial identity inseparable at the same time as each category is progressively dissolved.

The novel's protagonist, David, is thus a product of converging identities, both racial and sexual; his emergent sexual identity is both heterosexual and homosexual; his racial identity, which appears to be prototypically that of the all-American (blond) boy next door, grows increasingly less "white" as David admits that even his whiteness is a myth, an illusion, yet an *integral component* of the mask he wears in order to "pass" as straight. As David's true identity is revealed, all the aspects of his identity as a white, heterosexual male that appeared to be stable are put into question; it is a performance that is doomed to fail if, as Judith Butler writes in

Bodies That Matter, "for a performance to work, then, means that a reading is no longer possible, or that a reading, an interpretation, appears to be a kind of transparent seeing, where what appears and what it means coincide."[6] According to Butler, the successful performance is one in which "the body performing and ideal performed appear indistinguishable" (129). What we have, then, in *Giovanni's Room* is a body (in David) that endeavors to perform the social ideal of white, straight malehood, only to find that the ideal, for him, is that which is socially aberrant—the black, the gay, in short, all that his lover, Giovanni, comes to represent.

As I demonstrate in the first section of this essay, race is not here, as Butler argues elsewhere (18), a *product* of sexual encoding but an identification *entwined* with sexuality, both heterosexual and homosexual. Race, then, in my analysis, is not to be read as sexuate (to borrow Irigaray's term) but as a category through which certain bodies have been marked as desirable and undesirable; the undesirable is that which is reclaimed in Baldwin's novel. It is in this reclamation that the reversal of the colonial identification process is enacted.

This process has been described by Homi K. Bhabha as having three underlying conditions in the colonial context for "an understanding of the *process of identification* in the analytic of desire." Summarized and paraphrased, these are: 1) existence made possible through the interaction with (or gaze of) the Other; 2) the split-subject produced as an effect of desire for the Other; and 3) identification as "the production of an image of identity and the transformation of the subject in assuming that image"[7] in continuous distinction from the Other. The dependency between the Subject and the Other thus forms, as Fanon argued earlier, the articulation of any given, colonizing or colonized, identity. The objectified Other is the basis for a differentiation that permits the emergence of the Subject into the realm of "being." It is this "beingness" that Baldwin's David pursues so desperately as he recounts the story of his love affair with Giovanni. This desperate pursuit is foiled through the reversal of colonial differentiation, a process that I term "raciosexual amalgamation" and to which I will turn in the final section of the essay.

Baldwin's aim in this reversal is to reveal and relieve the Black (male) body beneath that of the articulation of the gay (ostensibly white) body, which itself relies upon the Black female body for its articulation (I return to this point in the first section of this essay). In so doing, he blurs the lines between race and sexuality, traditionally upheld in more recent critical inquiries, without, however, obscuring the role race plays in the process of (dis)identification between Self and "Other" (that which exists outside of the self and permits the self to define itself by distinction from what it perceives itself not to be). Baldwin's amalgamated body attempts to escape the historical bipolarization of sexuality first delimited by race and then articulated ideologically through discourses of sexuality. In other words, he undermines the manner in which racial differentiation has been historically established through the creation of sexual stereotypes buoyed by pseudoscientific discourses meant to render those constructions natural.

As Sander Gilman demonstrates in his essay "Black Bodies, White Bodies," racist discourse of the nineteenth century came to be constructed around the image of the "African Venus"—African women who were brought to Europe as "samples" of foreign exotica only to be ridiculed, demonized, and sexually stereotyped. Says Gilman: "The antitheses of European sexual mores and beauty is embodied in the black, and the essential black, the lowest rung on the great chains of being is the Hottentot."[8] Thus, Gilman writes that "Black females do not merely represent the sexualized female, they also represent the female as the source of corruption and disease."[9] The stereotyping and marking of African women's bodies as receptacles of depravity then served to mark the abnormality of the Black male body and its attendant sexuality. Not coincidentally, at the turn of the century, gay men of any race were believed to be "inverts," women trapped in men's bodies;[10] the model of sexual depravity that circumscribed gay representation would thus continue to rely on the overdetermined sexualization of the "black," represented by the African Venus, for its articulation of the gay male as a social anomaly, an inferior product of genetic mutation, a "prostitute" existing outside of gender convention. Through the trope of black identification, then, Baldwin's novel provides us with a subtle unveiling of the dynamics of Black gay identity in cultures (American and European), which revile both blackness and homosexuality while exoticizing both race and sexuality together and separately. The apparent absence of Black gay identity within the novel is a reflection of reality; its presence is too a reflection of a far-reaching denial of Black gay identity in American letters in the era of civil rights. And yet, it is in this historical moment that we see made paramount the issue of (in)visibility in African American literature, most notably in Ralph Ellison's *Invisible Man*.

In the second section of the main body of this essay, then, I turn to an evaluation of the literary metaphor of invisibility so well illustrated by

Ellison's novel. This metaphor held up a mirror to the condition of the African American (male) person in revelatory ways, indicting the process of alienation by which African Americans were systematically denied social enfranchisement. In this marginalization, racial politics of the time appeared to mirror sexual politics, relegating Black persons to the shadows of social life and denying their humanity in ways parallel to the ostracization of gays and lesbians who occupied states of "closetedness," denied the right to circulate freely and openly in society in ways that made visible their sexual identities. This is not to say, of course, that gays and lesbians were reviled in the same ways as were "visible" minorities such as African Americans, who could not "hide" their "difference"; my analysis focuses on how the underlying reasons for such ostracization resulted in making invisible the aforementioned groups of people in terms of their social and legal existence. Denied basic freedom and rights, then, people of color as well as gays and lesbians can be said to have occupied similar sites of marginalization in the United States in the mid-twentieth century. Perhaps more crucial to bear in mind in this context (as I have touched on in the previous section) are the reasons that the analysis of racial and sexuality oppressions have been left unlinked and unexplored.

I am proposing, then, that Baldwin's text can be engaged as a "miscegenated text" for its attempt to bridge and dismantle what have become increasingly fixed constructions of racial and sexual categories. Miscegenation tales, we should recall here, are those that positioned African Americans who were for all outward appearances white as the hero or heroines of stories that sought to humanize the Black person by appealing to the epidermal construction of race for a primarily white readership. Although much has been said about the problematics of employing "white" African Americans to humanize "blackness," I am in agreement with Valerie Smith when she claims that with respect to white-Black bodies:

[T]heir conditions are productive sites for considering how the intersectionality of race, class, and gender ideologies are constituted and denied; not only do these bodies function as markers of sexual and racial transgression, but they signal as well the inescapable class implications of crossing these boundaries.[11]

Keeping this assertion in mind, we should consider that the overdetermination of racial identification by skin color or African heritage (the one-drop-of-Black-blood rule of yesteryear, for example) has been utilised to make first physically visible, then socially and legally invisible nonwhite, non-European people. Though miscegenation tales of the turn of the century such as Frances Harper's *Iola Leroy* (1892) and the Harlem Renaissance novellas of Nella Larsen sought to complicate notions of racial identification by pointing out that physical markers of race were more or less insubstantial or often misleading, it is curious that it has been near impossible for these texts in fact to undo the ideology that sustains the necessity for physical differentiation. The charge of racial self-hatred notwithstanding,[12] it would be productive to begin to examine the hybridity inherent in such characters who are not simply "white" by color or "black" by heritage but a combination thereof; this is to say that as mixed-raced characters, they embody both white and Black cultural legacies with varying transmutations of whatever heritages miscegenation has brought together through their very bodies. Thus, when presented with a mixed-raced character, might we begin to see the European elements that make up that character as well as that which is being reclaimed as African? Further, might it be possible to read against the grain, to read such a character as white inasmuch as that character's consciousness is presented as such in representative works (the first several chapters of Harper's *Iola Leroy* are a case in point) and to then explore *how* the transformation of that consciousness occurs as a result of the character's acceptance of the transgression that has produced them? More pointed, might it be possible for a character who is not otherwised identified as "Black" to *acquire* that cultural knowledge (much as Iola does in Harper's text once she is apprised of her part-Black descent)? It is the transmutation of culture and heritage that is most essential to grasp in the present discussion, for it is this ultimate transgression, when engaged in with genuine intent (not to follow a hip-hop fad, for example), that will ultimately disrupt the barriers that have been erected primarily between races, genders, and sexualities to support an imperialistic, misogynist, and racist class system that necessitates the firm upkeep of those barriers in order to continue to function.

In the final section of this essay, then, I suggest further that the struggle of the novel's protagonist implicitly serves to inform more recent critical grapplings with the question of the postcolonial, that is, with the process of decolonization in contemporary societies. It does so in demonstrating that decolonization (and colonization itself) is a process that binds the subject to its "other," the colonizer with the colonized, and that the decolonization of the latter necessarily transforms the former. Baldwin exposes the symbiosis implicit in the colonial project and shows how that synergy can be put at the service of dismantling the hierarchical power structures that have come to dominate our relationships to one another across race, sex, class, and sexuality divides. As he does so, he explicitly demonstrates the need for the dissolution of labels that inaccurately define each of us and yet circumscribe our existence and limit our individual claims to personal choices and freedoms.

Living, as we are, enveloped in the legacy of entwined racism and homophobia, critics intent today on unpacking the politics of marginalization must refuse to consign to a footnote not only the ways in which racial discourse is differentially experienced across racial boundaries but the limited critical venues through which that discourse has come to be contested. The latter affect crucially our ways of apprehending the identity formation of those who cannot "pass" from one race to an other, from one gender to an other, from one sexuality to an other, and, who, in their manifest failure to transcend such polarized categories, nonetheless encompass aspects of each.

In order to move firmly toward such a transcendence (one that is neither romantic in nature nor oblivious to the forces of social and cultural reality) in the present essay, it is my intent to make use of parts of theoretical apparatus that might appear, at first glance, to be anathema one to the other: postcolonial theory, African American literary criticism, performance theory, gay and lesbian theory, and historical revisionist criticism. My purpose in doing so will be to demonstrate the extent to which many of these perspectives speak to the same subject, that is, the nature of power structures and how prejudice appears to serve the purpose of maintaining the hegemonic (im)balance of power in particular social contexts. Though few critics involved in these fields successfully cross the barriers of racial, sexual, sexuality or class differences, it will be my purpose to demonstrate the ways in which *joining* these perspectives can propel us to better understand how fear fuels the maintenance of these social barriers and can induce us to begin to dismantle each of them. Further, such an interdisciplinary approach should underscore the need to develop a more expansive and flexible critical discourse for the analysis of the imbrication (rather than intersection) of race, sex, sexuality, and class identities.[13] As Yvonne Yarbro-Bejarano notes in her essay "Expanding the Categories of Race and Sexuality in Lesbian and Gay Studies,"[14] "[t]he destabilization and expansion of regulatory categories of analysis will help us to produce more complex imaginings of ourselves in the world and the place of race in our lived realities as gendered sexual subjects" (133). Perhaps I would rephrase Bejarano's statement only slightly here so that lived reality would be foregrounded not as an effect of gender and sexuality mediated by race but as a lived reality in which race cannot be disengaged from our gender and sexual positioning in society; in this sense, the use of interdisciplinary critical tools will aid us in demystifying the process of identification and how it is that some of us may in fact be socially sanctioned to willfully "forget" or minimize our racial, gender, or sexual identities.

Ultimately, then, my reading of Baldwin's *Giovanni's Room* within this interdisciplinary critical frame seeks to demonstrate that the novel inscribes what Sandra L. Richards gestures toward at the end of her important essay "Writing the Absent Potential: Drama, Performance, and the Canon of African-American Literature" when she writes that in African American drama "the unwritten, or an absence from the script, is a potential presence implicit in performance"[15] and invokes the Haitian cult of twins, the "marasa," of which consciousness Vèvè Clark has written "invites us to imagine beyond the binary."[16] Although *Giovanni's Room* is not a piece of theater, it does engage in the act of ensnaring its readers in a productive performative exchange within which David's identity is realized through the textual repetitive motion of his memories and through the reader's perception of what is revealed in the textual gaps memory affords as the narrator's insistence on telling the story in a series of flashbacks leads us through a path of evasions and the subsumed process of the character's coming to identify with a nonself that he already embodies at the outset of the story. Thus, performativity, in my analysis, is to be read not as the by-product of, as writes Philip Brian Harper, "a mode of *theatrical* production" but as "a mode of *discursive* production."[17] Baldwin's complex presentation of David's inner struggle is to be read as the textualized grappling with the articulation of identity; in this sense, then, the text is "performative" as it enacts the very process of gender and racial identity formations in twentieth-century Western society. In the end, it is readers' unwillingness to disentangle themselves from David's need for self-deception that has limited more complex readings of the text. By placing the novel in the context of critical and literary perspectives articulated by Black gay men more recently (most notably in *In the Life* [1986] and *Brother to Brother* [1991] wherein the editors, Joseph Beam and Essex Hemphill, align themselves critically with the tenets of "multiple jeopardy" put forward in Black feminist criticism), in the con-

text of its historical position with respect to the African American literature of its time, and in the context of current gay/lesbian and postcolonial
studies debates, *Giovanni's Room* reveals itself as being among the first
textualizations of the Black gay experience. It is a text that moves "beyond
the binary" to situate itself also as a model of textualized amalgamation,
the very fusion necessary to unify the polarities that ultimately result in
the demise of that "Othered ideal" that is so reviled within the text—the
Black and gay self. What we are forced to read between the lines of
Baldwin's seemingly universal text of the (white) gay experience is thus
the subtext of the Black gay experience.

I AM THE MAN, I SUFFERED, I WAS THERE

One must note that despite the overt homoeroticism of the novel, Baldwin refused to label *Giovanni's Room* a gay text. He once categorically
stated that "it is not about homosexuality"[18] but rather that "it's what
happens to you if you're afraid to love anybody."[19] In a letter to his editor
in 1953, Baldwin wrote that "since I want to convey something about the
kinds of American loneliness, I must use the ordinary type of American I
can find—the good white Protestant is the image I want to use."[20] That
"type" has resulted in the easy dismissal of the novel in the assessments
made of Baldwin's vision for racial harmony in the United States. David
Bergman, for one, argues that "Baldwin's analysis of sexuality stands in
contrast to his analysis of race" and supports this claim with a faulty
interpretation of Baldwin's essay on André Gide, "The Male Prison."
Bergman contends that the essay exposes internalized homophobia on
Baldwin's part.

In "The Male Prison," Baldwin chastises Gide for having "outed"
himself while married to his wife, Madeleine; Baldwin criticizes Gide and
his marriage precisely because of its artificiality, its façade of heterosexuality maintained at the expense of Madeleine's sexual freedom. Baldwin
thus declares that the marriage is a misogynist sham by which Gide's wife
is kept entrapped in the prison of Gide's own internalized homophobia.
Hence, he writes: "When men can no longer love women they also
cease to love or respect or trust each other, which makes their isolation
complete."[21] In writing this, he sought, not as Bergman argues, to offer a
"paean to heterosexuality" (169), but to refuse to align male machismo
and misogyny with gay identity. As when he dealt with women's rights

within the parameters of racial equity (most notably in *If Beale Street Could Talk*), Baldwin uncompromisingly refused to participate in perpetuating the oppression of (it must be said, heterosexual) women (as Gide did in leading his double life with Madeleine) through the maintenance of heterosexist norms that also serve to deny the existence of gay male lives. Baldwin reveals his contempt for the masking of sexuality in the very structure of *Giovanni's Room*, in which his protagonist, David, literally uses women's bodies as shields against his own homoerotic desires.

David, an American in Paris, is waiting for his girlfriend, Hella, to return from Spain, where she has gone in order to "find herself." As he waits, David undergoes his own confrontation with self, falling in love with Giovanni, an Italian bartender. What ensues is their love affair, which they contain within the Parisian *demimonde* and the cramped quarters of Giovanni's rented room, a temporary residence "not large enough for two." [22] That room, of course, is the closet to which Eve Sedgwick refers in her work *Epistemology of the Closet*, when she writes that "[it] is the defining structure for gay oppression in this century," [23] the liminal space within which gays and lesbians have been forced to exist while remaining nominally hidden from mainstream society. In Baldwin's novel, the room, or "closet," represents David's limited capacity for love with either men or women, an incapacity spawned from an identity of self-loathing. David thus continuously alternates between feeling trapped by Joey (a childhood friend), Hella, Sue (a one-night affair), and Giovanni. After being with Sue in order to escape his love and desire for Giovanni, David thinks: "I hated her and me, then it was over, and the dark, tiny room rushed back. And I wanted only to get out of there" (133–134). Similarly, as he remembers his first gay experience as an adolescent with his friend Joey, David thinks: "I had decided to allow no room in the universe for something which shamed and frightened me" (30). With Giovanni, David briefly ceases to flee from his sexuality and reenters what, for him, is a room of shame and fear, for it is the world Giovanni inhabits, desperately hoping to be freed himself. As David explains, "I was to destroy this room and give to Giovanni a new and better life. This life could only be my own, which, in order to transform Giovanni's, must first become a part of Giovanni's room" (116).

As their relationship progresses, David reverts to his usual pattern of self-hate and flight. He "felt the walls of the room were closing in on me" (139), and his love quickly turns to hate: "I was guilty and irritated and full of love and pain. I wanted to kick him and I wanted to take him in my arms" (154). The room, the "closet," is presented by Baldwin as a psychological prison not unlike that faced by Ralph Ellison's protagonist in *Invisible Man;* it is in this parallel that we can begin to see the close connection between racial and sexual disenfranchisement.

Curiously, the relationship between race and (homo)sexuality has by and large been occluded or reductively associated one with the other in mainstream literary studies. Although critics strictly concerned with African American literature have for the most part kept a persistent silence on the issue of gay/bi/lesbian identity, some critics engaged in gay and lesbian studies have made a point of *invoking* race in the construction of gay and lesbian identity. In her compelling essay "Sexualities Without Genders and Other Queer Utopias," Biddy Martin asserts, for one, the claim "that race gets cast in the terms of fixity and miring in the same moves that gender and identity itself do."[24] Martin sets out, in part, to demonstrate the pliability of racial identity, that is, that race is not, in fact, "fixed" by demonstrating the extent to which gender "passings" (on the part of lesbians) mirror racial ones. She writes:

Racial passing, which is a crossing, and gender crossing, which may well operate as a passing (as a man), are required in this scheme in order to make visible any distance from what is otherwise the ground for differentiated figures. Such crossings have the potential to destabilize and collapse problematic boundaries. But we have to be wary of the tendency to make sexuality the means of crossing, and to make gender and race into grounds so indicatively fixed that masculine positions become the emblem again of mobility. Men do not seem gendered and whites are not racialized in accounts that make these issues too distinct.[25]

Arrestingly, Martin goes on to show that lesbian cross-identifications (Butler's butch/femme analyses and her theorem of the lesbian phallus are cited as examples) are mired in racial identifications and the need to "[render] lesbian desire legible."[26] As B. Ruby Rich delineates in her essay "When Difference Is (More Than) Skin Deep," race thus becomes the marker for a difference that can no longer rely on the gender difference for the articulation of gay/lesbian selfhood:

Race occupies the place vacated by gender. The non-sameness of color, language, or culture is a marker of difference in relationships otherwise defined by the sameness of gender. Race is a constructed presence of same-gender couples, one which allows a sorting out of identities that can avoid both the essentialism of prescribed racial expectations and the artificiality of entirely self-constructed paradigms. The possibility exists, then, for a kind of negotiation of identities not found elsewhere. . . .[27]

I suggest that this sense of unexamined or subversive potential is persistently foreclosed in gay/lesbian studies (as Yarbro-Bejarano, whom I cited earlier, notes): though it may be true that the use of racial markers in same-sex relationships may come to redefine our sense of gender constructions and gay or lesbian identity, those racial markers tend to remain fixed, unquestioned, and reinscriptive of racial stereotyping. Thus, while Rich would argue that at times "racial difference itself [seems] to call lesbianism into existence," I argue that it does so at the expense of erasing the black body, which is now transformed into *the* site of sexual transgression. Hence, the black body remains objectified at the service of the articulation of a primarily *white* gay and lesbian identity, leaving in the margins that which might make intelligible the *black* gay and lesbian identity.

The problematic use of the black body as site of both gender and sexuality transgression is most apparent in the work of Judith Butler, who, in pursuing the metaphor of passing as the performance of sexed identity in *Bodies That Matter,* analyzes the film *Paris Is Burning* for "what it suggests about the simultaneous production and subjugation of subjects in a culture which appears to arrange always and in every way for the annihilation of queers, but which nevertheless produces occasional spaces in which those annihilating norms, those killing ideals of gender and race, are mimed, reworked, resignified" (124). Central to this exploration is the foregrounding of the affirmation to be found in the film, which Butler defines as "the creation of kinship." Kinship, in Butler's appraisal of a film that centers on drag balls created for and by primarily Latino and African American gay males, eventually comes to replace race itself. Butler critiques both the filmmaker and bell hooks's analysis of the film for defining the men in the film as "black"; "neither," she says "considers *the place and force of ethnicity* in the articulation of kinship relations" (my emphasis, 134). Kinship here functions as a disassociation, on Butler's part, from racial identity because she objects to the conflation of Latino identity with African American identity; though such a conflation may be unwarranted, it is difficult to understand why kinship should come to replace the racial identifications that the subjects of the film appear to be reconfiguring without, yet, abandoning them. Ethnicity appears to be posited by Butler, in my opinion, as a dearticulation of race, although its emergence here is a function of a difference-from-blackness rendered visible through the Latino presence; the ethnicity Butler wishes to foreground nonetheless reiterates current racial demarcations, disallowing for the plausibility of "black" ethnicity and permitting ethnicity to circulate as a term that is nothing more than code for "nonblack," if not completely and assimilatively "white." It is true for a number of the Latino gay males in the film that they are both Latino *and* Black, while those who do not *appear to be* of African descent clearly do not define themselves as "white."

This inability to do away completely with the oppressive structures of racialized identity is the reason that, for Venus Xtravaganza, a preoperative transsexual featured in the film, it is so essential to pass both as white and as female to attain some measure of class privilege. While Butler admirably delineates the ways in which internalized homophobia and racism contribute to the unmaking of Xtravaganza (her premature death at the hands of a white, male client), she is less able to confront the situation of the Black gay men in the film, specifically, the survival of Willie Ninja. Ninja, Butler claims, "can pass as straight; his voguing becomes foregrounded in het video productions with Madonna et al.; and he achieves postlegendary status on an international scale. There is passing and then there is passing, and it is—as we used to say—'no accident' that Willie Ninja ascends and Venus Xtravaganza dies" (130). A more focused analysis of the role race plays in this context would reveal a less reductive conclusion, that is, that Venus Xtravaganza dies precisely because she attempts to coopt the spaces of white womanhood with a body that is neither entirely white nor entirely female. Ninja, however, cannot (and the film makes this visibly evident) pass as white, an impossibility that means that were he to emulate "women," he would have to pass as a Black woman (I also think that the time frame in which Ninja might conceivably have been "read" as straight is quite narrow: he was known to be a part of the gay ball scene long before he appeared in Madonna's videos, most notably 1991's *Vogue*, which was followed, in the same year, by the film *Truth or Dare*, which revealed him, along with most of Madonna's dancers, to be gay to a perhaps unsuspecting straight audience). As Butler herself notes, that identification is empty of empowering potential, for it "falsely constitutes black women as a site of privilege" (131). Ninja survives, not "accidentally," because of a recognition that male power for a Black male in contemporary American society ensures a measure of survival. Ironically, then, it is in the *failure* to transcend his "blackness" that Ninja might be said to "survive" while, for Xtravaganza, it is the ability to (temporarily) *secure* that transgression that ultimately ushers in her demise. This is not to say that Ninja's survival is the effect of a fixed racial identity; more precisely, it is a survival that hinges on the *perception* of fixity within the discourse of dominant, white society for its articulation.

What has all this to do with Baldwin's *Giovanni's Room* and the racial identities figured within the novel? Simply put, Baldwin's ambivalently identified protagonist, David, relies on similar, but inversed, racial categories to safeguard his identity as a white, heterosexual male. Like Venus Xtravaganza, David attempts to pass; the body he identifies with is a source of privilege that has, for most of his life, been accorded him without question: As his self-perception begins to fail, he ultimately edges toward self-destruction, attempting to regain that illusory, fictive body as the source of his identity. It is in David's inability to embody those categories fully that his Black gay body begins to be revealed and the reversal of the colonial process is put into motion.

In the novel, the trope of blackness is rearticulated in the context of gay existence, and the most desired and yet the most disparaged character are one and the same, the Italian Giovanni. In the European context, it might be said that Giovanni is marked as "black" just as Italian immigrants to the United States were, in the late nineteenth and early twentieth centuries, raced as nonwhite if not as people of "black" origin. But it is not this facile explication of Giovanni's Mediterranean "otherness" and its concomitant potential for exploring the evolution of racialization and ethnicity in the European and American contexts that appear most important in the text. It is Giovanni's *association* with this signifying racial or ethnic difference, its impact on his exoticization in the gay circles within which he finds himself in the Parisian *demimonde*, and, ultimately, the narrator's *identification* with this exotic Other that propulse the entire narrative into a tenuous imbrication of raciosexual constructions of identity that cannot be denied. It is not possible, however, to comprehend how such an imbrication takes place and serves to destabilize the colonial identification process without taking stock of how the novel is situated in its own historical period within the canon of African American literature.

To continue, then, I now turn to situating the text historically to reveal the way in which Baldwin's David is implicitly positioned as a "Black" character despite his surface appearance of "whiteness." Such an exercise reveals why, in 1956, Baldwin would have found it so necessary to remove his characters from the American setting George Chauncey describes in his *Gay New York* as "the most visible gay world of the early twentieth century . . . a working-class world, centered in African-American and Irish and Italian immigrant neighborhoods and along the city's busy waterfront" (10). Why did Baldwin find it impossible to combine within the text an evaluation of both Black and gay identities and deem it necessary to remove his characters to "another country" and the waterfront of the Seine? The next section demonstrates that it is necessary to provide a bridge between author and text in order to appreciate fully the narrative exposition of sexuality within the novel and its raced implications. Furthermore, by exposing the intertextuality present between the novel and Ralph Ellison's *Invisible Man* as well as Baldwin's short story of 1951, "The Outing," we can arrive at a new reading of the text that brings us closer to releasing its encoded depiction of the complexities of Black gay existence.

JUST ABOVE MY HEAD . . . ?

Through the vehicle of his 1952 novel, Ralph Ellison introduced to the American world of letters a concept of social marginalization or invisibility entrenched in the discourse of (American) racism; in particular, the metaphor of invisibility used throughout his work centered on describing and coming to terms with the peculiar alienation and denigration that were the daily portion of the average African American man as he attempted to emerge from the confines of a segregated nation. As Ellison's invisible man, unable to assimilate convincingly into the world of his oppressors or that of the politically militant "brotherhood," struggles in his abandoned cellar to formulate a new ideal identity, he becomes the prototype for the foiled desires of the post-"New Negro" African American male. Ellison writes of his aims here some thirty years after the publication of the novel:

[M]y task was one of revealing the human universals hidden within the plight of one who was both black and American, and not only as a means of conveying my personal vision of possibility, but as a way of dealing with the sheer rhetorical challenge involved in communicating barriers of race and religion, class, color and region. . . .[28]

Ellison did so by plumbing the depths of denied humanity. The source of both frustration and liberation, the state of invisibility described in *Invisible Man* results from just such denial. Ellison's metaphor thus carries with it the same sense of alienation described by Essex Hemphill, an alienation that demands that a particular raced and eroticized sector of society be treated as second-class citizens. One could argue that in Hemphill's case and for most Black gay men and women, sexuality adds another dimension to this alienation, that of suffering ostracism from within the African American community as well. Nonetheless, what is crucial to take away from Ellison's metaphor, in the present context, are the ways in which racial demarcation curtails the possibilities of assimilation and results, in his character's case, in a movement "underground," that is, to a space of self-negation (the cellar) similar to the disavowal of gay identity (the closet); in both situations, this movement underground is a self-protective measure against social constraints. A parallel structure might be that of the discourse of miscegenation most prominently voiced in African American literature in response to social mores from the 1920s to the early 1970s.

As Philip Brian Harper has shown in his important essay "Private Affairs: Race, Sex, Property, and Persons," the historical stigmatization of miscegenation in the United States between Euro-Americans and African Americans was at its base a social construction invested in the commodification and exploitation of Black bodies. In his analysis of Francis Harper's turn-of-the-century miscegenation tale, *Iola Leroy* (1892), Harper thus concludes:

[M]iscegenation, insofar as it implies the reconceptualization of a nonwhite individual not as a privatized object but as a private subject (by definition entitled to hold private property), represents a profound threat to the political status quo and thus becomes a source of anxiety throughout "official" culture.[29]

This source of anxiety is mapped onto the Black body. As a consequence, those bodies which attempt to transgress the boundaries of race and sexuality, that make that Black body intelligible to begin with, become the object of close scrutiny. This scrutiny (negative in nature, of course) is present precisely because the act of miscegenation literally renders the permeability of racial and sexual boundaries tangible; transgression then becomes actionable rather than remaining a lofty, hypothetical goal for those who would benefit from the destabilization of hierarchically constructed social classes. For Harper, *Iola Leroy* presents compelling evidence for connecting racial oppression with oppressions meted out because of one's sexuality:

[I]t seems to me that if we interrogate the apparent parallel between the political significance of mixed-race relationships and that of homosexual identity in the light of the economic dimension of the concerns I have examined, we may discover that antimiscegenation sentiment and homophobia—or at any rate, the versions of them prevalent in the United States—derive their impetus largely from a common organizing principle: the sanctity of the private realm as a means of controlling the flow of economic capital.[30]

That flow is, of course, regulated through the heterosexual contract to benefit white males, an identity synonymous with imperialism and colonialism. Thus, to extend Harper's insight further in the context of my present analysis, I argue for understanding this parallel as impacting not only the economic constraints imposed on Black bodies for the benefit of white ones, but the basic process of identification itself. Furthermore, though I am sympathetic to the implicitly Marxist analysis proferred by Harper, I think it somewhat reductive to argue for the dissemblance of the "sanctity of the private realm"; since the advent of the colonial process (through which so many cultures have been decimated or otherwise inter-rupted), that sanctity (and privacy) cannot be said to exist for those positioned as the Other regardless of the success of their attempts to transgress the boundaries that make possible the construction of their identities as Others.

Nonetheless, the denial of a private sense of identity has lead many to hide their "true" selves, selves otherwise criminalized in colonial societies (and here I do mean to include present-day America). This denial of identity, both racial and sexual, however, cannot forever be sublimated, for to continuously deny the self is to ensure one's spiritual and sensual death, if not one's actual physical demise. Thus, as Ellison's invisible man struggles with his identity as an African American male and retreats from society, he concludes: "Here [underground] . . . I could try to think things out in peace, or, if not in peace, in quiet" (558). He soon discovers that going underground will not solve his impending loss of identity in Ameri-can society. For this reason, he ultimately declares, "I must come out, I must emerge" (567). The act of self-revelation, of "coming out," holds the promise of providing the invisible man with the means to propel himself into the "real" world and shed the all-consuming self-hatred and shame imposed on him from without that have contributed to his with-drawal from society and community; that "outing" will not, however, release him from the erasure he will continue to face in a society that plays at acknowledging his humanity and ultimately denies it. Thus, the novel ends without the actual fulfilment of this promise.

Similarly, David in *Giovanni's Room*, knowing too well the conse-quences of transgressing social constraints, is contained in Giovanni's room. The room thus appears to be a place of refuge in a world that accepts few contradictions within the same being, only bipolar identities, the "straights" and the "folles"—the latter, drag queens of the Parisian underground, whom David so abhors as he begins to identify with them on a common ground. David belongs to neither world and to both; he is a bisexual character (thus occupying a space of hybridity not unlike that of the "miscegenated" character), unable to accept that he is capable of loving a man as fully as, indeed, he has loved a woman. David's internalized homophobia keeps him in denial. Giovanni, on the other hand, "had great plans for remodeling the room" (96), of "pushing back the encroaching walls, without, however, having the walls fall down" (152). Giovanni's hopes for such a transformation, in the face of David's growing loathing, are slim. The physical privacy of Giovanni's room offers no protection to either character from the limitations of each's psychological response to marginalization: Giovanni's desperation, David's shame. Though David also comes to realize the necessity of emerging from that room to claim the identity of the "othered ideal" he himself has colluded in rendering invisible, his fear propels him to foreclose his own process of emergence.

Though *Invisible Man* is ostensibly focused on the negation of racial identity and *Giovanni's Room* on the negation of sexual identity, juxtaposing the trials of the two protagonists in terms of their identity struggles against Euro-American social mores proves productive. "Minority" identity, in both novels, is posited as the primary source of alienation for those seen as "Others" within mainstream American life. And, in both, marginalization results in the spatial containment of the "hated" identity, a containment that threatens to annihilate both protagonists and forever sever them from their communal and national home/land. The connections between these novels become all the more apparent when the authorship of *Giovanni's Room* is seriously taken under consideration in the analysis of the work's multiple aims. For, though *Giovanni's Room* is a prototypical gay "coming out" story, it also functions as Baldwin's "coming out" novel, a clear declaration of his own identity as a gay author; furthermore, it encodes, even as it distances itself from, Black signifiers (as I demonstrate in the final section of this essay) in the process of articulating the parameters of gay identity and alienation. In so doing, it joins Ellison's *Invisible Man* in arguing against the stereotyping of Black males and for the freedom of the individual's right to constitute his or her own identity; it goes beyond Ellison's text in bridging the gap that has become apparent in current theorizing of the body in race and sexuality discourses, respectively, in American culture. That bridge is in fact hinted at with Baldwin's dedication of the novel to his then lover, the white and bisexual Lucien Happersberger, followed immediately by a quote attributed to Walt Whitman: "I am the man, I suffered, I was there." An extratextual sign, to be sure, but a significant one nonetheless. To those critics who charged that Baldwin knew too little of the gay experience to write as cogently about it as he did on the issue of race, this autobiographical inscription served as a legitimizing warning, if not as an explicit manifesto of Baldwin's own Black gay identity.

The rich intertextuality between *Giovanni's Room* and Baldwin's short story, "The Outing," reveals a further attempt on his part to have readers work at releasing the racial subtext evident in the novel. Written five years earlier than *Giovanni's Room*, "The Outing" provides the former with its texture: the characters in the short story appear to be the prototypes for the later incarnations of David and Giovanni. The Baldwin biographer W. J. Weatherby, for one, suggests in *James Baldwin: Artist on Fire* that the final scene of the short story became the basis for an expanded revelation of male gay desire in the later novel.[31] "The Outing" is the story of the friendship between two Black adolescent boys—Johnnie and David—their love, and the "threat" of gay desire exposed between them. In the story, the two boys attend a church picnic presided over by Johnnie's father. The main event of the picnic is the presentation of a butterfly-shaped pin from the boys and Johnnie's brother Roy as a birthday present to Sylvia, a girl on whom each appears to have an adolescent crush. Of the three, David is the most romantically interested in Sylvia. Still, as the action of the story progresses, he is shown as capable of evoking a profession of love from a boy, Johnnie.

The similarities between the characters are indeed striking: the two Davids are alike in that they both encompass bisexual lives and act out their desire and love for members of both sexes while making a commitment to neither; both are unable to fully express their gay identities as they fear being stigmatized within their communities. Their sexuality is thus distorted, since both are entrapped within the parameters of what Adrienne Rich has termed compulsory heterosexuality (later updated by Judith Butler as "the heterosexual imperative") and are unable to separate heterosexual desire from their masked homosexuality. Further, Johnnie, like Giovanni, is acutely and desperately aware of his David's inability to reciprocate love fully, to risk social disapprobation in order to express gay desire. In "The Outing," however, Johnnie is aware of the social stigmatization that surrounds homosexuality in a way which Giovanni refuses, in the novel, to concede (even though he falls victim to the most extreme expression of homophobia in his execution). Not surprisingly, then, Johnnie's thoughts, at the point at which he consciously comes to term with his homosexual desire for his friend, echoes those of David in the novel. Baldwin writes:

Johnnie felt suddenly, not the presence of the Lord, but the presence of David; which seemed to reach out to him, hand reaching out to hand in the fury of flood-time, to drag him to the bottom of the water or to carry him safe to shore . . . [he] felt for that moment, such a depth of love, such nameless and terrible joy and pain, that he might have fallen, in the face of that company, weeping at David's feet.[32]

We need only recall here David's words: "Giovanni was dragging me off with him to the bottom of the sea" (152), and "watching his face, I realized that it meant so much to me that I could make his face so bright. I saw that I might be willing to give a great deal not to lose that power" (110). Johnnie's despair may parallel that of Giovanni, but his words are David's when the latter speaks of his feelings for Giovanni. Both characters are in awe of their lovers; both enshrine the object of their desires; both make futile attempts to deny that desire. The intertextuality in evidence here suggests to me that Baldwin is pointing out that gay desire is not, as Frantz Fanon and other Pan-Africanists would argue, the purview only of "white" cultures; it crosses all racial demarcations and categories. The transgressiveness of raciality subtly hints at the permeability of racial identities and suggests further that the identification of David in *Giovanni's Room* with "whiteness" is also the result of a permeable effect, that his racial identity need not be so rigidly cast, especially when his experience mirrors that of the Black gay youth depicted in "The Outing."

The main difference between the two texts is that Johnnie finds himself faced not only with the knowledge of his gay identity but with the overt condemnation of that identity within the Black church, which struggles to instill racial pride in its followers at the expense of multiple manifestations of difference within its congregation. Johnnie's gay desire thus creates in him an acute alienation from his community, which, as a Black adolescent already marginalized from mainstream American society, he cannot afford to sacrifice. David in *Giovanni's Room* is spared this dilemma in his very expatriateness, but he too undergoes an alienation from family and community; he is unable, specifically, to connect with his father as the chasm of his sexuality creates a void of silence between the two. David says about his relationship to his father: "now that he was trying to find out something about me, I was in full flight from him. I did not *want* him to know me. I did not want anyone to know me" (25). Johnnie's alienation in the "The Outing" is similarly characterized as an abyss, "depthless and terrifying . . . encountered already in dreams" (43). Through that terror, Johnnie is relegated to the shadows of the "closet," denied entry into his own dreams, his own "Giovanni's room": "for where there had been peace there was only panic and where there had been safety, danger, like a flower, opened" (47).

Ellison's "invisible man," Baldwin's Johnnie, as well as David and Giovanni, become "closeted" as each grows into a silence constituted by the dominant white, heterosexual society which others their identities and ultimately erases those identities when their visibility becomes too apparent. Thus, Eve Sedgwick's assertion that, "closetedness itself is a performance initiated as such by the speech act of silence—not a particular silence, but a silence that accrues particularly by fits and starts, in relation to the discourse that surrounds and differentially constitutes it"[33] is applicable to more than the gay context, though she herself denies the implicit connection between the two states of oppression.[34] This "closetedness," this silence, is, in effect, a sign of invisibility that extends Baldwin's text from the African American literary context of the mid-1950s associated with Ellison's text (since the latter demonstrated that the "stigma" of race is paradoxically that which makes possible the social invisibility of the "black") to the post-1960s gay American scene. It can be argued that the language that has more recently rendered gay marginalization visible is, in fact, borrowed from the African American experience.

George Chauncey demonstrates in his *Gay New York* that the image of the "closet" was not widely used before the Stonewall riot of the late 1960s and writes: "Many gay men . . . described negotiating their presence in an often hostile world as living a double life, or wearing a mask and taking it off" (6). In 1895 Paul Laurence Dunbar articulated the compulsory sublimation of identity for African Americans living during the Reconstruction Era in his poem "We Wear the Mask," in which he wrote: "We wear the mask that grins and lies, / It hides our cheeks and shades our eyes—/ This debt we pay to human guile."[35] Frantz Fanon was to make use of this metaphor of the mask in the 1940s and 1950s to theorize about the psychological impact of racist ideology that demanded that the person of African heritage deny his or her skin, the history of its stigmatization, in order to affirm the "civilized" culture of "whiteness." Similarly, as early as 1902, the concept of "double consciousness" articulated by W. E. B. Du Bois linguistically inscribed the social exigencies of being both African and American in a society that defined the African as subhuman and thus as un-American. African Americans were thus forced to assume a double life in which they continually negotiated their African heritage in the face of enforced assimilation into a culture that denied them the right to affirm and reconceptualize their "deviant" identity. Chauncey speaks also of the historical roots of the phrase "coming out" as "an arch play on the language of women's culture . . . the expression used to refer to the ritual of a debutante's being formally introduced to . . . the society of her cultural peers" (7) in the years prior to World War II; that language, however, also came to define the African American experience in the post-World War II years, as is evidenced by Ellison's use of the phrase in the final pages of his novel as the civil rights movement gained its full momentum in the twentieth century: "Thus, having tried to give pattern to the chaos which lives within the pattern of your certainties, I must *come out*, I must emerge" (emphasis mine, 565). Individuals of African descent thus enacted the very modes of survival— of masking, of doubleness, of coming out—that have come to be identified most recently as being indicative *only* of gay/lesbian oppression.

The very title of Baldwin's short story "The Outing" demonstrates his use of the phrase "coming out" to expose multiply signifying levels of visibility and invisibility. Literally, the phrase refers to the activity of the Black church picnic, the setting for the story; figuratively, it describes David's "coming out" as a believer within the Black church—if he agrees to do so, he will be granted permission to court Sylvia and thereby affirm his heterosexuality—and identifies the phrase with the assertion of African American communal cohesion. Johnnie, on the other hand, is forced to sublimate his desires as he observes David's pursuit of Sylvia; his "outing" takes place not in the public arena but in private, with David, when on the return home from the picnic "Johnnie moved and put his head on David's shoulder [and] David put his arms around him" (47). Johnnie's identity is thus masked in friendship, unvoiced, and is forced underground. In keeping with the motifs of alienation present in the Black male literary tradition of the day, the invisibility endured by Johnnie as a gay man within the Black community mirrors the invisibility endured by Black men in white mainstream society. His "coming out" is, in the end, left unresolved within the scope of "community" because of the overdetermination of Black sexuality. It is this stereotyping process that has led to the obfuscation of the implicit connection between Black and gay liminality, especially with respect to the text of *Giovanni's Room*.

Baldwin's deliberate "masking" of race within the novel results from the overt denigration of people of African descent in the decades preceding the 1950s, which in turn led to the suppression of sexual identity within the African American community. Since African Americans had been viewed, from times of colonization and enslavement on, as "oversexed"—again in keeping with the eroticization of the Black Venus figure—the Harlem of the 1920s and 1930s was situated as the primary social site of exotic/erotic pleasure by heterosexual and homosexual white patrons alike. Writes George Chauncey:

Like the straight white slummers who made Harlem's jazz clubs and speakeasies their playground, gay white men visiting Harlem were leaving behind the communities and families who enforced the social imperatives that normally constrained their behavior. But unlike the white visitors, black gay men and lesbians had to negotiate their presence in the shops and churches of Harlem as well as its clubs. (248)

Gay life was more visible in Harlem than in other New York communities because of its conflation with a constructed "Black" or African sexual licentiousness rooted in the colonial era. In addition, the Baptist (Black) church, as Baldwin shows in "The Outing," sought to desexualize and "purify" the African American community of this stigmatization by "rail-[ing] against the homosexual 'vice' growing into the neighborhood" (Chauncey 254).[36] Baldwin responded to both the racist sexualization of African Americans by the white community and the homophobia of the African American community by removing from the surface the appearance of race in *Giovanni's Room*. Baldwin, in effect, assumed "the mask of the invisible man"[37] and imposed it on his characters. From within this deception, however, he took care to code his text as a Black gay work of literature through the intertextuality of the work, as I have discussed, and, as I demonstrate later in this essay, by revealing David's process of coming to self as his identification with the Black (and gay) identity perceived as the cradle of debauchery in the social milieus of the time. The difficulty in analyzing Baldwin's text along these lines of identification proves to be a product of a lack of critical language sufficiently engaged with theorizing about the complex dynamics of multiply oppressed identities.

Such an engagement has perhaps been explored more convincingly in the arena of postcolonial studies, which has had to contend with a variety of racial, gender, and sexuality constructions in a vast geography of colonial contexts beyond U.S. borders. Frantz Fanon's homophobia notwithstanding,[38] it is most likely an understatement to state that his work has provided the core for the ongoing excavation of the power dynamics now perceived as having molded the identities embodied by colonized and colonizing subjects.[39] The colonial project, by design, Fanon claims, was meant to create in the colonial subject a sense of nonbeing, of inhumanity, which could be alleviated only through the assimilation of those cultural markers that appeared to define the colonizing powers. Ironically, those in a position of cultural and social dominance come to define themselves through the objectification of their subjects rather than through an autonomous identity construction. Diana Fuss writes accurately that "Fanon sees the Other for what it is: an ideological construct designed to uphold and to consolidate imperialist definitions of selfhood" (21). The inferiority of one "race" therefore legitimates the superiority of an other; the inferiority of the "black" legitimates the superiority of the "white." One might add two similar bipolarizations to this litany: the supposed inferiority of "woman" to "man" and of "homosexuals" to "heterosexuals." In each of these cases (although Fanon certainly does not do justice to the final two dyads), identity relies on a fragile imbalance of power; this fragility, I suggest, is the base for the position I am herein advancing, that critical analysis involved in dissecting the liminal must now take seriously the points of connection and disconnection in and among a variety of social relationships informed by matrices of power, which are uneasily disentangled one from the other. In other words, it is no longer sufficient to observe the similarities between different types of social marginalizations (racism, let us say, or sexism, or homophobia) but dismiss them as noncontiguous; the true task before us, in terms of deflating the harms committed against those who are defined as social "minorities," as anomalous bodies, is to reify those similarities and demonstrate how they feed one into the other. Each, I contend, is rooted in the history of imperialism, which is itself mired in the derogatory stereotyping of the intellect and sexuality of the "dark Other." I suggest further that "blackness" in this context—that of cross-racial and cross-cultural oppressions—operates as the principal trope of inferiority, the marker by which all minorities are measured and through which many are typified, historically, the "black" person (most often described as male, but more often than not feminized or, in fact, a female, such as in the case of the Hottentots), has been positioned as the most inhuman of minorities and, as we have seen, perhaps the most perverse.

THE EVIDENCE OF THINGS NOT SEEN

To this point, I have shown that the critical tools at our disposal are most often inadequate for examining the ways in which *Giovanni's Room* transgresses racial bounds. I have sought to show the ways in which the characters of this particular text are depicted as occupying spaces of disenfranchisement, which are known to encompass the lives of both Black and gay individuals in mainstream Western (American) society; I have hinted at an encoded Black gay presence in the novel beyond that which is made plausible merely through substitution (i.e., the possible substitution of gay identity in the novel for "black" identity) and asserted the necessity of using postcolonial theories, with respect to their treatment of identity, to reveal the amalgamated character of the novel as well as the novel's contribution to the demystification of Black gay life. This demystification can be arrived at by taking note of Baldwin's complex imagery of darks and lights, used in concert with David's identification process.

We should recall here the identification process described by Bhaba in "the analytic of desire" whereby individuals apprehend their own identities through a differentiation from a body they have "othered" (assimilated as "not me") and then come to desire in order to complete the sense of self. Finally, in that desire, the self (or subject) comes to a point of creating an image of whom it believes itself to be that distinguishes it from the other and bestows upon it license to subjugate the Other who tacitly fails to live up to that image. In *Giovanni's Room*, David pursues this image desperately as he begins to apprehend the process of identification and its basic fallability—its sociocultural construction, which otherwise appears to be an effect of nature.

The narrative, which is a product of David's memory, attempts to recast David's identity as a white heterosexual male through the to-and-fro motion of his recall. David's exorcism is nonetheless a foiled attempt at performing the identity that has enabled his safe existence; in this way, he enacts the cycle of performativity Judith Butler defines as "not a singular 'act'" but "a reiteration of a norm or set of norms" (12), a repetition that provides the illusion of a fixed identity. David thus begins, at the end of his tale, by foregrounding both his racial and his sexual identities. In the very first page of the text, he tells us:

I watch my reflection in the darkening gleam of the window pane. My reflection is tall, perhaps rather like an arrow, my blond hair gleams. My face is like a face you have seen many times. My ancestors conquered a continent, pushing across death-laden plains, until they came to an ocean which faced away from Europe into a darker past.

A page later, he describes his journey from the south of France to Paris, hinting at his yet to be unveiled gay identity: "There will be a girl sitting opposite me who will wonder why I have not been flirting with her"; finally, he affirms his heterosexuality by presenting, for the first time, his female love interest as he speaks of the house he is on the eve of departing: "My girl, Hella, and I rented it in Paris, from photographs, some months ago. Now she has been gone a week. She is on the high seas now, on her way back to America" (8). Throughout his narrative of gay desire, David repeats this tripartite enunciation: seeking to embody the ideal identity he finds imaged in his reflection, splitting off from that identification as he realizes his gay desire, and, finally, affirming a sense of self produced through the gender difference ("to be" as Bhabha states "*for* an Other" [188], in this case the Other being "woman"). He engages in this process in order not to remain in the space of indeterminacy signified in the position of the split subject, the space that in colonial contexts could be depicted as that of hybridity or *métissage*, which prevents the absolute "difference-from-Other" identification. As David becomes more explicit in revealing his affair with Giovanni—describing an adolescent fling and his renunciation of gay identity at that time, describing his life in Paris with Hella and her departure for Spain, describing life in Giovanni's room and his flight from that room in order to rejoin Hella—his repetitious cycle fails to convince. David's is a failed performance in every respect: he can no more assume the mask of normative heterosexuality than that of "whiteness."

David's failure is revealed through the complex inversion of whites and darks associated with the space that contains his marginalization, Giovanni's room. David describes his journey through this room, as follows: "Everyone, after all, goes the same dark road—and the road has a trick of being most dark, most treacherous, when it seems most bright" (36). The fulfillment of (gay) desire is imaged not as a triumph but as a fall, its brightness made "dark" by the concomitant by-products of homophobia: "closetedness," marginalization, self-abnegation, and social invisibility. Giovanni, the object of this desire, is himself cast at the crossroads of "light" and "dark": "so winning, all of the light of that gloomy tunnel trapped around his head" (59). Giovanni circulates throughout the novel as this pseudo Christ-like figure, a halo of bright light encasing his spirit until the very moment of his "crucifixion" on the guillotine. David, who admits to playing the role of Judas to Giovanni in his refusal to be true to his desire, projects his identity-struggle onto the very setting for the expression of that desire: the room's walls are "a dirty, streaked white" (113) and its windows "of ice and fire" (115) are "obscured . . . with a heavy, white cleaning polish" (113). Giovanni's attempt to normalize and safeguard the relationship is acquired through an elaborate "white-washing" of his surroundings, a whitewash that is just that—a false and tenuous covering up of a darkness that cannot be entirely effaced, that is, Giovanni's presumed nonwhite ethnic identity (his Italianness), his gayness, and David's fear of the difference(s) Giovanni embodies and compels him to emulate. For, if David begins his tale by showing himself the product of forebearers who, having colonized the American continent, look now into its darker past, ostensibly toward the East and eventually back to the African continent, then Giovanni comes to occupy that Otherness that lies in the face of David's gaze.

The disruption of the ideal identification process implicit in the colonial situation (for the colonizer rather than for the colonized) is underscored by Baldwin's refusal to reaffirm David's (white) racial identity throughout the novel. No mention is made of David's physical appearance, other than at the end of the tragic tale, especially from the perspective of his lovers. On the other hand, David's male lovers, Joey and Giovanni (whose names are clearly variants of each other), are carefully defined as "quick and dark" (11) and "dark and lionine" (39), respectively. If anything, Baldwin's placement of David in the role of "white conqueror" operates as a metaphor in the novel for privilege, a privilege that is maintained through David's "othering" of both male lovers in order to preserve (like Gide) his white, heterosexual male identity. It is precisely this ambiguity, this lack of absolute racial and sexual marking, that connotes David's (mis)identification and his gradual assumption of the identity he rejects in Giovanni.

David eventually finds himself embodying the position of an amalgamated racial and sexual self, neither completely white nor completely black, neither completely heterosexual nor completely homosexual. In this, the text approximates a narrative of the postcolonial experience, the disjuncture between the identity of the enslaved, then freed, colonial object. "In the postcolonial text," writes Bhabha, "the problem of identity returns as a persistent questioning of the frame, the space of representation where the image ... is confronted with its difference, its Other" (189). This interrogation fractures the image created by the repetition and reiteration of constructed race, gender, class, and sexuality norms and reveals as Butler points out with respect to the subversions brought to life in *Paris Is Burning*, that "the ideal that is mirrored depends on that very mirroring to be sustained as an ideal" (14). In *Giovanni's Room*, it is Giovanni himself who unveils David's desperate need to sustain the ideal image he has of himself; in one of his final conversations with David, he exclaims:

You love your purity, you love your mirror—you are just like a little virgin, you walk around with your hands in front of you as though you had some precious metal, gold, silver, rubies, maybe *diamonds* down there between your legs! You will never give it to anybody, you will never let anybody *touch* it—man *or* woman. You want to be *clean*. (187)

David's "purity" is clearly acquired through the power of the phallus situated bodily between his legs and figuratively in his deceptive narrative, the linguistic inscription of his need for phallic identification (it must be noted here that the power of the phallus is not simply "male" but essentially *heterosexually* male). At length, it is David's mirror that betrays him.

David sees himself through a reflected image twice more after the narrative's opening paragraph. In the second instance, "outed" by a gay acquaintance, Jacques, as he realizes David's desire for Giovanni as the two first meet, David faces his shame and fear: "I stared at the amber cognac and at the wet rings on the metal. Deep below, trapped in the metal, the outline of my own face looked upward hopelessly at me" (76). David's image emerges from below the "amber" contained in his glass and reflects his imminent descent into the claustrophobic darkness of Giovanni's room. Significantly, when Giovanni later reveals the conflict between himself and the bar owner, Guillaume, he will eventually murder, the two seal their union in despair with a shared glass of cognac; at this moment, Giovanni comes to reflect his room as "his eyes darkened" and "he looked again towards the windows" (143). Giovanni's identity is constituted through his objectification as David's desired Other, while David increasingly assumes an identification with that Other. Thus, in the final pages of the novel, David turns to his mirror for an affirmation of his straight white male identity; what he finds there imaged is not the blond Adonis who greeted readers at the onset of the text but the "dark light" of Giovanni. It is at this point in the novel that the colonial process of identification is effectively reversed as David comes to assume the identity of the Other, who now takes the place of the ideal image to become what I have termed the "othered ideal."

David tells us:

I begin to undress. There is a mirror in this room, a large mirror. I am terribly aware of the mirror. Giovanni's face swings before me like an unexpected lantern on a dark, dark night. His eyes—his eyes, they glow like a tiger's eyes, they stare straight out, watching the approach of his last enemy, the hair of his flesh stands up. (221)

In a last attempt to preserve his privileged identity, David temporarily sees his own body as it once was (and may remain, if his flight from self ever proves successful), "dull and white and dry" (222). But it is soon replaced again by Giovanni's "Othered" body as the latter journeys toward execution:

The body in the mirror forces me to turn and face it. And I look at my body, which is under sentence of death. It is lean, hard, and cold, the incarnation of a mystery. And I do not know what moves in this body, what this body is searching. It is trapped in my mirror as it is trapped in time and it hurries towards revelation ... the key to my salvation, which cannot save my body, is hidden in my flesh. (223)

In the end, David's transmutation into Giovanni's reflection reveals that he has become his own Other. David occupies the space of complete raciosexual amalgamation, for he is both Subject and Object, Self and "Other," colonizer and colonized: he moves beyond the space that contains the splitsubject he embodies through most of the narrative.

In this earlier split-subject state, he reflected the "idea of man as his alienated image, not Self and Other but the Otherness of the Self inscribed in the perverse palimpsest of colonial identity" (Bhabha 187); having moved past the identification of Giovanni with perverse, "dark" sexuality, David reaches out for forgiveness and redemption. In this, he fails to uphold the "image of post-Enlightenment man tethered to, *not* confronted by, his dark reflection, the shadow of colonized man, that splits his presence, distorts his outline, breaches his boundaries, repeats his action at a distance, disturbs and divides the very time of his being"

(Bhabha 187). It is in the very confrontation of "his dark reflection" that David finally comes to an acceptance of self along indistinct and unfixed racial and sexual lines and ends the distortions implicitly revealed through the memory of his embattled desires. So, too, then, are we, as readers, forced to realize that David's reversal of the colonial identification process has already taken place when we are drawn into the narrative; the initial reflection we are offered is a false one, as false as David's flight from self. What becomes most important, then, in the closing pages of the text is that we accept David for who he has become, the "dark Other" (his own "dark reflection"). Through David's amagalmated raciosexual self, we are brought squarely into the realm of the Black gay experience, an invisibility made real and linguistically intelligible in the mirror of David's fear.

The text of *Giovanni's Room* compels us to make connections between Black and gay identity, to see that the marginalization imposed on both sectors of society, and especially on those who occupy both spaces at once, is a reflection of a deeply rooted antagonism against the "perverse" in society, the dominated and, hence, colonized object(s) of derision. In so doing, we move closer to apprehending the dynamics of the uses and misuses of power in conditions that bear the mark of colonial domination; we can discern the ways in which we, as social beings, participate in the active suppression of the Others within and among us. As Baldwin himself once wrote: "[I]n the same way that to become a social human being one modifies and suppresses and, ultimately, without great courage, lies to oneself about all one's interior, unchartered chaos, so have we, as a nation, modified and suppressed and lied about all the darker forces in our history."[40] Echoing Ellison, Baldwin argues here (as he did throughout his writing career) against the social and individual amnesia that plagues American society and provides the fuel for the continued ostracization of those bodies who fail to be able to sustain the privileged identity of the white, heterosexual male self.

Though it does so elusively, *Giovanni's Room* thus presents the double bind of Black gay existence in which homophobic oppression can never be escaped by retreat to the homosexual closet or (racist) stigmatization escaped by "coming out." It depicts the life of the brother/outsider described by Essex Hemphill when he writes: "I am most often rendered invisible, perceived as a threat to the family, or am tolerated if I am silent and inconspicuous. I cannot go home . . ." (231). Though David ultimately "finds himself" in Giovanni's reflection and his body, he is nonetheless left to wander aimlessly without a return to the America he once fled. This end is not unlike that of "The Outing," in which Johnnie hides his gay desires for his friend David and finds himself alienated from the Black community. Both characters are homeless, for they must survive and live in a social matrix that refuses to accept the "Other" as part of the Self, the hybrid, the dark, as "normal," rather than as a "perversion" of normalcy. They are illustrative of what was once (and may still be) the Black gay experience in "America": they are Baldwin's invisible men, biding their time before they emerge.

NOTES

This essay is dedicated to my good friend Stavros Stavrou, who read and commented on its earlier drafts and tirelessly endured discussions of its themes over several years of correspondence. I am also thankful to the following people for providing comments at various stages of my writing process on *Giovanni's Room* and for sharing with me their expertise in various fields, from Victorian literature to drama: Ron Huebert, Florence S. Boos, Roseanne L. Quinn, and Karen Shimakawa. Finally, my thanks to the readers and editorial board of *Genders* for their learned guidance through the revision process that was necessary to produce the final form of this essay.

My use of the word "Black" throughout this essay, when capitalized, is intended to reflect the contemporary usage of the term by African Americans to denote a politicized racial class.

1. Joseph Beam, *In the Life*, ed. Joseph Beam (Boston: Alyson Publications, 1986).

2. Audre Lorde, *Sister/Outsider* (Freedom: Crossing Press, 1984), 116.

3. Beam, *In the Life*, 13. (The phrase alludes to the 1982 anthology edited by Gloria T. Hull, Patricia Bell Scott, and Barbara Smith, titled *All the Women Are White, All the Blacks Are Men, But Some of Us Are Brave* [Old Westbury, N.Y.: Feminist Press, 1982].)

4. Ibid., 14. Further references to this work will be included parenthetically in the text.

5. Harryette Mullen, "Optic White: Blackness and the Production of Whiteness," *Diacritics* (summer/fall 1994): 89.

6. Judith Butler, *Bodies That Matter: On the Discursive Limits of "Sex"* (New York: Routledge, 1993), 129. Further references to this work will be included parethentically in the text.

7. Homi K. Bhabha, "Interrogating Identity: The Postcolonial Prerogative," in *Anatomy of Racism*, ed. David Theo Goldberg (Minneapolis: University of Minnesota Press, 1990), 187–88. Further references to this work will be included parenthetically in the text.

8. Sander Gilman, "Black Bodies, White Bodies: Toward an Iconography of

Female Sexuality in Late Nineteenth-Century Art, Medicine, and Literature," *Critical Inquiry* 12, no. 1 (autumn 1985): 212.

9. Ibid., 231.

10. George Chauncey, *Gay New York: Gender, Urban Culture, and the Making of the Gay Male World, 1890–1940*, (New York: HarperCollins, 1994), 48. Further references to this work will be included parenthetically in the text.

11. Valerie Smith, "Reading the Intersection of Race and Gender in Narratives of Passing," *diacritics* (summer/fall 1994): 57.

12. Valerie Smith comments in her aforementioned essay that Hazel Carby's response to her own work has been to elucidate the possibility that such texts examplify "the problematics of black self-loathing that may well have contributed to the overrepresentation of such figures in black narratives" (57).

13. Such an approach has been put forward along these lines by Earl Jackson Jr. in his *Stategies of Deviance: Studies in Gay Male Representation* (Bloomington: Indiana University Press, 1995), when he discusses the science fiction of Samuel Delany in the context of Delany's coming to the genre through his *racial* identification with the supernatural creations he found as a child in the pages of Robert A. Heinlein's *Starship Troopers*, a text others have identified as a gay text. Delany, Jackson argues, is intent on creating within the pages of his own fiction characters who embody black and gay identities even as they exist beyond the social mores of "earthly" human identification. For Jackson, Delany "radicalizes the space opera by *synthesizing* his conceptual motifs with the structural components, this serves to *dissolve* the connection between the intellectual pleasures and politically conservative heritage of science fiction" (95). Since science fiction offers an "independence from mimetic faithfulness to the world as it is," continues Jackson, it opens the door to the kind of transgressive literature Delany creates, which positions the Other (people of color and women) at the center of his literary vision. My claim, then, is to argue for a similar synthesis of theoretical motifs and structures in the present analysis in order to dissolve the (dis)connection between the psychoanalytical modes of identification and those constructed through the history of imperialism. The present study should demonstrate that it is not necessary to have to turn to science fiction in order to achieve this dissolution. The "world as it is" might be transformable in the here and now rather than through the imaginary world of science fiction.

14. Yvonne Yarbro-Bejarano, "Expanding the Categories of Race and Sexuality in Lesbian and Gay Studies," *Professions of Desire*, ed. George E. Haggerty and Bonnie Zimmerman (New York: Modern Language Association of America, 1995), 124–35.

15. Sandra L. Richards, "Writing the Absent Potential: Drama, Performance, and the Canon of African-American Literature," in *Performativity and Performance*, ed. Andrew Parker and Eve Sedgwick (New York: Routledge, 1994), 83.

16. Ibid., 83.

17. Philip Brian Harper, " 'The Subversive Edge': *Paris Is Burning*, Social Critique, and the Limits of Subjective Agency," *diacritics* 24, no. 2–3 (summer/fall 1994): 93.

18. Dan Georgakes, "James Baldwin . . . In Conversation," (Interview) *Black*

Voices: An Anthology of Afro-American Literature (New York: New American Library, 1968), 666.

19. Quoted in David Bergman, *Gaiety Transfigured: Gay Self-Representation in American Literature* (Madison: University of Wisconsin Press, 1991), 165. Further references to this work will be included parenthetically in the text.

20. Karen Thorsen, "James Baldwin: The Price of the Ticket" (New York: WNET, American Masters Series, 1989), n.p. And yet, the novel was to some extent autobiographical in nature, as Baldwin's biographer W. J. Weatherby notes in *James Baldwin: Artist on Fire* (New York: Dell, 1989): "[I]n portraying various characters, [Baldwin] had used aspects of people he knew in the American colony in Paris. He wondered if they would recognize themselves. He depicted the bars and typical regulars in the Parisian underworld. He also drew from the emotional side of his own life in the French capital, even though he didn't portray anyone directly" (133).

21. James Baldwin, "The Male Prison," in his *Nobody Knows My Name: More Notes of a Native Son* (New York: Laurel, 1961), 132. Further reference to this work will be included parenthetically in the text.

22. James Baldwin, *Giovanni's Room* (New York: Dial Press, 1956), 112. Further reference to this work will be included parenthetically in the text.

23. Eve Sedgwick, *Epistemology of the Closet* (Berkeley: University of California Press, 1990), 71.

24. Biddy Martin, "Sexualities Without Genders and Other Queer Utopias," *diacritics* 24, no. 2–3 (summer/fall 1994): 105.

25. Ibid., 110.

26. Ibid., 111.

27. B. Ruby Rich, "When Difference Is (More Than) Skin Deep," in *Queer Looks: Perspectives on Lesbian and Video* (New York: Routledge, 1993), 321.

28. Ralph Ellison, *Invisible Man* (New York: Vintage, 1972), xviii. Further reference to this work will be included parenthetically in the text.

29. Phillip Brian Harper, "Private Affairs: Race, Sex, Property, and Persons" in *Professions of Desire*, ed. George E. Haggerty and Bonnie Zimmerman (New York: MLA Publications, 1995), 224.

30. Ibid., 225.

31. Weatherby, *James Baldwin*, 71.

32. James Baldwin, "The Outing," in his *Going to Meet the Man* (New York: Laurel, 1965).

33. Sedgwick, *Epistemology of the Closet*, 3.

34. Sedgwick appears to adopt the (African American) concept of invisibility to define the psychology of the gay "closet" at the same time that she declares that this space cannot encompass the social experience of racial marginalization. She writes: "Vibrantly resonant as the image of the closet is for many modern oppressions, it is indicative for homophobia in a way it cannot be for other oppressions. Racism, for instance, is based on the stigma that is visible in all but exceptional cases" (75). Sedgwick defines the difference between the two oppressions in terms of the physical evidence of minority status; this difference results in

Sedgwick's subordination of the effects of racism to those experienced because of homophobia. In truth, the most pervasive forms of homophobic and racist oppression render the racial minority and the gay/lesbian minority invisible legally, economically, and socially, by denying them their humanity. It is this overlapping reality that is excised in current queer theory but has been exposed by lesbian theorists such as Audre Lorde, Barbara Smith, and Minnie Bruce Pratt, whose experientially based writings have been labeled essentialist, practical, and, as such, antitheoretical in order to be dismissed in elitist feminist and queer circles. As these latter feminist theorists have pointed out time and again, it is the state of multiple oppression that now presents the most significant stumbling block for bridging analyses of race, gender, class and sexuality productively.

35. Paul Laurence Dunbar, *Majors and Minors: Poems (1895)* (Miami: Mnemosyne Publishing Co., 1969), 21.

36. Curiously, the historical evidence from this period (Chauncey 254) points to the overt condemnation of lesbian sexuality rather than gay male sexuality, since it was perceived as more detrimental to the perpetuation of the race; this suggests that within the African American community, the ideology that condemned Black sexuality through the African female body proliferated and was sustained.

37. Essex Hemphill, "Introduction," in *Brother to Brother: New Writings by Black Gay Men* (Boston: Alyson Publications, 1991), xvi.

38. Diana Fuss writes of Fanon's limited treatment of homophobia in his works: "For white men homosexuality is a pathological condition; for black men it is 'a means to a livelihood,' a by-product of colonialism in which black men from the colonies are forced into homosexual prostitution in the metropolis in order to survive economically" (32); for Fanon, then, homosexuality is a by-product of colonial domination whereby white males may exploit black males in order to dominate what they most fear, black male sexuality, but it does not occur to him that black males can, in fact, *choose* to enact gay desire for either black or white males, in or out of the colonial context.

39. Henry Louis Gates Jr. has noted that in recent years, Frantz Fanon (the man and his works) has been claimed by many areas other than postcolonial studies. In his essay "Critical Fanonism," Gates claims that Fanon "has now been reinstated as a global theorist, and not simply by those engaged in Third World or subaltern studies" (457). This renewed interest in Fanon demonstrates, in my mind, the necessity for a more cohesive concentration on the dynamics of the colonial project across the disciplines. Gates claims that the "current fascination for us has something to do with the convergence of the problematics of the colonialism with that of subject-formation" (438). This "something to do" might well be the result of increased decolonization, which has forced those in positions to dominate out of those positions and necessarily into a state of reevaluation concerning their identity as colonizers. This reevaluation is produced by the colonized who no longer accept the role created for them in the hegemonic chain of power. I should add also that though some of the essays from which I quote (by Diana Fuss especially) can be seen as belonging to this new critical tradition, I do

not see my present work as engaged in "critical Fanonism" but as a continuation of the work being done in African diasporic studies since Fanon, most especially French-Caribbean criticism, which owes an enormous debt to Fanon's work.

40. James Baldwin, "The Creative Process," in *Creative America* (New York: Ridge Press, 1962), 41.

SEVEN

Homosexuality and the Uncanny
What's Fishy in Lacan

Thomas E. Yingling

To claim that Jacques Lacan fails in the realm of sexual politics would come as no surprise to anyone familiar with his work or with the large body of feminist critique and appropriation it has generated. But gay theorists and critics have by and large bypassed Lacan's work; when psychoanalytic principles are invoked in gay studies, as they have begun to be in a few texts brave enough to confront the legacy of disciplinary violence never out of sight when psychoanalysis considers same-sex desire, it is most often Freud whose writing has drawn attention. Nor is this surprising if we consider that Jacques Lacan had seemingly little to say about this topic, with which Freud was relatively obsessed. Lacan's more general silence on the issue *is* surprising, however, if we consider that during the period of his writing, same-sex practices had become culturally and politically viable and visible in a manner unthinkable in Freud's era. But perhaps we can read Lacan's text for semes of homosexual desire, subjectivity, or possibility that do not appear as such on its surface— perhaps, that is, there is a discourse of the homosexual that appears throughout Lacan's text as an unspoken analog to the phallic structures of masculinity. (I mean here less to claim that male homosexuality is something radically other than masculinity than to further explore how— for Lacan at least—masculinity is possible only in dialectical relation to a subordinated feminine Other, a paradigm of identity unable fully to account for same-sex sexual practices and desires.)

In particular, I am interested in how the Imaginary is sublimated in structures of identification based on a third term denominated as the

Symbolic or the law or culture, and how the Symbolic structures of heterosexual masculinity require that oral and anal drives (especially as these might take same-sex objects) be placed under patriarchal regulation. I refer later in this paper to Manuel Puig's *Kiss of the Spider Woman*, but I want first to examine some of Lacan's statements about male homosexuality and anality in order to read how the former is in fact erased from the psychoanalytic discourse he produces.

In "The Signification of the Phallus," Lacan remarks that "male homosexuality, in accordance with the phallic mark which constitutes desire, is constituted on the side of desire, while feminine homosexuality, on the other hand, as observation shows, is oriented on a disappointment that reinforces the side of the demand for love."[1] I don't wish to follow this out too minutely (the seeming negative evaluation of lesbian desire follows closely from Joan Riviere and a whole history of narratives about lesbianism as lack or disappointment in psychoanalytic discourse), but what this seems to do is construct female homosexuality as a relation to the Other (Lacan's notion of demand as opposed to desire)—that Other whose prototype is the Mother: thus, in Lacan's "observation," we find a specular relation of woman-to-woman as the basis of female homosexuality—an Imaginary relation that seeks to or does refuse the Phallus and the patriarchal obligations of the Symbolic.

Masculine homosexuality, on the other hand, is a matter of phallic desire for Lacan—by which, of course, he does not mean genital phallic desire but a move into signification, into that process wherein the Phallus reveals itself as signifier. And the Symbolic is associated with the Oedipal in Lacan, so he reads masculine homosexuality as inevitably Oedipal and feminine homosexuality as a refusal to enter Oedipal time, as a refusal to accept castration. But because the genital stage supersedes all other stages in the process of ego development, even this refusal is Phallic for Lacan since there is only one genital stage, only one libido: the masculine. What is most interesting to me here (and there are a number of interesting things about this: "masculine/feminine" and not "male/female"; an insistence on the difference—but to what end?)—what is most interesting is the question of what happens to the drives and pleasures of the Imaginary *for masculine homosexuality* as it moves (however lamely or incompletely) through Oedipal confrontations and resolutions into the Symbolic? And what, specifically, happens to anal desire?

I ask this last question not just out of a desire to shock or indulge but because anal pleasure is the single most interdicted of those pleasures open to male bodies in our culture—and, I argue, is also the "thing" still that defines homosexuality. If the Phallus is the fetish, and masculinity the reified identity it signifies, the single most unthinkable event for the masculine is anal penetration *as pleasure* (masculine culture can envision anal penetration—it has, in fact, numerous fantasies of such, but these fantasies are violent; they are rape fantasies). I don't wish to claim here that if the New England Patriots suddenly began butt-fucking on Sunday afternoons instead of playing football, we would cease to live in a patriarchal or oppressive culture (but I might pay money to see it), nor do I wish to claim that anal desire is the "real" psychic or somatic condition of male homosexuality (Guy Hocquenghem seems to claim this in *Homosexual Desire*).[2] But it seems clear that those who are marked by a desublimation of anal desire will remain the abject of this culture as long as the structures that interdict that desire remain uninterrogated. Do we need examples from the parables of manhood to establish that anal pleasure is the unthinkable of our culture? Take Tom Wolfe's *The Right Stuff*, a fable of national destiny, masculine energy, spermatic daring (what else but sperm *is* the "right stuff?" all of those phallic projectiles writing history).[3] In its only anal moment, Scott Carpenter suffers the humiliation of a medical anal examination, a moment structurally akin to losing the space race. Or take Stanley Kubrick's *Full Metal Jacket* (1987), in which the only recruit who fails to be indoctrinated into the killing machine *becomes* instead a literal piece of shit (always suggested in the sergeant's rhetoric but successfully internalized and acted out only by him), killing himself on the toilet that marks his "worth" in this masculine economy. That these examples are military is no surprise, and we return to this in discussing *Kiss of the Spider Woman* later, but let me quickly emphasize that phallic strength, and the masculinity of which it is synecdochic, is structurally incompatible with anality in these narratives. Anality must be sublimated into a genitally organized ego: that is the imperative of masculinity; that is the outcome of a narrative that requires movement through oral and anal phases into genital organization as consonant with passage into (and hence out of) the Oedipal—and the very possibility of identification.

This is not always the case in homosexual desire, and it is not always the case in gay art. Jonathan Weinberg has suggested that we read the thematics of trash and refuse (dirt defined as "matter in the wrong place"), cans and holes in Jasper Johns's work as signifiers of what psychoanalysis has called "the anal character."[4] For Weinberg, these are signs not only of some secret desire within the artist but also of our culture's "derivation of values: why is one object better than another, why is one thing money and the other thing shit, why is one kind of work art and another just production."[5] Weinberg notes as well that cans and johns—the artist's name—are themselves signifiers of excremental process, and I would like to take this insight into cans and refuse as signifiers of the anal to a passage in Lacan, whose name interestingly enough breaks into "la can" (like "le car," a nicely gallicized and, in this case, feminized phrase signifying excremental process): that famous story of the sardine can that does not see him.

You may recall this; it is in *The Four Fundamental Concepts*, in a section concerned with the gaze—which, I remind us, is also Phallic. But what we read in this story as Lacan narrates it is the opposite of phallic power and authority. It is, rather, an experience of abjection, of being shit, of being—as he says—"out of place in the picture." Briefly, the narrative is as follows:

I was in my early twenties or thereabouts—and at that time, of course, being a young intellectual, I wanted desperately to get away, see something different, throw myself into something practical, something physical, in the country say, or at sea. One day, I was on a small boat, with a few people from a family of fishermen in a small port. At that time, Brittany was not industrialized as it is now. There were no trawlers. The fisherman went out in his frail craft at his own risk. It was this risk, this danger, that I loved to share. But it wasn't all danger and excitement—there were also fine days. One day, then, as we were waiting for the moment to pull in the nets, an individual known as Petit-Jean, that's what we called him—like all his family, he died very young from tuberculosis, which at that time was a constant threat to the whole of that social class—this Petit-Jean pointed out to me something floating on the surface of the waves. It was a small can, a sardine can. It floated there in the sun, a witness to the canning industry, which we, in fact, were supposed to supply. It glittered in the sun. And Petit-Jean said to me—*You see that can? Do you see it? Well, it doesn't see you!*[6]

Lacan does not find this amusing, although Petit-Jean and the others do. Lacan:

The point of this little story, as it had occurred to my partner, the fact that he found it so funny and I less so, derives from the fact that, if I am told a story like that one, it is because I, at that moment—as I appeared to those fellows who were earning their livings with great difficulty, in the struggle with what for them was a pitiless nature—looked like nothing on earth. In short, I was rather out of place in the picture. And it was because I felt this that I was not terribly amused at hearing myself addressed in this humorous, ironical way. (95–96)

Now the "little story" here is not Petit-Jean's but Lacan's—and the sardine can is a sign of refuse, the issue of size being quite important: belittled by someone whose very name is "little," like a sardine, the littlest and—idiomatically—the most anonymous of fish. This "little story" is thus a moment of abjection for Lacan, a moment when he does not signify—either for the can or for those working in the canning industry. (Lacan's nods to material history are interesting but far too brief). It is appropriate, therefore, that the narrative turns on the citing of another piece of garbage floating aimlessly on that sea that "wasn't all danger and excitement" (95), not all about male heroism (except, of course, the male heroism of bodily labor, something Lacan is here also marginalized from). It is a moment of nonbeing for the young intellectual—of being neither subject nor object—and we should not be surprised to read here signifiers of the anal, since abjection takes the anus as one of its naturalized sites on the body. What I am arguing for is not that this marks an unconscious homosexual site in Lacan (I'm not sure what the purpose of such an argument might be). Instead, I am arguing that a signifying practice expresses (and perhaps it is right to call this an unconscious expression, since it is veiled rather than explicit) how the anal is itself abjected from narratives of personal history and development: "I once was a lost and forsaken young intellectual whom even diseased fishermen might laugh at, and while this made me feel like shit, I now tell it as a story about a certain little can and a certain little john."

The anal is for Lacan just such a sight of abjection, of that which is expulsed from the body. Occasionally, this may be inverted, and then we have the rhetoric of shit as gift, of oblation (the most disgusting bodily product is turned into a precious commodity). What we never find in Lacan is an understanding of how the anus might appear as a sexual organ, as a site—that is—of bodily jouissance. Neither phallus nor its lack, the anus cannot be accommodated in an economy of desire whose generative fictions require that sexual difference—and therefore identity—be located at the site (and sight) of the genital.

One could do here an entire Deleuzean critique of the notion of organs as originary of the desire they are claimed to articulate, and while such a critique would be instructive in bringing the question of desire back to material relations, I haven't time—I want to turn to *Kiss of the Spider Woman*. (I am speaking here of the novel and not of the film). In Puig's novel, we are treated to a rather complicated dance of desire wherein it is impossible to say who seduces whom: Molina seduces Valentin, fulfilling his desire for a masculine lover, and Valentin seduces Molina (perhaps) and thereby secures the passage of information to his revolutionary cell. What is clear is that this occurs through an interesting negotiation of oral and anal drives. Much of the text, and much of the seduction, occurs through eating and feeding—more precisely, through Molina playing a maternal role; the whole question of withholding information (Molina is charged to "get" information out of Valentin if he is to be released) is, of course, anal in its psychoanalytic references. (Freud: "Only a few minutes after laughing about the absurdity of an infant purposely holding back his stool to thwart his parents, the same man told a story that provided a perfect illustration for Freud's theories: 'Do you know, there just occurs to me, as I see the cocoa in front of me, an idea that I always had as a child. I then always pretended to myself that I was the cocoa manufacture Van Houten . . . that I possessed a great secret for the preparation of this cocoa, and that all the world was trying to get this valuable secret from me, but that I carefully kept it to myself.")[7] The ultimate moment of intersubjectivity in the text occurs when Valentin begins to make love to Molina. During anal sex, he even says, "For just a second, it seemed like I wasn't here . . . not here or anywhere out there either. . . . It seemed as if I wasn't here at all . . . like it was you all alone. . . . Or like I wasn't me anymore . . . as if now, somehow . . . I . . . were you." (That last shift gets him off the hook, I'd say).[8] This moment is interesting in part because it breaks the pattern of defining desire through orality (speech breaks down in this section as well), and it seems that the anal moment here is indeed outside the disciplinary and panoptic eye of the prison, a moment of some pure intersubjective desire that defines the radical potential of male homosexuality.

But in reading the novel this way, we have forgotten something—it is not the act of fucking that determines "love" for Molina but something else: a kiss. When Valentin later offers a kiss that he had formerly refused out of disgust, Molina is convinced to carry the information to his colleagues when he is released. Hence we are returned to the oral, and to an entire regime of signification and representation that the novel has already read for us as deeply ideological (in the contest over "meaning" in Molina's narrations of films, we have come to be skeptical of "the kiss" as a sign in romance, yet it determines the outcome of the text in this case, producing on Molina's body not just desire for another man but a fantasy of martyrdom, of feminine masochism, of his own eventual death). The kiss secures this, and while I don't want to say that oral drives are always in the service of dominant culture, we can see here that the moment of transgression (of refusing the police equation of anality with information) is recuperated into dominant representational practice. Both oral and anal drives are part of the Imaginary, and both are desublimated in the text, but betrayal occurs here through the linkage of orality and representation. It is that moment when the possibility of homosexuality's denial of the structures of the Symbolic is returned to it; in the end Puig's vision is one in which there is no escape from the Symbolic. From the powerful political and psychic oppressions of phallic order, there are only reprieves.

I want to close by abruptly asking whether this novel—or this talk or this conference—is subversive—and if so, subversive of what? I do this partly in response to a student's claim that *Kiss* is not a subversive text because it leaves economic structures largely in place and concentrates only on the issues of sexuality and gender, and also because I think it is always an appropriate question when the word "political" is invoked these days. This comes to us as a political question because of a certain Marxist critique of this text—and of gay politics in the United States more generally—that suggests neither is transformative. But while I would argue that this discourse or the subversion of versions of patriarchal identity that occurs in homosexual relations (when that occurs in homosexual relations) is not transformative of all social relations, we must remember that sexuality is dialectical—therefore, to the extent that it is transgressive, its subversiveness does not stop at the fictional borders we mark as "gender relations," for that fiction does not stop at *any* border but crosses into all arrangements of social power and control.

So where do we locate "true" desire in this text? There is the desire to be a woman, the desire to be subsumed into filmic romance—to be kissed, the desire to overthrow the government. Oral, anal, political desires. What we need to see, I think, is that to privilege one form only is to fall into that trap marked out here as totalitarian: the kiss of the spider woman draws one into a web of desires—sometimes conflicting, often inchoate. Desire becomes the site of sublimity: and here we must read the revolutionary's point—that that happens only in a specific historical matrix. And here too we must read the tragedy of the text: there is no escape from the Symbolic, only momentary reprieves.

198 **THOMAS E. YINGLING**

NOTES

This essay was originally presented at the Gay and Lesbian Studies Conference at Harvard University in October 1990. Notes were assembled where possible by Robyn Wiegman.

1. Jacques Lacan, "The Signification of the Phallus," *Ecrits: A Selection*, trans. Alan Sheridan (New York: Norton, 1977), 290.

2. Guy Hocquenghem, *Homosexual Desire*, trans. Daniella Dangoor (London: Allison and Busby, 1978).

3. Tom Wolfe, *The Right Stuff* (New York: Farrar, Straus, and Giroux, 1979).

4. Jonathan Weinberg, "It's in the Can: Jasper Johns and the Anal Society," *Genders* 1 (March 1988): 53, 42.

5. Ibid., 51. One might argue with Weinberg here that "anal character" in psychoanalytic discourse usually signifies sublimated drives and not, as the case of Johns appears, the wholly de-sublimated.

6. Jacques Lacan, *The Four Fundamental Concepts of Psycho-Analysis*, ed. Jacques Alain Miller, trans. Alan Sheridan (New York: Norton, 1981), 95. Further references to this work will be included parenthetically in the text.

7. Quoted in Weinberg, "It's in the Can," 50.

8. Manuel Puig, *Kiss of the Spider Woman*, trans. Thomas Colchie (New York: Random House, 1979), 219.

EIGHT

The "Phallacies" of Dyke Comic Strips

Gabrielle N. Dean

On the cover of *Hothead Paisan Homicidal Lesbian Terrorist* 11, a quarterly comic book by Diane DiMassa, the eponymous heroine wields a pair of pliers as long as she is tall and a specimen jar containing a diminutive penis. The cover, which also announces itself as a "Tweested Eeshoo" ("Twisted Issue"), thoroughly anticipates its contents. Inside, Hothead captures, tortures and kills three rapists—an explicit enactment of a theme that runs throughout her comic strips: castration as a fantasy of insurgent political action, a direct assault on the patriarchal order in its most vulnerable place.[1]

That DiMassa, and Hothead, have no doubts about the coincidence of patriarchy and the penis is most clear in the following issue, 12, which lacks the usual page of letters from readers. Instead, DiMassa suggests and preempts the reactions of some readers to issue 11 in the opening frames of the strip: a series of stereotypical "straight white males" (bankers, tough guys, regular joes, slackers, hippies) are outraged by 11, but their outrage must be translated. A blank-looking man with a tie proclaims, "I'm just a regular guy doin' the best I can! What's this got to do with ME?" but his appeal is captioned, "I am basically unconscious. The living dead. I'd like to do a Bud Lite commercial someday." A pair of male twins with crew cuts and cavernous mouths declares, "It's offensive!!!" and "Yeah! That last issue wasn't funny!!!" but DiMassa interprets, "Angry women are absolutely terrifying beyond belief to us. Please don't." A bald, mustachioed man with crossed eyes and a furious furrowed brow commands us to "Stop acting so hysterical," but his real meaning is noted below: "You have no feelings, and if you do, they don't count." But having once established a range of stereotypes by carefully differentiating these portraits, DiMassa immediately effaces their detail and individuality. She illustrates the collective uniformity of these men by grouping them together, behind a fence, along with their remarks ("I can buy and sell you!!" or "Relax! Real women ain't like this!")—and then zooms out to reveal the location of the fence: a monumental, phallic pillar on a pedestal, marked with a placard that says, "For God, For Country, For Penis," from which emanates a cloud of heavily inked "Whines"—the final transcription of the masculine complaints. DiMassa's scheme acknowledges and then delegitimizes the symbolic power of the "straight white male"; moreover, the "translation" of his outrage, first into reductive expressions of fury and fear and finally into a mere whine, implies that the artist has an access to his language that even he does not possess. Most strikingly, however, his ultimate displacement is completed not through language but through graphic castration. The perspective zooms out again, to impart the parting joke: two grinning dykes with a classic cartoon box of TNT blow up the phallic monument and then burst into laughter, which overtakes entire frames with big "HA"s (*HHP* 12, 1–3).

For theorists, the strategy is only a bit different. Some feminist theorists claim, in tandem with DiMassa, that the psychoanalytic phallus is, after all, a penis, thus reinscribing the gendered basis of power hierarchies, access to language, and normative sexuality. And yet, in a move again comparable to DiMassa's graphic castrations, feminist theorists have also attempted to "blow up" this coincidence, to enlarge and explode it, to produce transgressive possibilities for women, often using the Foucauldian concepts of discourse and resistance to read Freud and Lacan against themselves and effectively rewrite feminine sexuality, perversity, and subjectivity. As the heated keystone of the larger debate about the compatibility of psychoanalysis and feminism, the argument about the coincidence of phallus and penis revolves around Lacan's notion of the organizing principle of the phallus: that it functions as the signifier of the lack that inaugurates subjectivity and thus constitutes an attempt to stuff that absence with language. Lacan insists that the veiled phallus—veiled to hide the inability of the phallus to accommodate the referential surplus that always exceeds signification—not be associated with any particular organ, neither the penis nor the clitoris. Various feminist critics of Lacan have noted, nevertheless, that his writings depend on the continued association of masculine authority with the symbolic order, ensuring the significance of the phallus in/as the "Law of the Father." This coincidence has also served as the occasion to make psychoanalytic theory work toward feminist ends, by suggesting that gender and the meanings attached to "sex" are themselves discursive products of the symbolic order that might therefore be discursively unsettled.[2]

But does feminist theory's appropriation of the tools of the father really change anything? Or are these tools, even in feminist hands, finally capable only of reproducing the status quo? Likewise, do DiMassa's pictorial castrations make a difference, or do they, by virtue of the fact that Hothead castrates over and over again, simply reinforce through repetition the dominance of the phallic? I argue that Hothead and other dyke comic strips do in fact articulate a countersubjectivity, a relation to the symbolic order that is, at times, successfully oppositional. This subjectivity does not—indeed, it could not—function by outright negation of the existing symbolic order; instead, I propose, it employs the fetishist's strategy of disavowal to imagine not one but a multiplicity of lesbian phalluses—what could be called, to be clever, "phallacies." Comic strips are particularly effective in this endeavor because of the material and economic circumstances of their production. That is, the medium of the comic strip—a series of graphic panels that sustains a narrative supplemented (not primarily organized) by the word, and particularly the comic strip's comic book form (a low-tech, inexpensive commodity that circulates on unofficial and unanticipated routes)—offers a unique forum for the disavowal of the Law. In their deliberate exploitation and development of abject figures, and as a medium that forces text as well as image into a visual reading, comic strips permit an articulation of dyke subjectivity that might otherwise be too dangerous. Because they are a phenomenon of popular culture, because they are historically "kids' stuff," because they are cheap and unregulated, and because they are, figuratively, illiterate, comic strips do not directly challenge entrenched symbolic systems but engage in a kind of guerrilla practice. Dyke comic strips visibly dislocate the phallus, and thus the chain of meaning emanating from its fixed position. They illustrate the phallus's transferability and transform it from the primary instrument of signification into a body, an incorporated assemblage, that signifies identity and desire. To uncover dyke comic strips and discover the countersubjectivity I want to find there, I first briefly differentiate comic strips from other media—film, printed text, and photography, especially pornography (with genealogical as well as material relations to comic strips)—to illustrate what comic strips accomplish technologically and mark their unique genealogical location. I then propose an explanation for the operation comic strips perform on/with dyke subjectivity; finally, I examine the work of three comic strip artists, Diane DiMassa, Alison Bechdel, and Fish, to demonstrate how each body of work engages the symbolic order in order to disavow it, with more and less efficacy, and reproduce the dyke in her own image.[3]

What do comic strip dykes do that other dykes don't? This question requires an investigation of dyke comic strips as a medium and as a cultural phenomenon. The comic strip dyke occupies an overdetermined site, a place crossed by technological, economic, and historical vectors that contribute to her present-day guises, functions, and performances. Since it is not my goal here to provide a full genealogical account of the comic strip dyke, I simply sketch, as it were, what seem to me to be the most important outlines that frame and produce her. First among these are the operations of the comic strip as a medium.

As in traditional narrative cinema, comic strips generally plot a diegesis that is advanced both linguistically and visually, through the constant interplay between these two elements. Like the conventional porn layout, however, in which a series of photographs follows a loosely connected sexual narrative, the comic strip story proceeds via framed imagery; the individual image is of primary importance and allows readers to produce their own fantasy narratives. Indeed, any single image can form the basis for a story. But a photograph—especially one designed to provoke a sexual response—is particularly amenable to narrativization, by virtue of its ability to appear to document a fleeting moment and thus its implication in a sequence of events. Comic strip panels recall the photographic image in their faithful reproduction of the "same" in frame after frame and in the customary modes of cartoon composition, which purport to be as "immediate" as a sketch. And, of course, comic strips rely on written text; they appear on paper and in books, newspapers, or bound pamphlets and thus emulate the most widely accessible versions of written, generally printed, text. Moreover, the appearance of "graphic novels" such as Art Spiegelman's *Maus* and the rendition of literary texts into comic strip forms underscores the relation between comic strips and printed text.[4] These culturally dominant media construct the way the comic strip, a series of framed images accompanied by text on paper, can be read.

However, it is as something to be read that comic strips are crucially different from the traditional forms of narrative cinema, photo porn, and printed text. While comic strips advance a narrative through written text and graphic imagery, while they simultaneously point to the narrative powers of the individual image, they also seductively reveal the very mechanisms of their production. Even in mainstream hero and newspaper comics, in which the unvarying reproduction of characters, the conformity of drawing styles, the even regularity of the handwritten text, and the uniformity of framing devices camouflage the manual labor that is their source, the convention of the artist's signature always reminds the reader of the mechanics of the comic strip's production and reinforces the notion of the comic strip as an individual artistic creation—though its claim to artistry may be merely its unerring consistency. Even if "Stan Lee" is ultimately a pseudonymous vacuum, a signifier without a signified, the appendage of his handwritten signature nevertheless invites speculation: who is he? and how does he do it?

The artist's signature is not the only mechanism at work in the revelation of the materiality of the comic strip, however; equally important is the reader's presence, an essentially interpretive presence, which is designated in the very composition of the conventional comic strip, and especially in the comic book. Comic strips do not create the illusion of seamless continuity; there are crucial interruptions, both temporal and visual, between sequences, as readers must wait for the next installment; between the actual images, separated by the frame; and within each frame, as scenes and characters are manipulated. Each comic strip panel amounts to a synchronic overlay of the pen-and-ink equivalents of the cinematic camera "shot" and screenplay "scene"—a scene played out in a single shot. This very compact rendering of visual narrative results in disjointedness, requiring the reader simultaneously to connect the images along the lines of the story and read the images against the story in order to get the visual jokes. The pleasure of reading a comic strip is more than the pleasure of illustration; this competition between text and image, a demand for visual acuity and interpretative expertise on the part of the reader, constructs the reader as authoritative. The reader's authority is augmented by the materiality of the comic strip; it is literally in her hands, permitting a degree of interpretive control: the reader can linger, skip pages, regard the image close up or at a distance in search of clues. Comic strip creators cater to the reader's interpretive control and the material limitations of the medium, rather than vice versa; the last panel on the recto page is usually emphasized, punctuating the story and providing an impetus to read on, while the first panel on a page often recaps, either textually or visually, some element from the previous panel. In fact, the typical length of a comic book strip is one verso and one recto page, so the entire strip can be visualized at once. In longer strips the rhythm of the story line often accommodates the page format and is thus, to a certain extent, dictated by anticipation of what the reader might do. The traditional forms of the comic book (a series of comic strips) and the comic strip (a series of blocked-out panels to be read left to right, top to bottom) write in the reader's place and interpretive authority.

"Alternative" comics, also called "new" or "underground," accentuate the presence of artist and reader through unusual or uneven framing devices, individualistic drawing and writing styles, appeals to the reader that puncture the illusion of a discrete narrative world, and story lines that invoke taboo, autobiographical, or subcultural subject matter. Moreover, some alternative comic strip artists deliberately draw attention to their failures to achieve technological perfection, as if to insist that the comic strip is a handmade object. Diane DiMassa, for example, marks the site of a technological flaw—the wavering line of a frame—with an aside to the reader pointing out, "You can't see it, but there's a big blob of white-out there!" (*HHP* 12, 9). Julie Doucet, creator of the *Dirty Plotte* series, reveals herself as a cartoonist in a sequence depicting her daily morning drawing routine in which she is practically illiterate; she sits on the toilet mumbling "WXQVV AGAIN GTBK!!" and rips up her sketchbook yelling "NOO!! AWW FFUCK SHHIT OFF!! XZWTKK!"[5] Unlike comparable cinematic, photographic, literary, or other artistic genres that also, in the mode of postmodern self-reflexivity, exhibit the mechanics of their production (such as grainy film stock in independent films or the visible black frame of the negative in photographic prints), alternative comics are in fact mass-produced, inexpensive, and available through accessible distribution networks; yet they retain a subcultural status. Likewise, although photo porn is produced and disseminated along similar channels, alternative comics are positioned as artistic productions, whereas pornography must transmogrify into "erotica" in order to achieve a similar standing.[6]

Indeed, unhinged from the unique circumstances of their economic and cultural circulation, the attention to unmasking that is the identifying sign of alternative comics would mean very little. North American dyke comic strips in particular represent an entity that can signify only at the juncture of several concatenated discourses: the topoi and economies of alternative comics, post-Stonewall "gay" and dyke cultures, and feminism.

Comic strips, since their inception in the late nineteenth century, have reproduced dominant arrangements of gender, sexuality, race, and class in their authorship, dissemination, and presumed readerships—but a lively and prolix underground has, almost from the beginning, garbled these arrangements; "comic strips" constitute a discourse with both an official line and an unofficial response, alternately repudiating and directly mining cultural veins of pornography, horror, adolescent deviance, and countercultural politics.[7] The underground that essentially reiterated the mainstream male dominance of the medium received a feminist retort in the 1970s with the creation of several comic books for women, notably *Wimmin's Comix*. More recently, the heterosexist presumption of both mainstream and alternative comics has been challenged by explicitly "gay" comics, a phenomenon most concretely represented by the appearance in 1989 of an anthology called *Gay Comics*.[8] The naming of this phenomenon attests to the historical tendency of alternative comic strip writers and readers to be organized as specialized "communities" (i.e., fanboy conventions, comic strip/skater connections, comic book buying, selling, trading networks), a tendency that also is constitutive of "gay" culture, specifically urban post-Stonewall culture. It is, in fact, this tendency of ours to organize in communities that makes our comic strips economically viable, as they are easily distributed and consumed through existing publications and locations, such as bars and bookstores, which have been crucial in the formation and definition of communities.

Comic strips with dyke characters first emerged in the context of feminist comics in the mid-1970s; after the decline of specifically feminist comics that same decade, dyke comic strips also began to appear in the context of "gay" comics. Dyke comic strips, therefore, are the product of a queer coupling, born from two comic strip subcultures with divergent and significant relations to pornography. Gay male comics often accentuated the (gay male) body as an object of desire or even functioned as pornography, most prominently in the work of Tom of Finland. But dyke comic strips' feminist origins also place them in the historical midst of a debate that was crucial in the construction of American feminism, that is, the so-called "sex wars"—the often contentious examination of the interstices of sexual practice and political theory, with a focus on the production, use, and proliferation of pornography.

This conflict over the representation of sex distinctively stages the development of dyke comic strips by delimiting the topical repertoire to "identity" and referring only obtusely to "desire." Most dyke comics from the 1970s through the mid-1980s focus on "lost history," coming out, meeting friends and girlfriends, and other elements of social life; sex is described but usually not depicted, especially not in a way that could be used to incite sexual desire.[9] Certain aesthetic characteristics of comics facilitate this disavowal—their newsprint surfaces and black-and-white linear images are in stark contrast to the glossy color photos of publications (such as *Playboy* or *Penthouse*) wherein lesbian sex is packaged for the viewer, presumed to be a straight man. But paradoxically, "desire" must be represented in order to carry out the project of dyke "identity"—an imperative made acutely apparent in any juxtaposition of dyke comics to their gay male counterparts, which often investigate an identity formed in relation to sexuality.[10] Thus, the image of the dyke in her comic strip setting is historically designed not to represent a sexual object but to be a fetish; that is, the comic strip dyke registers the symbolic structure of normative heterosexuality in which (presumably) she could be read only as a sexual image that (presumably) would erase lesbian desire by supplanting it with male heterosexual desire. Dyke "identity" in the comic strip, imaged as a stereotype, becomes a fetishistic substitute for desire, a code of disavowal that can be cracked only by the initiated.

Fetishism is, Freud insists, an exclusively masculine perversion, since it is a reaction of the male child to the fact of his mother's castration in order to disavow the possibility of his own.[11] Subsequent attempts to revise this thesis, to make a case for female fetishism, have produced the notions that the "female fetishist is a woman who responds to her mother's desire by wanting to be her (missing, absent) phallus"; that it provides a "paradigm of undecidability" with which "women can effectively counter any move to reduce their bisexuality to a single one of its poles"; or that it is possible through an assumption of the masculinity complex, in which a woman "disavows women's castration, but this castration is her own, not that of the phallic mother."[12] None of these explanations of female fetishism adequately addresses lesbian desire, which is not necessarily bisexual, an expression of a masculinity complex, or a figment of maternal desire. I am not attempting to theorize here what provokes or sustains lesbian desire; rather, I am suggesting that "the problem" with lesbian desire is its unrepresentability. Lesbian desire is, in Judith Butler's terms, symbolically possible only in the abject form of the "phallicized dyke," who serves to enforce normative heterosexuality.[13] To acknowledge lesbian desire is to be thrust into the morph of the phallicized dyke, foreclosing the possibility of reciprocal desire; the threatened effect is estrangement from the social and from language and thus psychosis. Disavowal is not only possible for the subject of lesbian desire, it is absolutely essential; the simultaneous acceptance and repudiation of the symbolic order in which she would be abjected is the very premise of her subjectivity.

The "phallicized dyke" is a stereotype; her function as such is to serve as a representation of the abject, a figure who enforces the Law as an object of repudiation. Homi Bhabha demonstrates the instability of the stereotype in the colonial scene:

Although the "authority" of colonial discourse depends crucially on its location in narcissism and the Imaginary, my concept of stereotype-as-suture is a recognition of the ambivalence of that authority and those orders of identification. The role of fetishistic identification, in the construction of discriminatory knowledges that depend on the presence of difference, is to provide a process of splitting and multiple/contradictory belief at the point of enunciation and subjectification. ... It is a non-repressive form of knowledge that allows for the possibility of simultaneously embracing two contradictory beliefs, one official and one secret. . . . [14]

Bhabha's fetishized stereotype—an image, an ideal, an object of ridicule, and an agent of the Law—threatens to disintegrate the distinction between identification and repudiation.

The stereotypes used to enforce normative heterosexuality differ from those set up to guard colonial authority in that the fetishized body on which the stereotype depends is not a "raced" body but a "sexed" one, i.e., one distinguished by the absence or presence of the penis that installs sexuality as well as sex—although both are marked in an economy of specularity and certainly overlap, as I discuss later in this essay. The task for the subject of same-sex desire is to occupy the stereotype, in the sense of a military occupation, a guerrilla colonization; to fetishize this fetish, the stereotype, in order to both identify with it and reject it. In inhabiting a prescribed performance, a performance whose reiteration is demanded by the symbolic order, the subject's own ambivalent processes of identification and disavowal can derail this reiteration and animate instead toward unanticipated ends, abject desires. The appeal of the dyke comic strip is in its repetition of stereotypic figures—figures, however, without form, which are literally empty, not fleshed out, revealing their status as impossible and unlivable ideals. They are abject figures, but in their material representation on the flat, spartan page of the comic strip, they are stripped of their horror even as they articulate it. Thus the enforcing power of the stereotype vacillates. The repetition of these figures, more-over, threatens with each reproduction to dilute or augment the unstably signifying figure of the abject. And finally, the reader's ability to "occupy" the outlines of the stereotype, to claim and refuse the figure as her own in an alternating circuit of identification facilitated by the technological and genealogical characteristics of dyke comic strips, presents another instance of the stereotype's instability and thus another pleasure for the reader's fetishizing imagination.[15]

Within the context of dyke comic strips, then, who is this "phallicized dyke" and what does s/he do? The three bodies of work I examine suggest an assortment of guises in which she appears. Hothead Paisan performs the role of the stereotypical "phallicized dyke" as the threat of castration which constructs relations to the phallus and thus gender; yet her personi-fication of this abstract threat reveals the tenuousness of the distinction that castration supposedly imprints on the body. In her wildly popular *Dykes to Watch Out For*, represented here by the collection *Spawn of Dykes to Watch Out For*, Alison Bechdel suggests a dyke body politic that is fragmentary and composite, a social vision in which the "phallus" is the organizing unity of dyke utopia—but is predicated, tellingly, on dis-avowal. And in various comic strips by Fish, the dyke is literally "phal-licized"; phallic simulacra are incorporated into the dyke's sexual reper-toire, positioning "it" as a transferable instrument of bodily pleasure with multiple significations. In other words, all three comic strips inscribe visible substitutes—fetishes—that operate as the phallus, illustrating the ambivalence of the distinction between "having" and "being" the phallus that subtends the normative sex and gender systems in the Lacanian scheme: masculinity as a "having" that induces a desire for the lack that is feminine "being." Installing plural and fetishistic phalluses, dyke comic strips thereby expose and exploit a set of "phallacies," multiple gaps or *méconnaissances*; in so doing, they articulate a mode of dyke subjectivity that counters the conditions of its being.

Hothead Paisan seems at first to perfectly embody the phallicized dyke without shifting the framework set up by normative sexuality. She is at the mercy of her own rage against society, which she expresses by castrat-ing men who are exaggerated stand-ins for the patriarchal order. The strip oscillates between horrifying/satisfying scenes of castration, as Hot-head's rage gets the better of her, and her regret—over losing control, not over the loss of the penises. Moreover, Hothead is a somewhat butch androgyne, and she is attracted to femmes, thus conforming in almost every respect to the stereotypic "phallicized dyke": her refusal to assume the feminine position defined by castration results in a "figure of excessive phallicism . . . devouring and destructive, the negative fate of the phallus when attached to the feminine position . . . [implying] that there is no other way for women to assume the phallus except in its most killing modalities."[16] Hothead's rage is never unrequited, since various instruments of destruction miraculously appear on her body or in her immediate surroundings—guns, bicycle pumps, knives—but her equipment is always used to castrate. In other words, in an initial reading, Hothead's castrating acts seem to indicate either a bad case of penis envy or a lethal masculinity complex.

These diagnoses, however, cannot account for Hothead's desire for self-control. Castration is not fulfilling; indeed, it is often figured as an obstacle, rather than as a liberatory decapitation. *Hothead Paisan* 9 begins with a visitation by an angel, an identical Hothead with wings, who pleads with Hothead to "find some love in your hearts"(*HHP* 9, 2). (Does the plurality of her address suggest that Hothead is representative of all dykes? humankind?) Hothead is then accosted by a devil, a ribbon of smoke who resembles her rageful appearance, who doesn't "speak" but shows her newspaper headlines: "It's Open Season in Colorado," "Man Opens Fire on 'Feminists' in Classroom," "Man Rapes and Kills Six-Year-Old Daughter"(*HHP* 9, 4)—signs of the symbolic which, after an inner struggle, precipitate Hothead's return to her regular scene. This acknowledgment of her division into two, her "better half," an imaginary imago, who advocates tolerance, and her "evil twin," who conjures up the symbolic order in order to provoke Hothead's alienated rage, throws the phallus into question: is it Hothead's appropriated phallic instrument, used to castrate and thus by implication "feminine" and transferable? or is it Hothead's elusive self-mastery, the control that would appropriate the ordering principle of the phallus? In *Hothead Paisan* 10 Hothead is reproached in a dream for her useless behavior, and this episode suggests that what Hothead needs is self-control (*HHP* 10, 13–15).

Hothead's elusive self-control is figured both as something she lacks and as something she has but is always (in danger of) losing; that is, as both castration and castration anxiety. Hothead, then, doesn't seem to miss an absent penis, nor does she believe herself to possess one. Instead, Hothead dislodges the phallic from the penile: she insists on their coincidence and then, emphatically, she severs their connection. Hothead's rage is constituted not by a desire for the phallus but by a desire to resignify the phallus; she wants control over signification, specifically over her own means of signifying. In other words, she wants to "be" the phallus but not in the matrix presumed and imposed by normative heterosexuality: she wants self-control, not femininity. As a monster, she is out of control, fragmented, unassimilable to a totalizing specular ideal; the dyke who stands before the Lacanian mirror, when she refuses to accept castration, is threatened with yet another cut, this time from the signification that her image could otherwise assume. Castration doesn't get her what she wants—hence the repeating scenes of castration—but because she castrates in order to "be" rather than "have" the phallus, she disrupts the scheme that sets up gender and sexuality. In other words, the phallus is, as Butler argues, "fundamentally transferable"; that is, it is always being removed from its "proper" location, so "castration," that which installs the subject's relation to the phallus, is also, paradoxically, the vehicle by which the phallic regime is undone.[17]

Hothead, then, exceeds the outlines of the abject "phallicized dyke," because as the image of disavowal—an image that simultaneously castrates, is castrated, and fears castration—Hothead functions as a fetish. Cast as a stereotype, Hothead overdramatizes the role, revealing that the very circumstances that supposedly animate that stereotype, the relation to the phallus via castration, are ambivalent, capable of contradictory significations. Finally, Hothead the hero also signifies equivocally. Her fixation on anger is evidence of her alienation from the symbolic order; her rage represents the inevitable response to this exclusion but the representation of this rage reinscribes her alienation. Although Hothead is never caught or punished, her performance is unnerving. DiMassa mitigates the reader's identification with Hothead by drawing her as a primitive caricature; Hothead, her acquaintances, her targets, and her cat are rough, stylized compositions lacking the illustrative details that would allow the reader to place them in a realistic setting. Hothead's castration narratives are fantasy, but ones in which prohibition is as prominent as desire; that is, her own ambivalence about the long-term usefulness of her project, her desire for self-control, reinforces the ambivalence of readers who don't really want to identify with her or live out these experiences, because total identification with Hothead would incorporate a sacrifice of symbolic subjectification—it would align the reader too closely with Hothead's alienation and her lawlessness. To appreciate Hothead's rage, and yet to distance oneself from it, refuse it, acknowledge its existence as cartoon only, presents the reader with a vicarious, safe expression of rage, a disavowal that serves as a symbolic representation of the identifactory disavowal undertaken by she who claims dyke identity.

Hothead Paisan 12, in which DiMassa projects the responses of readers horrified by the excessive castrations of 11, ends with a feminine "utopia," complete with environmental renewal, floods of menstrual blood, a Native American Earth mother, and an Asian moon woman. This scenario, however, remains incomplete; DiMassa depicts the fantasmatic havoc wreaked by angry women and then reverts to "reality," so that the final frames of the issue show Earth mother Coco and moon spirit Loon-Chi resolved to fix the world in the near future (*HHP* 12, 10–17). Although DiMassa cannot sustain this vision from within the scene of castration, the sequence of these events suggests that "castration" is the antecedent to "utopia." And in Alison Bechdel's *Dykes to Watch Out For*, this promise is carried out. *Dykes to Watch Out For* attempts to rewrite the Law of the Father as dyke domesticity in which difference, as a vector of unequal access to signification, ultimately disappears; the phallus here is nowhere visible as a bodily projection but is the organizing principle of community, which uses the portrayal of difference, paradoxically, to signify sameness. But Bechdel's utopic feminist fantasy, like DiMassa's, cannot successfully evade the differences that threaten to reproduce inequality within the dyke community. Anxiety about the surrounding symbolic order is displaced onto the very images that are set up to thwart it; the comic strip image of the dyke utopia is ultimately a fetish predicated on a disavowal of difference.

In contrast to Hothead's rebellious appeal, *Dykes to Watch Out For* serves as the prima donna of dyke comic strips; collected into five volumes, the weekly comic strip focuses on the lives of a group of friends and their trials in love, at work, and especially, at home. The action centers on Mo, Bechdel's admitted alter ego, whose anxieties about patriarchal injustice are lovingly skewered by her friends and housemates, the Asian American New Age Sparrow, Ginger, an African American Ph.D. student, and Lois, the permanently horny lezzie-boy. The cast of characters has hospitably expanded to include a wide range of stereotypic characters, presumably representing the scope of "the lesbian community." In Bechdel's collection *Spawn of Dykes to Watch Out For*, in which the pregnant Latina C.P.A. Toni and her partner Clarice, an African American hot-shot lawyer, prepare for the birth of their baby, the characters are introduced and labeled with epithets as brief and emblematic as the ones I have given them here; each character, including Mo's ex-lover, the chubby, incisive social worker, and her new love interest, the disabled, quick-witted bookstore worker, is given a specific identity that more or less dictates her behavior throughout the narrative.[18] While the story line in this particular collection culminates in the birth (at a birthing center, of course) of Clarice and Toni's baby, the real focus is on the interactions between characters as they are deployed in situations imitative of "real life" in the community: working at the women's bookstore, eating at the women's cafe, bussing to the March on Washington, sitting around the kitchen table kvetching about sex.

The careful inclusion of all "kinds" of dykes, along with Bechdel's illustrative attention to body size and race, as portrayed by hair and facial structure, results in a kind of compendium of dyke typologies. The well-intentioned diversity of the characters nevertheless produces a cast of stereotypes: none of them is complete in her own right, but together they produce a puzzle-picture of the community of choice. The reader's identificatory pleasure depends not on her assimilation of any one character as an ideal; the brief dimensions of each character, delineating race, job, marital status, and personality, are easily "outstripped," as they are designed to be. Rather, the reader's pleasure lies in identifying with the "whole" body, with the notion of family queerly and politically recast, and in her concomitant ability to identify its operative parts.

Presented with this perfect wholeness, who would not reject the fragmented and unidentical parts that are presumed to precede it? The strip "No Place Like Home" (60) reviews the motives for the deliberate replacement of the dyke utopia for the patriarchal family, suggestively rewriting the Mirror Stage—the phase that, according to Lacan, institutes subjectivity when a child sees in her reflection a unified, obedient, and idealized body. To emphasize the preferability of the dyke body politic, "No Place Like Home" depicts Toni, Clarice, Lois, and Mo with their families of origin on New Year's Eve; all four families are either outright homophobic or malignantly clueless, and the heroines are stripped of the ability to signify as dykes. Leaving a home that denies or abuses one's sexual identity for the unity of the dyke family is, by implication, inevitable and unproblematic. It is at this point, however, that the ordered dyke family reveals its instability, for the price of unity is the disavowal of difference, here racial difference—a standard foil for the deflection of anxiety in places where gendered hierarchies and normative sexuality are questioned.[19] In place of the heterosexual, reproductive family ordered by the father and thus by the phallus, the dyke family, the "family of choice," is unified by political concerns, habits, values, a unity that would clearly be threatened by racial friction. The dangers of racial difference are anxiously represented and symbolically repressed; while Mo and her cohorts express their dismay at racist atrocities, one of the many evils of the patriarchal regime, conflict among them generally concerns personal relationships independent of socially constructed differences— the house is messy, someone is grumpy, girlfriends are arguing. In this dyke idyll, the reproduction of the family as the family of choice does not entail a reproduction of the ills of the larger social context. This representation of racial harmony construes the reader as racially "neu- tral," which works out, as it often does, to mean white; this scenario is quite possibly neither familiar nor appealing to real dykes of color. Racial equality within the scheme of the comic strip suppresses certain kinds of "difference" while pointing markedly to others: the characters have ra- cially defined hair and facial features but not speech, and racial conflict is a constitutive problem of the outside world, emanating from it but not intruding on the dyke domestic. The phallus is to be found on this unified body not as a Father or even as a penis (indeed, penises or simulacra are nowhere in sight) but as an organizing plurality; that is, the idyll of racial harmony is implemented by and requisitioned from each character.

The fear of power differentials that might reinstate the Law of the Father leads not only to the denial of racial difference but also to the invisibility of sex in this picture of the dyke family. In contrast to the invisibility of race, which takes the form of transparency, sex is coyly removed from view, as if a curtain has been drawn across certain scenes. While friendship, foreplay, physical intimacy, romance, and even child- birth are portrayed with detail in *Spawn of Dykes to Watch Out For,* sex is suggestively covered over in the manner of the romance idiom. So, for example, when Mo has a last fling with her soon-to-be ex-lover, the reader is shown hugs, kisses, frenzied undressing, and then a close-up on the faces of the two women, teary and concentrated (37). Not only are their bodies excluded from the pictorial frame, but bodily pleasure cannot be ascertained from their facial expressions, which register instead possi- ble sensational pleasure written over with grief: we don't really know if they get off or if they're simply overcome with emotion. Likewise, even Lois, who is coded as "queer" by her attire and promiscuity and thus subject to a different set of sexual mores, is only partially caught in the act behind a sofa (61). Clarice goes down on Toni but under the pretext of relieving her of the discomfort of nine months of pregnancy; moreover, her head blocks the reader's view (92). Ginger and Malika attempt to videotape themselves having sex, and their successful position is reproduced in indiscernible miniature on a TV screen (93). This consistent swerve from the explicit representation of sex enacts a kind of pornophobia in which any representation of lesbian sex is available for appropriation by the straight men, anxiously pointing to a symbolic order that hovers hungrily just outside the frame of the comic strip—the same kind of anxiety that results in the elision of racial difference.

Despite the tensions underlying Bechdel's democratic utopia—a sameness coded as invisible, racially white, and sexually "vanilla"—this fantasy of a different symbolic order does suggestively remove the organizing principle of community from an originary authority. The "phallus" is here everywhere and nowhere, an elision reflected in a corresponding elision between imaginary and symbolic—in distinct contrast to the Lacanian set up, which requires the separation of these realms. Lacan's unacknowledged superimposition of penis on phallus underlies the opposition of imaginary and symbolic: the phallus operates successfully in the symbolic but its dominance is vulnerable in the imaginary, where the narcissistic and antagonistic identifications that constitute the imaginary threaten to reveal the absence of the phallus and unhinge its primary significance in symbolic Law. The hierarchical and oppositional relation between symbolic and imaginary cannot obtain if the phallus is ambivalent.

If the phallus is the privileged signifier of the symbolic, the delimiting and ordering principle of what can be signified, then this signifier gains its privilege through becoming an imaginary effect that pervasively denies its own status as both imaginary and an effect.... In other words, what operates under the sign of the symbolic may be nothing other than precisely that set of imaginary effects which have become naturalized and reified as the law of signification.[20]

The comic strip is profusely illustrated with inside jokes that obscure this difference as effectively as those that mark race and sexual activity. Bechdel litters the panels with humorous, detailed references, visual and textual, to "lesbian identity" and to the specific temporality of the action. Lois, for example, perennially attired in leather jacket and t-shirt, is emblazoned with an official March on Washington t-shirt in a 1993 strip (75) and another that says "I fuck to come, not to conceive" (115) during the birth of Toni's baby. Bechdel is particularly adept at mutating headlines and titles to reflect the times and the identities purveyed by her characters; one newspaper's headline reads "Camel denies its 'Old Joe' ads target kids" in one panel, "Despite 7,800% increase in sales to minors since ads began" in the next, and finally " 'And we don't draw him to look like a penis either!' chairman insists" (23). But alongside this sly commentary reminiscent of DiMassa's fantasy headlines are titles and names of, references to, real cultural phenomena: *Vanity Fair* with Cindy Crawford shaving k. d. lang on the cover (93), the television show *Roseanne* (82), rented videos like *The Virgin Machine* and *Sammy & Rosie Get Laid* (53). Signifieds that do exist and those that exist only in the imaginary space of the comic strip intermingle freely, challenging the authority of the symbolic, and the reiteration of real dyke cultural productions extends to the reader the promise of membership in the dyke utopia. In this undifferentiated concoction of significant images, and in the erection of a dyke body politic, *Dykes to Watch Out For* attempts to write an alternative law, in which the phallus is resignified as a utopic assembly of parts.

Fish's comic strips, in contrast with DiMassa's and Bechdel's, take as their explicit subject the "lesbian phallus," in a transcription and exploration of fantasies that define the parameters of dyke sexuality vis-à-vis the phallus as a transferable instrument of pleasure that has "nothing" to do with men. Fish fetishizes the phallic instrument, not in order to disavow castration but in order to disavow the presence of the Father. Unlike Bechdel, Fish ignores the Father's watchful eye surrounding representations of dyke sex; by constraining her strips to sexual locales, she insists on the role of desire in the image of the phallicized dyke, who differs from Hothead in that she is ruled by sexual pleasure.

In endowing every dyke with a dick and tracing out multiple variations of this theme, Fish reproduces the phallus to the point of banality—much as mass production of the dildo "exposes the male organ as signifier of the phallus, and not vice versa, that is, the dildo exposes the cultural organ of the phallus as simulacrum."[21] This plethora of phalluses denies it the place of primary significance. Fish's characters, moreover, are not restricted to the use of the dildo in their appropriations of the phallus. While phallic simulacra do play a central role in the comic strip "One Fine San Francisco Evening..." the characters participate in sex acts involving leather belts, chains, whips, a vibrator, and hands, all of which serve to signify sexual and, within the economy of these pages, symbolic power.[22] Similarly, in the comic strip "Diggy Diver, Dyke on the Go, in Dildo Mania," Diggy interviews the female patrons of "the feminist sex shop" as to their dildo preferences—but is interrupted by the appearance of a desperate customer whose favorite appendage ("I've had this dick for seven—sob—years . . . it's like it's mine") has broken off at the crucial moment.[23] This epitome of what might be called lesbian castration anxiety is resolved with the advice of another customer in the store: purchase of "Dick o' death," the size of a small rocket. However, the apparently satisfying one-upmanship implied by the character's assumption of the gargantuan phallus is deflated in the very next panel, when the sales clerk at the store whittles a totem-like face into the discarded member and says, "I like to feed them to my blender ritualistically at dawn" (*BA* 22). Again, Fish suggests that phallic appropriation is not dependent on a piece of strap-on silicone, that the phallus is not necessarily a sexual possession but a tool for any desire.

Unlike DiMassa and Bechdel, Fish does not employ a set cast of characters or continuous situations; her work is connected instead by the theme of radical sexuality and by artistic and narrative techniques reminiscent of video pornography, condensed into the comic strip format—closeups, disembodied speech, and the rounded frames of the TV screen. In "One Fine San Francisco Evening . . ." the sexual narrative is depicted in staged scenes that are sexually explicit but not linear; the reader is responsible for connecting these scenes into the fantasy of her own making and is encouraged to do so by stylized but realistic depictions of anatomy, penetration and pleasure indicated by body fluids and facial expressions of fear, excitement, and ecstasy. The reader's role is fortified by the traditional comic strip device of speeding time through textual tags: "Thus the evening wears on . . . And on" (*RG* 15–17), obfuscating the presumed chronology of the narrative—the various sexual acts do suggest a sequence, but whether this sequence takes place over twenty minutes or ten hours is unclear. Fish further disrupts the power of the sexual and textual narrative by drawing her reader's attention to particular moments in the scene, often obscuring the specific sexual activity engaging the characters in order to emphasize body parts and sexual accessories in panels with "closeups"; these closeups, like their video counterparts, require a different "focus" and are drawn with veristic detail, in contrast to the caricature-like figures that surround them. Just as DiMassa uses caricature to provide a safe distance for the reader's identification with Hothead, Fish uses verism to suggest that the moment of closest identity between reader and comic strip spectacle occurs only as a product of desire.

These strategies of more and less realism, sexual explicitness drawn with attention to bodily pleasure but merely suggestive of specific acts, and video-porn devices such as the closeup, together set up a phallic economy in which the presence of the phallus as instrument of pleasure is indisputable but its form and application migrate and mutate. Or, since "the phallus can only play its role when veiled, that is, as in itself the sign of the latency with which everything signifiable is struck as soon as it is raised to the function of signifier," perhaps I should designate this migration and mutation as a game of hide-and-seek.[24] Sex in these comics both reiterates the (sexual) power of the phallus (-like) and dismantles it; veiling and unveiling are bodily functions independent of who exactly is being fucked and who is doing the fucking, thus obscuring the distinction between "having" and "being" the phallus and making light of castration, which does not here assume the same coercive meaning as it does in normative heterosexuality.

Like Bechdel, Fish is also attentive to racial differentiation and body type in her characterizations, but because her primary emphasis on sex relieves her of the responsibility of envisioning utopian social arrangements, Fish avoids the production of prescriptive and anxious diversity. Differences in race, age, and sexual position qualify the constitutive characteristic of the dyke, her possession of the phallus. The dyke's basic attributes as characterized in these comics—rebellious, tough, and, most of all, horny—are, like the cartoons they are, merely outlines, to be filled in by variations. Although Fish, like Bechdel, imagines a comic strip populated exclusively by dykes, the definition of this population as primarily a sexual one, and not a social, work-related, familiar utopia does not close down differences derived from experience in these realms simply because they are not opened up in the first place. This does not mean that Fish ignores the consequences of race or other marked differences, however. The participants of the sexual exploits in "One Fine San Francisco Evening . . ." are an African American femme dominatrix, her white butch assistant, and two butch bottoms, one black and one white. Although this strip initially depends on the standard motif of the "interracial relationship" to introduce racial difference, the neat pairing of black with white is soon disrupted by the variety of sexual combinations, arrangements that also revalue the stereotyped affiliations of race with particular sexual positions in interracial relationships. While Fish's representation of race relies on many of the same illustrative details as Bechdel's, she doesn't catalog racial or other differences; for example, in "Diggy Diver" some characters look distinctly African American, some white, and some, especially in the context of more clearly defined racial characteristics, seem to be racially indeterminate. In "One Fine San Francisco Evening . . ." the obvious absence of certain characters from the mix-and-match cast—where is the femme bottom? the African American butch top? where, indeed, are the Asian American or Latina or disabled characters?—reveals that the scene is not an exhaustive depiction of dyke sex, or even of dyke S/M sex. Instead, racial difference provides only one among many sets of differences to be rearranged within the parameters of pleasure in this comic strip. The sexual fantasy also presents a fantasy of traversible racial difference. The staging of fantasy thus differs from utopia, both materially and narratively, and Fish remains insistently fantastic—both *Real Girl 5* and *Brat Attack 4* feature sexual fantasy in action on their covers, and "Diggy Diver" and "One Fine San Francisco Evening . . ." begin and end in two notorious theaters of dyke sexual life, the room of the one-night stand and the feminist sex shop. These are sites where, like the "space" of the sex 'zine itself, identity positions—i.e., sexual positions such as top, bottom, butch and femme—are reinforced and transgressed for the sake of pleasure, for the investigation of desires. The incorporation of race into the scenario of sexual fantasy makes evident the extent to which race and other bodily attributes operate in the specular economy of desire but also injects the fantasy with irreducible elements of difference that circulate beyond its perimeter, that signify in other regimes—suggesting, finally, that fantasy depends on the exchange between imaginary identifications and symbolic significations.

Fish's comics explicitly fantasize dyke sex in order to play with the phallus, but this game is possible only by averting the surrounding gaze, by temporarily ignoring the uncontrollable significations that such play can produce. Is this yet another form of disavowal practiced by dyke comic strip artists and their readers? If so, how can a subjective position staked out in blind refusal of its context really signify; how can it be read? All three of the artists whose work I have examined here can be seen to construct a continuum of engagement with the political: DiMassa's Hothead launches headfirst into battle with a compelling if reductive version of sexual politics, Bechdel's cast of characters occasionally leave home to confront injustice, and Fish's perverts bring the political to bed. That is, each takes a different position with respect to the discursive networks that delimit and generate the dyke comic strip. As models of political engagement, they may not be truly viable, may not be capable of signifying on other pages. So, to restate the question with which I began, what difference do dyke comic strips make?

To answer, I turn again to the readers. Comic books aptly demonstrate the potential disparity between the community imagined by the comic strip creator and those of her readers, since the letters that frequently appear on the inside covers often belie any authorial intention in constructing a certain readership. *Brat Attack*, the now-defunct 'zine Fish edited, called itself "the zine for leatherdykes and other bad girlzzz"—but judging from their letters, readers included straight men, lesbian separatists, male-to-female and female-to-male transsexuals, lesbians who practice "vanilla" sex, and regular old S/M dykes (*BA* 46–47). Similarly, the readers of *Hothead Paisan* find all kinds of unanticipated uses for her; fan letters include paeans to Hothead's pet cat, Chicken, letters addressed "Dear Sir," letters that describe DiMassa as a "truly disturbed individual." For some readers, Hothead sets an example, but even these diverge: one woman writes in, "My local 'Queers R Us' store doesn't have the new issue—so I stabbed them in the head 25 times," while another says, "As a committed pacifist, I enjoy HH precisely because she feels the tension between an explosive, destructive anger and some sort of spirituality which tells her things can be done in a better way." For other readers, the purchase and ownership of the comic books themselves are a radical act: "I think my mom ritualistically burned all my Hothead's to make me Str8," or "I love writing GIANT ASS PUBLISHING really big on the envelope. My mail carrier is a born-again Christian" (*HHP* 9, 18–19). Readers' responses, even fan letters, sometimes seem to surround the comic strips' contents with a frame of disorder, misapprehension, and disagreement, but these artists continue to make "dyke comic strips," an act of steadfast determination in the face of contradictory evidence. But neither Fish nor DiMassa nor Bechdel, whose mainstream status effectively puts her on the front line of exposure to unsympathetic readers, actually turn from the material reality of comic strips, from the knowledge that comic strips circulate in unforeseen ways; instead, they reproduce and disseminate those responses that would at times seem to erase the very premise of the comic strip dyke. The reader's page is only the most visible assurance that the comic strip dyke articulates her countersubjectivity by seizing the words that would silence her. Taking hold of her sex, so to speak, the cartoon image of the phallicized dyke—her abject guise suggested as crudely as possible in cartoon form—installs her own pleasure on pages coded as childish, boyish, materially unappealing, artistically meaningless; in short, from a location deemed symbolically castrated and yet one that reproduces the phallus ad infinitum.

Of course, to be honest, and as is probably perfectly obvious anyway, my real reason for taking on the dyke comic strip and proposing for her an inventive articulation of subjectivity and a range of phallic dispossessions, "phallacies" made possible by disavowal, is my own attraction to her. Why am I so seduced by this seemingly innocuous, even vacuous, even at times offensive, form of entertainment? My pleasure has the flavor of sweet revenge. The comic strip dyke manages to wrest an "identity" from the very set of signifiers implicated in her abjection, she invests in her own "desire." In other words, she performs the same sort of reclamation palpable in the terms "dyke" and "queer." And this is also the reason it seems to me to be most useful to employ the arguably restrictive apparatus of psychoanalytic theory to approach dyke comic strips and to describe their operations. Although the theories of Freud, Lacan, and their exegetes might seem to outlaw "feminist psychoanalysis," nevertheless, such a thing has evolved and become an eminently useful, if not always concordant, device for the scrutiny of culture and a rich system of reference and metaphor. Because in some sense they signify that which dyke comic strips are up against, the theoretical words of the Fathers also supply, I think, a delightful opportunity to collaborate with dyke comic strips by engaging in guerrilla practices.

NOTES

Thanks to Norman Bryson, Kate Cummings, Tim Dean and Le'a Kent for their helpful comments on various versions of this essay, and to Nathan Kibler for generous access to his comic book collection.

1. Diane DiMassa, *Hothead Paisan Homicidal Lesbian Terrorist* 11 (New Haven, Conn.: Giant Ass Publishing, no date), cited hereafter within the text as *HHP* followed by the number of the issue and page number.

2. I am only briefly rehearsing here the barest terms of this debate. Indeed, the debate itself seems to be constituted in terms of its rehearsal, one that, in recent years, has generally opened the question in order to decide in favor of the usefulness of psychoanalysis for feminist theory. For more thoughtful reprisals, see Jane Gallop, "Phallus/Penis? Same Difference," *Women and Literature* 2 (1982): 243–51, revised and reprinted in *Thinking Through the Body* (New York: Columbia University Press, 1988) and her *Reading Lacan* (Ithaca: Cornell University Press, 1985); and Kaja Silverman, "The Lacanian Phallus," *Differences* 4, no. 1 (1992): 84–115, and *Male Subjectivity at the Margins* (New York: Routledge, 1992). For the implications of the phallus/penis debate for lesbian sexuality, see Judith Butler, "The Lesbian Phallus and the Morphological Imaginary," *Differences* 4, no. 1 (1992): 133–71, revised and reprinted in *Bodies That Matter: On the Discursive*

Limits of Sex (New York: Routledge, 1993); Heather Findlay, "Freud's 'Fetishism' and the Lesbian Dildo Debate," *Feminist Studies* 18, no. 3 (1992); and Teresa de Lauretis, "Film and the Visible," in *How Do I Look? Queer Film and Video*, ed. Bad Object-Choices (Seattle: Bay Press, 1991), 223–84.

3. I will continue to use the word "dyke" to identify the readers and the writers of, and the characters in, the comic strips I discuss. It is a term used in the comic strips themselves and one I apply to myself, an avid comic strip reader. "Dyke," like the comic strips I examine, exists uneasily between "gender" definitions of sexuality and "sexual" definitions of sexuality, as articulated by Eve Kosofsky Sedgwick (see Eve Kosofsky Sedgwick, *Epistemology of the Closet* [Berkeley: University of California Press, 1990], 88), that is, in some overlap of space between "lesbian" and "queer." This is not to imply that all those who would call themselves lesbians would call themselves dykes, or that all those who would call themselves queers would call themselves dykes, or that "lesbian" and "queer" are mutually exclusive. The term "dyke" foregrounds the definitional instability of the sexuality name game, and this seems to be the best strategy for the moment. Rather than attempting to characterize the diverse range of possible identifications inhering in and facilitated by these comic strips, I am admitting that range even while I constrain it to "dyke" territory. However, I use the word "lesbian" to indicate same-sex desire between women, in order to differentiate "desire" from "identity."

4. Art Spiegelman, *Maus: A Survivor's Tale*, vols. 1 and 2 (New York: Pantheon Books, 1991). Graphic novels include texts originally conceived as comic strips, such as *Maus* or the samurai stories of Stan Sakai (Sakai, *Usagi Yojimbo* [Seattle: Fantagraphics, 1995]), and texts created as collaborations between an artist and a writer, books such as *Brooklyn Dreams* and other issues in the Paradox Press series (J. M. DeMatteis and Glenn Barr, *Brooklyn Dreams* [New York: Paradox Press, 1995]. Graphic novels also include traditional literary texts that have been adapted to comic strip form, such as the Classics Illustrated series for children, which includes *Hamlet* and *The Scarlet Letter*, among many others (William Shakespeare, *Hamlet*, adptd. Steven Grant and Tom Mandrake [New York: Berkley Publishing, 1990] and Nathaniel Hawthorne, *The Scarlet Letter*, adptd. P. Craig Russell and Jill Thompson [Norwalk, Conn.: Classics International, 1994]), and adaptations of adult novels, such as Paul Auster, *City of Glass*, adptd. Paul Karasik and David Mazzucchelli (New York: Avon, 1994).

5. Julie Doucet, *Dirty Plotte* 3 (Montreal: Drawn and Quarterly, 1992), 2–3.

6. In a complete genealogy of dyke comic strips, it would be essential also to trace the relations between alternative comics and 'zines, comic strip pornography and the photo novella. 'Zines, for example, often include comic strips (see, for example, Fish, ed., *Brat Attack* 4 [San Francisco: Brat Attack, 1993], and *TeenFag Magazine* 2 [Seattle: Chow Chow Productions, 1993]) and circulate in many of the same economic networks and kinds of subcultures as alternative comics, as does comic strip pornography. In fact, comic strip pornography would have to be classified as a subgenre of alternative comics, but one with different alliances to mainstream pornography and art. Photo novellas also present interesting categorical questions with respect to comic strips, film, and photography. But for my

purposes here, I am restricting my consideration of the cultural context of alternative comic strips to more dominant cultural forms.

7. Roger Sabin, *Adult Comics, An Introduction* (New York: Routledge, 1993).

8. Robert Triptow, ed., *Gay Comics* (New York: New American Library, 1989). Of course, this title reflects a masculine predilection, as does the book. My quotational reiteration of the term is intended to expose this predilection.

9. See, for example, the work of Rhonda Dicksion, Andrea Natalie, Noreen Stevens, Kris Kovick, and Jennifer Camper, in Triptow, *Gay Comics;* Roberta Gregory, "Bitchy Butch," *Gay Comics* 15, ed. Andy Mangels (San Francisco: Bob Ross, 1992): 11–15; Mel Gebbie and Dot Bucher, eds., *Wimmen's Comix* 7 (Berkeley: Last Gasp, 1976).

10. Triptow, for example, in his introduction to *Gay Comics,* says, "Homosexual and bisexual artists are compelled to go public in gay comics for deep personal reasons. The point of art, after all, is to express one's inner self . . . art and humor are expansive influences; together, they can set you free," thus installing sexuality as the inner self to be expressed (Triptow, *Gay Comics,* 4).

11. Sigmund Freud, "Fetishism," *The Standard Edition of the Complete Works of Sigmund Freud,* trans. and ed. James Strachey (London: Hogarth Press, 1991), 21: 152–57.

12. Naomi Schor, "Female Fetishism: The Case of George Sand," *Poetics Today* 6, no. 1 (1985) n 2, 303; Ibid., 306; Elizabeth Grosz, "Lesbian Fetishism?" in *Fetishism as Cultural Discourse,* ed. Emily Apter and William Pietz (Ithaca: Cornell University Press, 1993), 113.

13. Butler, *Bodies That Matter,* 96.

14. Homi K. Bhabha, "The Other Question: Difference, Discrimination and the Discourse of Colonialism," in *Literature, Politics & Theory,* ed. F. Barker, P. Hulme, M. Iversen, and D. Lexley (New York: Methuen, 1986), 167–68.

15. This formulation shares with that of Teresa de Lauretis, in *The Practice of Love: Lesbian Sexuality and Perverse Desire* (Bloomington: Indiana University Press, 1994), an emphasis on the relation between disavowal and lesbianism. I am proposing an association between disavowal and the dyke's power, or lack thereof, to signify, however, while de Lauretis is describing the dynamics of desire. De Lauretis suggests that "the lesbian fetish is any object, any sign whatsoever, that marks the difference and the desire between the lovers" (228) but especially masculinity, since "the lesbian masculinity fetish does not refuse castration but disavows it; the threat it holds at bay is not the loss of the penis in women but the loss of the female body itself, and the prohibition of access to it" (243).

16. Butler, *Bodies That Matter,* 102–3.

17. Ibid., 62.

18. Alison Bechdel, *Spawn of Dykes to Watch Out For* (Ithaca, N.Y.: Firebrand Books, 1993), cited hereafter within the text.

19. See Richard Fung, "Looking for My Penis: The Eroticized Asian in Gay Video Porn," Judith Mayne, "Lesbian Looks: Dorothy Arzner and Female Authorship," and Kobena Mercer, "Skin Head Sex Thing: Racial Difference and the Homoerotic Imaginary," in Bad Object-Choices, *How Do I Look?*

20. Butler, *Bodies That Matter,* 79.

21. Cathy Griggers, "Lesbian Bodies in the Age of (Post)Mechanical Reproduction," in *The Lesbian Postmodern*, ed. Laura Doan (New York: Columbia University Press, 1994), 121.

22. Fish, "One Fine San Francisco Evening . . . ," *Real Girl* 5 (Seattle: Fantagraphics Books, 1993): 20–25, cited hereafter in the text as *RG*.

23. Fish, "Diggy Diver, Dyke on the Go, in Dildo Mania," *Brat Attack* 4 (San Francisco: Brat Attack, 1993): 20–22, cited hereafter in the text as *BA*.

24. Jacques Lacan, "The Signification of the Phallus," in *Feminine Sexuality: Lacan and the Ecole Freudienne*, ed. Jacqueline Rose and Juliet Mitchell (New York: Norton, 1985), 82.

NINE

An Anatomy of Absence
Written on the Body, The Lesbian Body, and Autobiography without Names

Leigh Gilmore

What do Lesbians do in bed?
"Tell them," said Sophia, the Ninth Muse.
Tell them?
There's no such thing as autobiography, there's only art and lies.
　　　　　　　　　　　　　—Jeanette Winterson, *Art and Lies*

As a response to the injunction to tell what lesbians do in bed, "[t]here's no such thing as autobiography, there's only art and lies" is a curious reply. Winterson seems to suggest that the autobiographical lies immediately behind, or within, questions of sexuality and sexual how-to. What lesbians do in bed is a personal question, a subjective question despite its generalizing tone and capital L, an autobiographical question. Yet immediately after coming to the fore, the autobiographical is made to recede behind, or within, "art and lies" as if the question of sexuality must be routed through autobiography on its way to somewhere else. The circuit from sexuality to autobiography is made with dazzling brevity on the way to "art and lies," and in this moment autobiography is negated and absented in the place perhaps where one is most likely to look for it. The autobiographical trace is significant here, for it indicates the way autobiography is embedded in both sexuality and artifice, and even provides a way to think of how they are related. Autobiography keeps turning up (or disappearing) in weird places, threatening to throw the inquiry off, or the inquirer. "There's no such thing as autobiography" echoes the fervently whispered "there's no such thing as ghosts" as a denial in the presence of uneasy, even downright panicky, belief. There is something discreditable about both autobiography and ghosts—those figures of absence and haunting—and despite the presumed truthfulness of one (autobiography) and the unlikeliness of the other (ghosts), one finds recurring assertions that they either do or do not really exist, as if the meaning of that existence were insistently and precisely in question. In facing the meaning of autobiography's existence, Paul de Man came up with tropes of absence and death.[1] Autobiography, as de Man notes, in its effort to represent life comes inevitably upon its own impossibility. In compelling the autobiographical voice, one speaks across a gulf to address an inanimate face, one's own, and urges it to speak. Such an attribution of face to voice is inexorably a de-facement for de Man, for the thing itself (you) is not "there" in the past or in the text just waiting to speak. It must be conjured zombie-like, and de Man's rather pessimistic if scrupulously deconstructive reading ends there as the self writing the text stares across an abyss toward the self in the text. There is a certain gothic quality to de Man's reading that allows for a link to Terry Castle's *Apparitional Lesbian*, in which Castle argues that the lesbian is typically represented as a ghostly presence, a specter whose haunting is evidence of both her derealization and her persistent presence.[2] In its frequent absenting from the scene of writing and its persistent interruptions of it, autobiography, like sexuality, is knowable both in and as absence as well as vivid, self-declaring presence.

Despite its former "little fish in a big pond" status in literary studies, autobiography has come into its own. It now serves as a useful site for all kinds of explorations into the representation of identity as a range of critics working on materials as diverse as popular culture, Native American symbols, African American oral narratives, scholarly discourse, and contemporary experimental writing rely on, even as they challenge, the critical insights produced through an engagement with autobiography. At the same time, the familiar division among critics and artists, practitioners, and activists has been blurred by their shared interest in and their experimentation with self-representational projects conceptually affiliated with autobiography.[3] What is striking about this convergence is the opportunity to perceive within it a reshaping of the discourses of self-representation, for autobiography as a genre possessed of limiting characteristics and a canon of representative works has not been the exclusive or, arguably, primary location of self-representation. Those performances in which the representation of identity is foregrounded often work against the conventions of autobiography, the hallmark of which is that the story can be told (and is perhaps best told) as a straightforward narrative with continuities of character, time, and place. Yet one need not work obediently within those conventions in order to produce a text in dialogue with autobiography; indeed, those resistant texts that we might even be tempted, following de Man and Castle, to call apparitional autobiography indicate how autobiography is recognizable only in its trace. Obviously, though, a text may admit the conventions of autobiography only to work against them and remain a recognizably autobiographical venture. For example, if one construes autobiography's reliance on referentiality and truth telling as formal conventions, those conventions may then provide an occasion for experimentation in which reliable reportage and historical verifiability recede as proof of autobiography. They are no longer the content that defines the project as autobiographical, but the residue left behind. Those previously stable, or at least familiar, coordinates of autobiography would then no longer offer proof of the autobiographical but rather act as the prompt for speculation precisely where proofs once unambiguously were.

The expansion of autobiography in this direction both adumbrates and enacts a horizon of possibility, powerfully suggested by Foucault, of a "developmental" project without a telos: "One writes in order to become other than what one is."[4] Within the purview of this Foucauldian possibility, autobiography can operate as a way of knowing focused on a radically scrutinized identity. What autobiography may offer to the experimental and speculative projects undertaken in this vein is less a unique activity than a mode of exploration; less, that is, a definable content than a way to explore how the contours of self-representation transverse and pervade multiple cultural productions. I have argued elsewhere for the conceptual viability and theoretical utility of broadening the scope of critical inquiry beyond the stricter limits of autobiography to observe how it is part of a larger discourse of self-representation.[5] Such an emphasis permits us to dislodge some cultural productions from categories or interpretive locations that restrict their meanings and to ally those productions with others, which are also being translated across boundaries of meaning, in an effort to explore how they challenge dominant notions about self-representation.

I offer this reading of Jeanette Winterson's *Written on the Body* and

Monique Wittig's *Lesbian Body* as experiments with and interventions in self-representation in order to explore the usefulness of a focus on self-representation for a discussion of the representation of sexuality and gender.[6] Both are interesting in this context because they play with certain expectations about how and whether lesbian authors write lesbian texts, and what such a claim might mean. In addition, both texts are more interested in proliferating questions around that query than in producing answers to it. That they do so, and how they do so, allows both to invoke certain interpretations, expectations, and conventions that attend autobiography even as they work those connections for productive kinds of dissonance. They allow the reading effects implied by autobiography to remain lively even as they press beyond autobiography's formal boundaries. I am describing Wittig's and Winterson's texts as being in implicit dialogue with autobiography in order to highlight how certain rhetorical conventions and cultural references or situations catalyze the expectations generated by autobiography; namely, that the writer has a truth to tell and is telling it about the writer's life. What in either text motivates this contextualization? That Jeanette Winterson's first book, *Oranges Are Not the Only Fruit*, was widely received as autobiographical has installed the expectation, confirmed by some reviewers and almost all my students, that subsequent texts by Winterson can be read within the context of an autobiographical project, even if Winterson wants to change the rules. That Monique Wittig's experimental text *The Lesbian Body* seems to name the author in the title leads many readers to affirm (or contest) the book as a truth text of lesbianism. What I would say is happening in both readings is that certain assumptions about truth, gender, and sexuality, and the representation of identity indicate that the texts are being read, in part, for their proximity to autobiography. Rather than pronounce such interests as false or limited, I want to let them provide a way into the trickier and more expansive discourses of self-representation and the issues raised there through their interrogation of identity as a function of representation, especially in their attention to the materiality of bodies and the relation of language to the coming-into-being of sexuality and gender.

Why choose autobiography, even provisionally, as a category through which to move these texts on the way to resituating them within the broadened category of self-representation? To begin, autobiography has participated in the production of cultural values around human worth since it has been named as such. Whether autobiography is pressed into service as the shining star of the Enlightenment (via Rousseau as an exemplar of self-consciousness) or its evil twin (via Foucauldian critiques of such a self and the limits on its consciousness), autobiography has been used as both proof text and limit case of what can be known and represented through the category, however contested and changeable, of identity. Whether identity is metaphorized as the self, the self-in-relation-to-others, the subject, the subject-in-process; in other words, as autonomous, relational, or persistently "other" that identity as it is represented in autobiography has been used in cultural narratives about success, fame, human value, social progress, and citizenship. Sexuality has been a crucial element in all these narratives, especially as it is used to underwrite the normalcy of gender hierarchy as either an inevitability through lack of critique or failed critique or an achievement through certain developmental narratives. This discourse on identity is saturated in a presumptive heterosexism that construes heterosexuality as the unmarked category of sexuality, that is, as a synonym for sexuality. Through their reinscription of heterosexism and gender hierarchy, autobiographies function as documents of cultural value. Autobiographies of famous men dominate the genre. The cultural value of these men's lives and the value of their autobiographies are elided: book and man are figures for each other, even *are* each other, as the focus on representation is obscured by the foregrounding of autobiography *as* identity itself rather than one mode of its construction. Due to the way in which some critics and readers minimize the constructedness of autobiography and the complexities of any kind of confessional or testimonial performance, a focus on self-representation emphasizes precisely what is always disappearing in discussions of autobiography, namely, that self-representation concerns representation and the values at any particular time and in any particular place attach to the identities of those who navigate these discourses in order to represent something other than the lives of famous men. The critical task as I see it, then, is to examine the meanings that subtend and structure representation when identity is at stake and at risk and to read certain texts for their ability to trouble and intervene in the dominant meanings that circulate through identity categories such as gender and sexuality. Although this may look like an exercise in seeing autobiography (or ghosts) where none was previously discernible, I hope it offers a way of reading what seems all too readily autobiographical (sexuality as confessional text) in a rather different way.

Jeanette Winterson's *Written on the Body* features an ungendered, unnamed narrator who falls in love with a married woman. Monique Wittig's *Lesbian Body* creates a lesbian world in which the lovers explore the possibilities of embodiment. Through an intertextual reading, it is possible to consider what Wittig's strategy of renaming and Winterson's strategy of not-naming reveal about gender, sexuality, and the modes of signifying them, in relation to self-representation. Both Wittig and Winterson deploy one of the most common tropes of autobiography: the intertwined figures of book and body. Wittig writes: "The body of the text subsumes all the words of the female body. . . . To recite one's own body, to recite the body of the other, is to recite the words of which the book is made up" (10). Winterson, too, offers this trope: "I like to keep the body rolled up away from prying eyes. Never unfold too much, tell the whole story. I didn't know that Louise would have reading hands. She has translated me into her own book" (89). Because the bodies in both are anatomized in less than familiar ways, the figure of the book and body suggest texts that one must labor to read well. Wittig names the bodies in question on the title page as "lesbian," and female pronouns appear in the text. The body is represented in the mode of becoming lesbian rather than in its possession of any particular parts that make it such. In Winterson, no gender references are permitted about the first-person narrator who nonetheless describes her or his sexual adventures with men and women in some detail. The body in both texts signifies gender and sexuality in shifting allusions to the transparency and opacity of what bodies can tell us about what we "see."

   In neither text is the relationship between body and sexual identity primarily referential or mimetic. There is no stable referent, either anatomical or metaphorical, that makes the bodies lesbian, no single practice or array of fetishes that proves the body's sexuality as lesbian. Rather, the relationship between identity (what can and cannot be rendered visible when "I am a lesbian" is or is not the primary signifier of sexual identification) and representation (how to tell a story with sexuality at its center without relying on a familiar way of representing sexuality) becomes the ground for an extended inquiry into the claims to knowledge made by the presence and absence of the names around and through which the body is made to cohere. Evidence of identity, therefore, is located in representational practices of *habeas corpus* (bringing out the body) that resist a legalistic imperative of proof in favor of signification, that is, of proximate and shifting signifiers that can be read relationally within and among texts. I invoke legal language here in order to signal that expectations about whether and how a text is autobiographical are often coded as expectations about whether an author is telling the truth, which is frequently elided with a judgment about how well the author can be said to conform to (or reproduce) hegemonic notions of appropriate identity. This expectation reveals that identity is a function of representation that is thoroughly imbricated in the juridical. Instead of judging whether the body is made intelligible within normative discourses of identity, I want to intervene in those judgments by turning the focus toward how these texts bring out the body. The question, then, is not whether the author is telling the truth but how the body is used as a truth-text and what truth-claims about identity are made through the body.

Wittig explores ways to signify "lesbian" through what we could call reanatomization, a comprehensive invention and display of and by bodies under the rubric of "the lesbian body." Her refusal of a patriarchal regime of names makes it possible for bodies to dissolve under that system of kinship, which depends on patrilineage as a system of meaning and value, and to reemerge through a matrix named "lesbian." That the name "lesbian" titles the project but is not reproduced on every page indicates that the power of this signifier lies in naming the whole text *The Lesbian Body*, rather than in any single or separable dimension of it. Bodies in this text are always coming apart. They are either described through a cataloguing of parts coming back together or of parts being disjoined limb from limb and limb from socket. The violence of this disarticulation and rearticulation points up the materiality of language (especially in Wittig's catalogues of body parts), the way language bears upon the body, makes it knowable (or unknowable).

In contrast to Wittig's experiment with the body under the name "lesbian," Winterson's ungendered, unnamed narrator declines such an utterance. If Wittig's lesbian body is rendered material by its name, Winterson's textual body coheres around the performative "I am a grieving lover."[7] An intertextual reading of Winterson's and Wittig's representations of bodies makes it clearer how Winterson's signification of desire without sexual identification can be read as a refusal of the patriarchal regime of names and the identities it compels. The body's intelligibility is risked in both; in Wittig by claiming and in Winterson by declining a sexual name. Both, however, work the body for its capacity to figure sexuality in terms that do not reproduce heterosexist claims to knowledge. Wittig's emphasis on naming as the mode through which the lesbian emerges makes it possible to ask of Winterson's choice of not-naming:

how, in the context created by reading the texts together, does absence signify?

In order to direct this question toward critical conversations beyond autobiography studies, we need only look to the work being done on the body and the performative and to some earlier work on the theoretical meanings of presence and absence initiated, from different but not irreconcilable directions, via deconstruction and feminist theory. A fairly diverse group of theorists informs my formulation here of how absence signifies. Feminist critics, for example, have undertaken a massive critical project of recovering and remembering the erased cultural productions and lives of women. Although some poststructuralist work on absence, notably by Pierre Macherey, Hélène Cixous, and Jacques Derrida, is written at a conceptual distance from the retrieval and archival work of lost, buried, and disappeared writers and subcultures, taken together these projects amount to a massive reconceptualization of evidence. Evidence, following these critical interventions, may be adduced in and as what is missing, through loss, omission, trauma, or some condensation of these and other phenomena. Interpretive practices have followed these projects and extended them by reading inferentially and circumstantially for remnants, traces, and fetishes of what has to be recognized as a revised real.

In the context I am describing, the revised real emerges through a reconceptualization of evidence. Representations of the real depend on and are a function of what can be claimed as evidence, in the case of self-representation, of identity, of *who* was *there*, of how identity can be rendered intelligible. Critical work on bodies is significant here for its claims about how bodies are read as and for evidence of the real. A newly fashioned matrix for reading bodies has merged insights about the body's materiality with claims about how the body performs meaning. Both emphases—on materiality and on performance—underscore how representations of the body are caught up in competing systems of meaning. Although an emphasis on how bodies perform gender, race, and sexuality contends with the insistence that the body possesses these attributes, these positions appear furthest apart in their most abstract formulations. They are surprisingly similar when they situate the body in a material realm of consequences. Whether the body possesses or performs race, gender, and sexuality, the material consequences nonetheless strike with similar intensity. Both *The Lesbian Body* and *Written on the Body* exploit the possibilities of how bodies possess and perform "identity." In both, the ways in which the representation of the body is its identity is of central concern. *The Lesbian Body* has been a part of feminist discourse about the body from the beginning of the recent interest in that topic. *Written on the Body* intersects with a later stage of this discourse and depends, in my view, on the thinking about the body that precedes it, including Wittig's *Lesbian Body* as its most salient precursor. *Written on the Body* is contemporaneous with a renewed interest in speech act theory, specifically, the performative as it has been theorized by Judith Butler and others. This interest in the performative links legal studies of injurious speech to the U.S. military's "don't ask, don't tell" nonpolicy, and to the contexts in which utterances must answer the question "who are you?" with a statement that begins "I am." In addition, both texts explore how and whether texts perform autobiography, how the lesbian author's sexuality motivates the reading of her text as autobiography, and how such impulses might be rethought.

Written on the Body extends the self-representational project Winterson initiated in *Oranges Are Not the Only Fruit*, published in 1985 when she was twenty-six, which won the Whitbread Prize in England for fiction. Yet the stability of "fiction" as a sufficient description of *Oranges* is called into question immediately because the constructed line between first-person fiction and autobiography is barely meaningful as a marker of generic territoriality. In *Oranges*, Winterson trades across this border through her combination of historical events and places (in her and her protagonist's lives) with allegory and fantasy. This intermingling of the imagined and the verifiable articulates a threshold between fiction and autobiography and serves as an entry point for the text into a category that expands on the generic limits of either. Both protagonist and author are brought up in Lancashire, the adopted daughter of an evangelical mother and barely visible father, and both are named Jeanette. In *Oranges*, young Jeanette is recruited into her mother's allegorical pact with the world. Here, she recites her origin story: "I had been brought in to join her in a tag match with the Rest of the World. She had a mysterious attitude towards the begetting of children; it wasn't that she couldn't do it, more that she didn't want to do it. She was very bitter about the Virgin Mary getting there first. So she did the next best thing and arranged for a foundling. That was me" (3). The mother expects the daughter to become an evangelist, and this plan proceeds more or less as anticipated until Jeanette falls in love with Melanie. Once she does so, what she is capable of seeing in herself and the local community of women believers alters. Subsequently, the lesbians in whose midst she has grown up are recognized as such. Jeanette realizes that she shares their sexuality, though what she will make of this at the end of the book is still an open question. She does not reject the carnival tent atmosphere of evangelism and the otherworldly orientation of her mother, but neither is she accepted by her mother, minister, and church as a lesbian. So in the way of the autobiography, the *bildungsroman*, the coming out story, and the heroic quest narrative, she must leave her home to find it. In this case, she heads off to university. The author's notes on the book jacket preview, condense, and displace the same lesbian pilgrim's progress.

Winterson's books and Winterson's body have been conflated by some reviewers and readers in an attempt to gender and name her narrator "lesbian." To do so, readers must detour through the autobiographical, a detour into the intelligible, whereby readers inscribe the identity of the author upon the dissonance in the category of identity in the text. Whereas *Oranges* blends allegory and fantasy as ways to reread the contours within an arguably historical and personal landscape, Winterson's own, her intervening works, *Sexing the Cherry* and *The Passion*, depart from the verifiable details of Winterson's life and engage history on a grander scale. In these intervening texts her penchant for allegory is untethered from the biblical and the autobiographical per se and channeled into meditations on space, time, and narrative. Her new interests resume and extend what can still be called an autobiographical task in *Written on the Body* insofar as Winterson's first-person narrator returns to some earlier preoccupations with identity and representation first explored via the autobiographical. Some reviewers have assumed that *Written on the Body* is a sequel to *Oranges*, both of which are claimed as *romans à clef*. This is less evidence of a critical consensus than a symptom of what kinds of questions get asked when a review is framed through autobiographical assumptions. In the *New York Review of Books*, Winterson's fictionalizing of the self-representational "I" has been reviewed as a literary device.[8] The unnamed and ungendered narrator is taken as an interesting conceit in a love story focused so centrally on the body and its materiality. After all, the reasoning goes, it's not as if Winterson is really hiding anything with this "I"; everyone knows she's a lesbian. While the autobiographicality of *Written on the Body* has not been particularly contested or even really puzzled out in the so-called straight press, some lesbian reviewers have had another point to make. Sarah Schulman, for example, finds the device of the ambiguous narrator an odd and rather unsuccessful refusal by Winterson to take the name of lesbian. For her,

Written on the Body is like "all fiction based somewhat on real life" and is marred by "lapses of discipline" such as "too many lines of recreated dialogue," which nonetheless make the "emotions richer, easier to recognize." Schulman considers the text flawed, if endearing.[9] Schulman solves the ambiguity of the narrator's gender by diagnosing *her* as "a confused, insecure lesbian who can't fully love the woman of her dreams." The problem here is not so much that the narrator isn't identified as a lesbian but that a lesbian author has an ambiguously gendered narrator. Both reviews concern sexuality, its visibility and what one makes of it. Yet both breeze past the constitutive and not merely perfunctory impediment Winterson sets in their path. There is a prior question here about autobiography as the generic grid of truth. To claim that the name "lesbian" would solve the questions of name, gender, sexuality, and identity evades the problematic within the representation of identity Winterson engages. In terms of names, *Written on the Body* already claims to be a novel. It is not the presence of the name "novel" through which this text enters into the problematic but through the absence of the name "autobiography" precisely in the places one wishes to find it. Were it present, all competing or disruptive knowledge of identity could be compelled to cohere under this name. Identity (the author's, the narrator's, the text's) would become knowable through a grid of intelligibility *already in place*.

I take *Written on the Body* as both a continuation and an expansion of Winterson's interest in self-representation, if in significantly altered terms. The question with which *Written on the Body* begins, "Why is the measure of love loss," expands upon one posed in *Oranges*, which concerns naming: "There are many forms of love and affection, some people can spend their whole lives together without knowing each other's names. Naming is a difficult process; it concerns essences, and it means power." Here, her question was: "But on the wild nights who can call you home? Only the one who knows your name" (170). In *Oranges*, Winterson sought an answer to "who can call you home?" in allegory and fantasy. That narrative moves between the coming out story, and its consequences for Jeanette, and parables in which she chats with advice-giving demons. While her interest in fantasy links *Oranges* to *The Passion*, *Sexing the Cherry*, and *Art and Lies*, a different connection links *Oranges* to *Written on the Body*.[10] In *Written on the Body* the various tensions and problematics are charted primarily not through the alternative plenitude of fantasy but in the linkage of love and loss. Fantasy's counterpart, anxiety, emerges in the responses induced by an unnamed and ungendered narrator. In *Or-*

anges, Winterson's questions about power, knowledge, and names; her recurring tropes of home, wild nights, love, and loss; and her exploitation of autobiographical echoes gesture explicitly toward self-representational discourse. In *Written on the Body,* however, Winterson extends the self-representational strategies of *Oranges* into the perverse strategy of not-naming.

The strategy of not-naming raises some related questions about identity and the mechanisms of identification through which identity is ascertained and secured: in what ways does a name indicate presence? Must the absence of a name be linked to loss? Or, to put it more precisely in *Written on the Body*'s terms, when and how can absence be read as something other than loss? When and how does absence signify what one does not possess, rather than what one refuses to give? Winterson's text works these questions for a range of possible answers. But there are prior questions here about names and their function within the field of representation. How, within the discourses of self-representation, do names signify identity? What does it mean for a name to identify a subject, to gender it, sex it, make it real? What are the definitional limits of "sex," "gender," and "sexuality" as evidence of the "identity" of an autobiographical subject? Ultimately, these questions focus on Winterson's text in a very particular way: they offer a map for the possibilities that attend the representation of identity when names are absent.

Written on the Body offers a hard case for testing the meaning of names. Immediately, the lack of disclosure or the seeming invisibility of gender foregrounds sexuality as a question. Without the name of gender and the identity it indicates, how are we to know this "I"? When we attempt to infer sexual identity from the narrator's lovers, we are offered bisexuality as a nonidentifying answer to the question of gender: the beloved is a woman, and the narrator has had some male and more female lovers. Gender and sexuality do not reduce to each other, nor do they confirm *an* identity for the narrator. The refusal to disclose gender, and the subsequent interpretation of sexuality as a question moves the reader briskly onto autobiography's familiar ground, where identity is implicated in questions of representation and ontology. What might seem so ontologically *there* as to defy the need of representation becomes, in this text, difficult to name. In this way, Winterson forces the autobiographical to divulge its weirdness and to open onto the wider, and wilder, field of self-representation through the questions mentioned earlier. Through her inquiry into naming, as it instantiates how identity is a function of representation, Winterson moves from a more expected to an unexpected location within self-representation.

The expected claims about names in autobiography emphasize their stabilizing function: a name identifies a person, a family, and a history and focuses attention on the solid corporeality to which it refers. Ultimately, the name seems to mark a ground zero of representational veracity: "who *is* the autobiographer?" can be answered by a simple cross-check and verification of the author's name and the protagonist named in the text. If they are identical, you have autobiography. But as Winterson suggests in *Oranges*, the stakes are too high for naming to function as a simple referential anchor that holds the world to the text through the name of the autobiographer: "Naming is a difficult process; it concerns essences, and it means power." Though this may sound like a young lover reaching for "deep meaning," as a comment on naming in autobiography it is suggestive. In autobiography, the name becomes a symbol not only of the past to which one may lay claim but of the past and the family that claim you. Such a symbol (and such families) may well be more threatening than comforting. After all, not everyone who writes autobiographically ends up embracing the name as a signifier of familial belonging. Some write in order to destroy the claims on them made by families, communities, and past experiences. Following in this vein in her feminist intervention in the history of ideas, Denise Riley finds an apt figure in Desdemona, whose life depends on what may be done to her through a name.[11] Desdemona's questioning and querulous signature, "Am I that name?," resonates here as a self-representational signifier that is different from the performative "I am that name," though comprehensible as part of the same signifying system. "Am I that name?" does not mean the obverse of "I am that name," not, that is, "I am *not* that which men say I am" but "am I?" a question that leads toward an interpretive context in which, presumably, those who know the answer can ensure the consequences that will follow. To find oneself named, pinned in place by that identification, and placed within a community, a family, and a home is precisely what many self-representational writers are trying to escape and not simply to represent. Thus, writers may engage the discourses of self-representation as much to lose a name as to find one. To lose a name is not merely to exchange one set of constraints for a less familiar one. To remove oneself from a familiar audience and community in an effort to find a more companionable home is not an easy task. Rather, to route self-representation more emphatically and precisely through representation necessarily engages the subject in an altered discursive project, the terms of which are not fully predictable. The writer may well need to reconstruct the very possibilities and grounds for community through this effort.

The terms in which Winterson casts this venture are more concerned with the anxiety provoked by the absence of the name than with sustaining the conceit of an unnamed, ungendered narrator. In other words, if not-naming were merely the coy pose of a clever writer, its ability to generate anxiety might well dissolve within a few chapters. Anxiety remains in lively play, however, because what is missing is the signifying chain of identity that presumably corresponds to a material reality in which identity as a signified coheres through the progressive, motivated, and linked signification of sex, gender, and sexuality. Autobiography not only depends on this signification, it seems to prove its reality. Winterson's strategic omission of the name strikes at the signifying seam between reality and autobiography. Winterson's installation of a speaking subject whose only name is "I" places the reader in a position to question which signifiers cause the subject to unravel and which to cohere, and in what contexts.

Through the absence of names, Winterson raises questions of identity that the presence of names does not really answer. Questions about the ascertainable identities of the narrator, the author, and the text are stabilized by names but are not identical to them. The questions lie there, redundant, seeking transparency. An answer would throw light but in doing so would obliterate the opacity through which this narrator emerges. Both the text itself and the *topos* of gendered and sexual identity here are "written on the body" in such a way that the body cannot simply offer a transparently visible or unambiguously legible proof of "identity," but that does not remove the problem of identification, of establishing how "we" know "one" (a woman, a lesbian, an autobiography) when "we" see "one." The body is usually thought to provide compelling, even irrefutable, proof of sex and gender, and ultimately of unique identity. The body coalesces under the name of sex. The erotic body is mapped through acts, zones, desires, all of which usually cite sex as identification. How, then, can a book on the body, a love story no less, avoid sexing the subject? While *Oranges* brings out the autobiographical body through naming it as female, as lesbian, as "Jeanette," *Written on the Body* traces a different path through self-representation. Winterson almost seems to be asking how much she can leave out and still conserve the autobiographical trace. The experiment here plays at the extreme edge because she chooses to omit both name and sex as she refuses to secure the body's identity beyond that of "lover." It seems improbable to pursue self-representation without names. It not only defies generic conventions and the expectations they install; it risks coherence altogether. But perhaps the limit of coherence at which Winterson plays through figures of the name and the body locates *the* risk worth taking precisely due to the functions both name and body have played in regimes of truth and identity, regimes in which autobiography itself has served.

Written on the Body attempts to map the boundary of representation—its limit—in relation to what can and cannot be known and uttered about the lover's body and between what can be represented through a lover's discourse and what, in the absence of the beloved, is lost and must achieve signification elsewhere. To do so, *Written on the Body* divides into three sections. In the first, the narrator recounts falling in love with Louise, who, when they meet, is married to Elgin, a cancer specialist. The narrator is a hero cast in the Byronic mold; there have been many lovers, mostly women, and many married women. There have also been many heartbreaks. The narrator fears that Louise, too, will become another figure in her romance narrative, but Louise defies expectation and, instead of kissing the narrator goodbye, declares that she is leaving Elgin: "My love for you makes my other life a lie." The lovers begin an idyllic stretch that ends abruptly in some awkward and rather implausible blackmail: Louise, it turns out, has leukemia. Elgin tells the narrator that Louise's symptoms have flared, that he and he alone can guarantee her state-of-the-art medical care, and that his connections offer the best hope for Louise's health. But there is a catch: he will not offer them unless the narrator vanishes. The narrator agrees, and the book breaks into its second part, a sustained meditation on the body. This section consists of four chapters devoted to the body. At their conclusion, the narrative of the first section seems to resume, though the ending invites a revision of this schema.

The excess generated by the absence around naming and gender finds explicit, even hyperbolic, representation in Louise and Elgin, the Married Couple. There is even a detailed account of how Elgin got his name, and he is rendered in stereotypical terms as Jewish. In a similarly schematic way, Louise's gendered representation is a proliferation of formalist attributes, even fetishes of gender: her red hair, her pale skin, her lovely home, her effects, all amount to a hyperbolic emphasis on her femaleness, on the necessity of saying "she" in reference to Louise. Louise pervades, even invades, the scene as a system of gendered signs. Signifiers of gender proliferate around her; she is an extension of and extends into her home. All this metonymic displacement allows the narrator to find fetishes everywhere: "She dribbled viscous juices down her chin and before I could help her wiped them away. I eyed the napkin; could I steal it? Already my hand was creeping over the tablecloth like something out of Poe" (37). The excessivity of Louise's gendering in the context of the narrator's self-representation casts Louise's "reality" into doubt. She is a gendered object in a hyperreal sense: she is almost a phantasm. Some names attach to her readily, but all depend on an interpretive context of sexuality that is structured through a significant absence. The problem of knowing Louise's name(s) is consistent with the problem of not knowing the narrator's; both concern the context in which gender and sexuality as evidence of each other is performed. Louise is not presented in a delimited way as a "married woman"; her desire is not thoroughly heterosexualized by this name, and therefore the narrator doesn't pop out from behind namelessness as a fella. Instead, Louise reacts unpredictably in relation to that name, and the reader is offered another possible name for the beloved. She's a real femme, that Louise. With the femme-ing of Louise comes the subtextual encoding of the Casanova-Narrator as butch.

Perhaps Castle's reading of the lesbian as apparition permits a two-step reading toward identifying the narrator: if Louise can be read as an apparitional lesbian, then the narrator steps from behind the curtain and reveals herself, too, as such. Louise's extreme womanliness is not precisely what Castle argues for as the lesbian's derealization, but it accomplishes the same spectralization of the character. Obviously, this is an inferential reading, a circumstantial reading, and it is consistent with the opening up of this reading practice rather than with the narrowing of the evidence into a single proof of the narrator's identity. But such an inference does not, finally, resolve the question. Do lesbians fall in love only with lesbians? Can a reading practice that seeks to open up the categories "married" and "woman" close down around the category "lesbian"? In other words, things get tricky here precisely because it is the ascription of names to identity, the very code of the juridical, that Winterson is scrambling. Castle's argument works best, I think, for texts other than *Written on the Body*, for in this case it is the unknowability that is interesting. Thus I see less a veiled derealization than a sympathetically posed question about realization. While Castle provides a way to identify lesbians in literature, I mean to emphasize here how *Written on the Body*'s signification performs in a different way. The absence of a referential ground zero for the narrator keeps the signification in play, renders interpretation necessary. If the narrator is not readily comprehensible as a "woman," she need not be incomprehensible as a lesbian, and this is the sort of linkage of gender to sexuality as the basis of identification and identity that Winterson wants to keep coming at throughout the text and not, particularly, to resolve. Her questions unfold in this way: must a reading of sexuality be routed through a gender proof? How great is the distance (interpretive, representational, self-representational) between the names "woman" and "lesbian?" These questions all concern the interpretive space opened up between sexuality and gender, between identity and names. And it is a space that Winterson will not suture.

Since Winterson will not suture this space, what meanings are generated and circulate here? The space ambivalently evokes both loss and omission; that is, the space of namelessness may seem like the space that marks where a name was lost as much as the space of its refusal or obliteration. Such ambivalence between loss and refusal leads in two directions. In one direction, if one believes that a name has been lost, then its former presence registers as that which one possessed or knew. A rupture between a "before" and an "after" evokes nostalgia. The "lost" name becomes a pretext for nostalgia, which gestures toward a narrative with an origin (toward myth) and installs the repetition of loss as a central motif, whether this is figured as the "return" of or to what was lost or as the repetition of its loss. In a different direction, namelessness memorializes another struggle. Here, the absence of a name signifies not loss but a successful evasion of the fixity implicit in naming, and a redirection of the representation of identity. Nostalgia and this provisional freedom from fixity are welded in *Written on the Body*, and both circulate through the representation of gender and sexuality.

In this context, Winterson's narrator raises the question of narcissism by turning from the other or others to the self, toward the narrator's own pain rather than toward an external love object. The narrator's own body is now where Louise's body can be known and, functionally, is. In this extreme incorporation that apprehends another as the self and that merges self and other to the point of absorption, Winterson seems to be flirting with something rather more controversial than character development. By coding the narrator as narcissistic, she gestures toward the discourses of sexology and their inscription of homosexuality as pathology, most notably, as narcissism, though I find no simple identification grid here (if narcissism, then lesbianism). The connection is implicit in the discourses of sexuality, and interpretive practices of reading for the possibility of lesbian representation make much of inference. The emphasis falls on interpretation. There is no way around it because there is no named "there" to which signification will attach or return. Assignation of signifier to signified (in the name of naming) would arrest the production of signification in which this text is engaged. Even as the specter of narcissism is raised, Winterson eludes the trap that Freud set because the subject to whom narcissism would attach engages self-representation differently. This isn't simply a story of "women who love too much" or "lesbians without very good boundaries." The text frustrates those conclusions, even as it suggests them, as Winterson constructs a discussion of the beloved's body by a lover without the name to which narcissism might attach.

Following the first section of *Written on the Body*, the narrator's body is removed from one narrative, a straightforward tale of complicated love, and another self-representational discourse in which to measure love and loss is called for. Winterson does all that can be done with the questions that I have suggested animate the first section of the book and then raises the representational stakes. The narrative breaks when Louise becomes ill and the narrator presumes to choose Louise's future for her. At this point, Louise's body is on the verge of becoming the body in pain and, as a body saturated in a materiality with consequences, a body that demands another discourse for representation. Winterson removes Louise in order to focus primarily on how the narrator experiences the pain of loss. The narrator has lost a body that in this text is primary. While it is not originary per se as either a maternal or infantile body, it is a primary love object nonetheless, and, insofar as it is absent, mourned, and central, is a fetish for the body logic that is generated by the context of a central loss.[12]

Following the opening, unnamed narrative section, there are four lessons in the anatomy of absence entitled "The Cells, Tissues, Systems and Cavities of the Body," "The Skin," "The Skeleton," and "The Special Senses." Each section begins with a *Gray's Anatomy*-like description: "THE CLAVICLE OR COLLAR BONE: THE CLAVICLE IS A LONG BONE WHICH HAS A DOUBLE CURVE. THE SHAFT OF THE BONE IS ROUGHENED FOR THE ATTACHMENT OF THE MUSCLES. THE CLAVICLE PROVIDES THE ONLY BONY LINK BETWEEN THE UPPER EXTREMITY AND THE AXIAL SKELETON" (129). What follows are reminiscences in the presumed present tense of narration from which the narrator has recounted the story. Memory combines with grief to produce a discourse in which the partial presences conjured by memory combine within the sliding invention of imagination. Memory goes beyond reporting and becomes self-invention. The turn toward the other via memory is a turn toward the self as the producer of counterimages and also as the locus of grief. The absence of the beloved within this present tense is now embraced and becomes the occasion for both memory and self-representation: "It was a game, fitting bone on bone. . . . Bone of my bone. Flesh of my flesh. To remember you it's my own body I touch. Thus she was, here and here" (129–130).

Even with this renewed emphasis on the materiality of the body, on the names by which the body can be described beneath the surface, sex is still not given. In addition, *Written on the Body* refuses to hint at sexual identification through sexual difference. Here is the narrator on the presumptive appeal of sexual difference: "I thought difference was rated to be the largest part of sexual attraction but there are so many things about us that are the same" (129). The invocation of sexual difference suggests the old chestnut that "opposites attract," which is shorthand for the logic of heterosexism in which sexual difference is the fetish that, ironically and illogically, grounds heterosexuality. In the narrator's embrace of sameness, an unmarked body offers no "clues" to gender and sexuality. Although this is the sentence I have heard quoted as "proof" that the narrator is a lesbian, consider how it continues to deflect that gaze and to pursue a discourse of sexuality different from one that assigns names to sexual identities. No erotogenics follows from conventionally sex-marked sites, body parts, zones—no penis, labia, clitoris, breasts, but also no anus, no nipples. No "source" sites or parts from which substitutes are drawn—the site of pleasure and pain is, more comprehensively, the body. If there is a fetish, and why wouldn't there be, it would be the body as the displaced locus of embodied knowledge, the material with which eros develops, the real that aches. If I say, as Winterson's narrator might, "I ache for you," do you want to know, precisely, what part hurts? Winterson's language helps to locate a different source of desire—the "I" rather than the specified, named person, who in desire has desire. It is not "Jeanette" or the genitals ("jeanette-als"?) so much as the self-representational "I," the capacity for saying "I," that constructs pleasure and pain.

Through its emphasis on the "I," the anatomy lessons continue to explore autobiographicality, if in terms different from those in the first section in which absences in the narrative could be filled, as some reviews of the text suggest, with information from Winterson's life. The lessons anatomize absence and indicate, however, that this is a self-representational project that capitalizes on the shared "I" of autobiography and first-person fiction in which the "I" forms an opening, an orifice through which the self-representational pours. It is impossible to say, though, which is hole (the self-representational? narrative?) and which is rim in this reading, because the "I" of the narrator generates meaning in both locations.[13]

Perhaps what is most pertinent to *Written on the Body* is the way in which this "I" functions as a body part in a way that is consistent with the text's erotogenics and is no more or less a mark of the real than the other body parts represented here. It is not that Winterson claims there is no materiality to bodies and sex; the representations of other characters besides the narrator suggest as much. Rather, the text makes it possible to consider the materiality of language through the representation of the narrator. The materiality of names does not totalize the materiality of bodies and sex, and the materiality of bodies and sex is not totalizable under names.

In this context, we can ask if Winterson succeeds in taking up the project that Judith Butler adumbrates in the conclusion to her essay "The Lesbian Phallus": "For what is needed is not a new body part, as it were, but a displacement of the hegemonic symbolic of (heterosexist) sexual difference and the critical release of alternative imaginary schemas for constituting sites of erotogenic pleasure."[14] Butler rereads narcissism and the phallus to uncover two things: 1) that Freud links pain to love when he detours through hypochondria in his discussion of narcissism, and 2) that Freud's and Lacan's use of the phallus depends not on the equivalence or nonequivalence of phallus to penis but on the logic of expropriability and substitution. That is, the phallus is not the signifier of the signified worth having but the signifier of investiture. As such, according to Butler, other phalluses or other assignations of the phallus are certainly possible and would become productive of other imaginary morphologies. Through this reading, Butler makes clear that the lesbian phallus is not a new body part but a signifier of alternative morphologies, of imaginary bodies with pleasures that are not predicated on their reproduction of what she calls the "hegemonic symbolic of (heterosexist) sexual difference." To enlist Butler's reading in reading the body logic I am describing in *Written on the Body*, the "I" does not underwrite the coherence of the body any more than any other body part does, though, taken together, all gesture toward a materiality that motivates signification. They refer less to a total object of which they are all parts than to the function that produces them, here a representation of the body and a materiality of sex rendered without the names of sexual difference-as-identity.

At this critical intersection, Wittig's work offers a significant counterpoint to Winterson's. Compare the interpenetrative possibilities in the named lesbian body in Wittig to the unnamed in Winterson. A representative moment in Wittig: "The women lead m/e to your scattered fragments, there is an arm, there is a foot, the neck and head are together, your eyelids are closed, your detached ears are somewhere, your eyeballs have rolled in the mud, *I* see them side by side, your fingers have been cut off and thrown to one side, *I* perceive your pelvis, your bust is elsewhere, several fragments of forearms the thighs and tibiae are missing. . . . *I* announce that you are here alive though cut to pieces, *I* search hastily for your fragments in the mud, m/y nails scrabble at the small stones and pebbles, *I* find your nose a part of your vulva your labia your clitoris, *I* find your ears one tibia then the other, *I* assemble you part by part, *I* reconstruct you . . ." (79–80).[15] The beloved's violent bodily dispersal and her recuperation are repeated throughout the book. The lesbian body is capable of infinite disarticulation and reassembly under the name of lesbian. Wittig's pleasure in cataloguing the lesbian body, its organs, functions, and intimate anatomy form the rhetoric of a series of prose poems or block-style fragments. Without the name of "lesbian," this body does not cohere. It would merely be destroyed, its resurrection outside the logic of identity explored in this text. However, the grieving lover may always collect the beloved and restore her to health within the embrace of the lesbian body as a system of representation.

In this sense, Butler's reading of Lacan can illuminate what Winterson and Wittig are doing with names. As Butler points out in her reading of Lacan: "For Lacan, names, which emblematize and institute this paternal law, *sustain* the integrity of the body. What constitutes the integral body is not a natural boundary or organic telos, but the law of kinship that works through the name. In this sense, the paternal law produces versions of bodily integrity; the name, which installs gender and kinship, works as a politically invested and investing performative. To be named is thus to be inculcated into that law and to be formed, bodily, in accordance with that law" (72). This presumption of bodily coherence through sex and the name are refused and reworked by Wittig's and Winterson's (if in a very different way) inscription of the lesbian body. Without the phallus, without genitals or hierarchized erogenous zones, Wittig gives us a body ripped and ripping open that nonetheless persists under the name of "lesbian." A name is generated here that is also part of the pieces from which all of the lesbian body may be reworked. Its pleasures are in its continuity. Winterson's narrator declines the performative because the narrator's identity cannot logically be identified by that utterance. To declare a name and a gender would give the narrator the status of all narrated objects, including Louise, and the project would implode. Winterson gives us bodies in pain: the text of Louise's leukemic body is set beside the narrator's grieving figure.

It is important to raise again, and in altered terms, the question of why the refusal of names, especially in a climate of detection, is significant. When we remember how emphatically the name goes to kinship, and how the enforced linking of names to kinship structures makes legally binding familial ties out of arrangements like marriage and, through this construction, legalizes acts that would be crimes were they committed against non-kin, we might well conclude that the call *for names* is less about establishing referentiality than it is about ensuring the kinship structures and juridical discourses that follow from them. Names for identity and body parts belong to an order of signification that is a social order. To resist these specific names, at the very least, is to resist that social ordering. In *The Lesbian Body*, the resistance to the social ordering that includes patriarchal kinship focuses on linking changed names to a changed body and, implicitly, to changes in the social body. The patrilineal names are refused, along with the regimes of the body they impose. Wittig breaks down the body and catalogues it, reanatomizes it as lesbian, and undertakes an epic and violent reworking of the acts of love, embodied knowledge, and their complex pleasures. In the absence of patronymic traditions, the body breaks down. In fact, bodily integrity itself is risked. This makes possible the emergence of an altogether different bodily coherence, one not organized around the phallus as the symbolic signifier of value.

I should clarify here that my interest in psychoanalysis is subordinate to my interest in Butler's reading of it. I intend her reading to operate as a pivot, a way to turn from psychoanalysis, while acknowledging its relevance, toward an alternative reading. A Lacanian morphology misses the pressure points of Wittig's experiment, for although it could be suggested that Wittig seems to start and stay within the logic of a return to the mirror stage by representing a body in pieces, it seems more plausible that the lesbian body as *le corps morcelé* is on the verge of cohering differently. Through this representational location and tactic, Wittig undertakes a sustained project in signification. Her emphasis does not fall simply upon putting the body together differently; that is, she is not trying to come through the mirror stage *to* and *as* something/someone/someplace different. Rather, the project is sited there and stays there, inhabiting its function and techniques and working the contours of signification for the persistence and appearance of the disallowed—the lesbian body, a body the subject is prohibited from forming. The repetition is key here. Wittig can disassemble and reassemble the lesbian body from any part. Thus, a psychoanalytic reading reaches a particular limit when confronted with *The Lesbian Body*. As an alternative to a Lacanian reading and as a supplement to Butler, I suggest that the logic through which Wittig's lesbian body coheres is fractal.

Fractal geometry offers a way to describe irregular shapes (sometimes called "pathological" in Euclidean geometry) that are self-similar, i.e., are shaped identically at their micro and macro levels. Fractal geometry has been used, for example, to demonstrate that the shape of the English coastline at one-hundred-mile segments or at one-mile or one-foot segments is identical to its overall shape. The point in my reading of *The Lesbian Body* as a shape that is comprehensible through fractal geometry is to claim that part of the body does not stand in for or represent the whole (as through synecdoche); rather, as I read Wittig, that the lesbian body at every order is identical in morphology to every other order of magnitude. Each part is identical to any other part in shape, and therefore the body can be recognized as lesbian from *any* fragment and can also regenerate the largest organization of the body from any fragment. The parts of the body, then, do not cleave easily from nor refer to a whole body, as in synecdoche; rather, from any body part, including the "I," the whole project of writing autobiography without names could be generated.

In *Written on the Body*, the grieving lover has absented herself from the wounded beloved and cannot recollect her. Parts and functions of the body become occasions for meditations on loss without the prospect of reconstruction. Whereas Wittig has refused patrilineal names and instituted a discourse of the endlessly explorable lesbian body, Winterson seems to go under its interdict and loses a name. Winterson's narrator cannot reach the beloved but can only move further away, study books on grieving, and wait. The narrator is returned to one body: the narrator's own. This "I" 's discourse on the body does not bridge the violence of separation but leaves the "I" on one side of the abyss with only the body s/he can touch as evidence of the other's presence . . . and absence. There are similar tropes in both texts, but one difference remains the place of the name and the morphological equivalence between identity and name that both will claim. For Wittig, "lesbian" is the signifier of bodily coherence that incorporates violent dismemberment but permits the pleasure of putting the body back together. Without the signifier of lesbian in *Written on the Body*, the lover's identity persists through and as the absence of Louise, a monument to breaking up: "I am alone on a rock hewn out of my own body."

Following the four lessons on the anatomy of absence, *Written on the Body* returns to the story. It is March, and Elgin has promised to call with news about Louise's condition. But something has shifted, and it is not just what was left of the plot. Interruptions in the style of the lessons recur in the narrative as it drives toward an ending that is distinct from the story-telling style of the first section and informed by the self-reflexivity of the second section's excursion into the body. The ending reflects on the process of writing, and the identity that emerges from this shift in the third section is the author-identity, which, Foucault argues, is always disappearing: the identity signified by the autobiographical performative "I am writing."

The third section breaks from the confines of story telling to become more self-reflexive, almost an allegory on story telling, and finds Winterson resuming her interest in fantasy. The differing forms of the sections offer differing strategies for writing on the body and as such form an experiment in alternative morphologies (of the lover's body, of the body of the writing, of sexuality). Whereas the first section is more conventional in narrative terms, and the second section meditates on anatomy and absence, the third section is disorienting in terms of time and in its willingness to turn phantasmatic Louise loose as the uncanny. When the narrator finally decides that she must find Louise and set it all right, the narrator's attempts to track her down turn up only traces and dead ends. The places where the narrator might find Louise are now, more than ever, the narrator's own body. Yet Louise, phantasmatic in the first section and spectral in the second, is now, curiously enough, "back."

Louise returns in the penultimate paragraph, paler and thinner, but alive. But the shimmering real into which Louise enters is loaded with signifiers of writing and textuality. Winterson concludes:

> This is where the story starts, in this threadbare room. The walls are exploding. . . . I stretch out my hand and reach the corners of the world. . . . Beyond the door, where the river is, where the roads are, we shall be. We can take the world with us when we go and sling the sun under your arm. Hurry now, it's getting late. I don't know if this is a happy ending but here we are let loose in open fields. (190)

In its conclusion, *Written on the Body* appears to be more prequel than sequel to *The Lesbian Body*. The lovers have reunited, and their bodies grow to incorporate the world, which can now contain them both. Here, to be "let loose in open fields" may signify the same expansive and fictive desire for limitlessness that namelessness has signified throughout the text. Winterson's refusal to anchor the narrator through the name "lesbian," or her textual practice through the name "autobiography," has allowed for a particular inquiry into the limits of intelligibility within the representation of identity. Nonetheless, the ending turns back on the project itself as the narrator wonders, "I don't know if this is a happy ending."

This hesitant moment may well suggest the next best question to pose within the terms of what I have been describing as Winterson's project. We should allow this moment its charm: could a narrator who asks "Why is the measure of love loss?" resist asking whether the story has a happy ending? Still, and with no damage to pleasures besides charm, I am concluding that *Written on the Body* allows for an exploration of figures of facticity. Winterson has assembled a code for reading around the nexus of identity. She plays with the semiotics of naming as an i.d. code and investigates the slippage between names and things in a way that reworks the meanings among sex, gender, sexuality, and autobiography as problematical, uncertain, even enigmatic. To emphasize the connection to Wittig, we should remember that Wittig has argued that women are made knowable through the category of "sex" as a forcible interpretive act and that "sex" is a category she considers thoroughly political, without ontology, and constituted through a violent assault on the grounds of ontology.[16] For her, "[t]he category of sex does not exist a priori, before all society. And as a category of dominance it cannot be a product of natural dominance but of the social dominance of women by men, for there is but social dominance" (5). "Sex" as it prefigures "gender" and the autobiographical body for women is not primarily, then, a lived construction so much as a nonlived obstruction.[17] Thus, to "be" a woman already indicates a kind of material violence. For some contemporary writers like Winterson and Wittig, autobiography as the narrative account of a woman's subjection is refused. That Winterson chooses to tell a love story focused upon the intensity of embodied longing, of sex, and of longing without a gender marker may mean less that the narrator doesn't feel like a lesbian than that she doesn't feel like a woman in precisely the way that Wittig refuses that identification. For Wittig, the name "lesbian" trumps patriarchal kinship, makes it impossible for it to tell its story. Ultimately, Winterson is more skeptical about whether a different name (and the substitute order it proclaims) escapes the juridical. In this she plays poststructuralist to Wittig's structuralist. For Winterson, a name is still a name, and, while namelessness may not smash the juridical, it sure throws a wrench in the works. Taken intertextually, Winterson's and Wittig's work frames a question for self-representation and lesbian representation: if the continued possibility of self-representation is currently being renegotiated through autobiography without names, is this a happy ending? "I don't know," as a self-reflexive signature of dubious tone, indicates the need to read absences and the resistance to conventions of autobiographical, gendered, and sexual representation as revisions of the real.

NOTES

I want to thank Chris Castiglia for conversations that inform my work at every turn. Thanks also to audiences at the Autobiography Conference at Hofstra University (1994) and the 1994 Gay and Lesbian Studies Conference (University of Iowa).

1. See Paul de Man, "Autobiography as De-facement," 919–30.

2. See her "Polemical Introduction" to *The Apparitional Lesbian* (New York: Columbia University Press, 1993) for a briefing on this thesis. The familiar term "thinly veiled autobiography" further suggests the ghostliness of autobiography. Readers look for the autobiographical everywhere, as if it were everywhere, and when they find a certain kind of text they suggest that its art is subordinate ("thinly veiled") to its real existence as autobiography. Writing, in this view, merely drapes the real recalling the metaphors of language as the clothing of thought.

3. As representatives of these interests, see the range of essays in Smith and Watson, eds., *Getting a Life* and *De/Colonizing the Subject*. In terms of art, an obvious example is Cindy Sherman, whose photographs of herself posed in the

styles of other places, forms, and times may be understood less as posing herself as others than as compelling others to pose as her.

4. "On écrit pour être autre que ce qu'on est." See David Halperin, *Saint Foucault*, 144 ff.

5. Such a category includes but is neither limited to nor defined through the same criteria as autobiography and covers, at least provisionally, cultural productions that have been unintelligible (hence dismissed or neglected) in other categories. See Gilmore, *Autobiographics*.

6. Jeanette Winterson, *Written on the Body*. Further references will be included parenthetically in the text with page numbers from the 1993 Knopf edition. Monique Wittig, *The Lesbian Body*. Further references will be included parenthetically in the text with page numbers from the 1986 Beacon edition.

7. See Judith Butler's recent focus on the performative which is drawn from speech act theory, esp. her "Critically Queer," 17–32.

8. Gabriele Annan, "Devil in the Flesh," 22–23.

9. Sarah Schulman, "Guilty with Explanation," 20.

10. Jeanette Winterson, *The Passion; Sexing the Cherry; Art and Lies*.

11. Denise Riley, *"Am I That Name?"*

12. *In this context, see Teresa de Lauretis's Practice of Love* for a discussion of loss and fantasy in lesbian representation and reading.

13. See Lacan's "The Subversion of the Subject" for a fuller discussion of this dynamic, esp. 299, 304, 315–16.

14. See her discussion in *Bodies That Matter*, 91.

15. *The Lesbian Body* was translated by David Le Vay, who is described in the foreword as an anatomist and surgeon.

16. Monique Wittig, "The Category of Sex," 1–8. Further references will be included parenthetically in the text.

17. See my *Autobiographics* (1994) for an elaboration of this point.

WORKS CITED

Annan, Gabriele. "Devil in the Flesh." *New York Review of Books*, 4 March 1993: 22–23.

Barthes, Roland. *A Lover's Discourse: Fragments*. Translated by Richard Howard. New York: Hill and Wang, 1985.

Butler, Judith. "Critically Queer." *GLQ* 1 (1993): 17–32.

———. *Bodies That Matter*. New York: Routledge, 1993.

Castle, Terry. *The Apparitional Lesbian*. New York: Columbia University Press, 1993.

De Lauretis, Teresa. *Practice of Love*. Bloomington: Indiana University Press, 1994.

De Man, Paul. "Autobiography as De-facement." *Modern Language Notes* 94 (1979): 919–30.

Foucault, Michel. "What Is an Author?" Trans. Josué Harari. In *The Foucault Reader*. Ed. Paul Rabinow. New York: Pantheon, 1984.

Gilmore, Leigh. *Autobiographics: A Feminist Theory of Women's Self-Representation.* Ithaca, N.Y.: Cornell University Press, 1994.

David Halperin, *Saint Foucault: Toward a Gay Hagiography.* New York: Oxford University Press, 1995.

Lacan, Jacques. *Ecrits.* Trans. Alan Sheridan. New York: Norton, 1977.

Riley, Denise. *"Am I That Name?" Feminism and the Category of "Women" in History.* Minneapolis: University of Minnesota Press, 1988.

Schulman, Sarah. "Guilty with Explanation: Jeanette Winterson's Endearing Book of Love." *Lambda Book Review* 3, no. 9 (Mar-Apr 1993): 20.

Smith, Sidonie, and Julia Watson, eds. *De/Colonizing the Subject.* Minneapolis: University Minnesota Press, 1992.

———. *Getting a Life.* Minneapolis: University Minnesota Press, 1996.

Winterson, Jeanette. *Art and Lies.* Toronto: Knopf Canada, 1994.

———. *Oranges Are Not the Only Fruit.* New York: Atlantic Monthly Press, 1987. First published by Pandora, London, 1985.

———. *The Passion.* New York: Vintage, 1989. First published by Bloomsbury Press, London, 1987.

———. *Sexing the Cherry.* New York: Vintage, 1991. First published by Bloomsbury, London, 1989. First published in the U.S. by the Atlantic Monthly Press, New York, 1990.

———. *Written on the Body.* New York: Knopf, 1993. First published by Jonathan Cape, London, 1992.

Wittig, Monique. *The Lesbian Body.* Trans. David Le Vay. Paris: Minuit, 1973. Boston: Beacon, 1986.

———. "The Category of Sex." In Wittig, *The Straight Mind and Other Essays.* Boston: Beacon, 1992.

Contributors

DENNIS ALLEN teaches courses in literary theory and in Lesbian and Gay Studies in the English Department at West Virginia University. He is the author of *Sexuality in Victorian Fiction*, and his essays on Queer Theory have appeared in *Modern Fiction Studies*, *Franco-Italica*, and *The Canadian Review of Comparative Literature*.

LAURA AURICCHIO is a doctoral candidate in the Department of Art History and Archaeology at Columbia University. Her dissertation addresses French women artists of the ancien régime.

JOHN CHAMPAGNE is an assistant professor of English at Penn State University, the Behrend College. A novelist as well as a critic, his most recent book is *The Ethics of Marginality: a New Approach to Gay Studies*.

MYRIAM J. A. CHANCY, an assistant professor of English at Vanderbilt University in Nashville, Tennessee, is a Haitian scholar and writer born in Port-au-Prince, Haiti, and raised in Canada. Her critical and creative work has appeared in a number of journals and anthologies, including *Frontiers* and *By, For, and About: Feminist Cultural Politics*. She is the author of *Framing Silence: Haitian Women's Literature of Revolution* and *In Search of Safe Spaces: Afro-Caribbean Women Writers in Exile*. Her essay is excerpted from her current work-in-progress, *"Visible Minorities": Translating Cultures in the Americas*.

GABRIELLE N. DEAN is a Ph.D. candidate in the Department of English at the University of Washington.

LEIGH GILMORE, an associate professor of English and of Women's Studies at Ohio State University, is the author of *Autobiographics: A Femi-*

nist Theory of Women's Self-Representation and coeditor of *Autobiography and Postmodernism*. Currently, she is working on a study of limit cases in autobiography and on obscenity law, self-representation, and sexuality in the United States.

CALVIN THOMAS has been an Emerson Distinguished Faculty Fellow in Modern Letters at Syracuse University and is presently an associate professor of English at the University of Northern Iowa. He is the author of *Male Matters: Masculinity Anxiety and the Male Body on the Line*, as well as articles in *NOVEL, Literature and Psychology*, and *New German Critique*. He is beginning work on two books, *Literature Beneath Itself: Critical Debasements of Modernity* and *Forgetting the Self: Zen and Postmodernity*.

ELAYNE TOBIN is the Cultural Studies Fellow at the University of Pittsburgh, where she is pursuing a Ph.D. in English. She is currently working on her dissertation exploring the role of biography in American middlebrow culture.

THOMAS E. YINGLING was an associate professor of English and director of graduate studies at Syracuse University at the time of his death in 1992. Author of *Hart Crane and the Homosexual Text*, he received his Ph.D. from the University of Pennsylvania. *AIDS and the National Body*, an anthology of his unpublished and uncollected writings, is forthcoming from Duke University Press.

ROBYN WIEGMAN is an associate professor of Women's Studies at the University of California-Irvine. She has published *American Anatomies: Theorizing Race and Gender* (Duke University Press) and coedited two volumes, *Who Can Speak? Authority and Critical Identity* (University of Illinois Press) and *Feminism Beside Itself* (Routledge).

Guidelines for Prospective Contributors

Genders welcomes essays on art, literature, media, photography, film, and social theory. We are especially interested in essays that address theoretical issues relating sexuality and gender to social, political, racial, economic, or stylistic concerns.

All essays that are considered for publication are sent to board members for review. Your name is not included on the manuscript in this process. A decision on the essay is usually reached in about four months. Essays are grouped for publication only after the manuscript has been accepted.

We require that we have first right to any manuscript that we consider and that we have first publication of any manuscript that we accept. We will not consider any manuscript that is already under consideration with another publication or that has already been published.

The recommended length for essays is twenty-five pages of double-spaced text. Essays must be printed in letter-quality type. Quotations in languages other than English must be accompanied by translations. Photocopies of illustrations are sufficient for initial review, but authors should be prepared to supply originals upon request.

Place the title of the essay and your name, address, and telephone number on a separate sheet at the front of the essay. You are welcome to include relevant information about yourself or the essay in a letter to the editor, but please be advised that institutional affiliation does not affect editorial policy. Since the majority of the manuscripts that we receive are photocopies, we do not routinely return submissions. However, if you would like your copy returned, please enclose a self-addressed, stamped envelope.

To submit an essay for consideration, send *three* legible copies to:

Thomas Foster
Genders
Department of English
Ballantine Hall 442
Indiana University
Bloomington, IN   46405

Subscribe to *Genders!*

For nearly a decade, *Genders* has presented innovative theories of gender and sexuality in art, literature, history, music, photography, TV, and film.

Today, *Genders* continues to publish both new and known authors whose work reflects an international movement to redefine the boundaries of traditional doctrines and disciplines.

Since 1994, *Genders* has been published as a biannual anthology, each volume focusing on a particular gender-related issue and offering original essays on the specific theme.

Don't miss the next edition of *Genders*. Subscribe today!

Please enter my subscription for the 1997 issues of *Genders* (2 issues, about 300 pages each) at the cost of $40.50 (shipping and handling are included in the subscription price):

Name _____

Address _____

City _____

State _____ **Zip** _____

I enclose ❑ check, ❑ money order (in U.S. dollars),
or please charge by bank card, ❑ MasterCard ❑ Visa

Account # _____

Expiration Date _____

Phone _____

Signature _____

Mail to:
New York University Press
70 Washington Square South
New York, NY 10012

Or call:
1-800-996-NYUP (6987)

Or fax:
212-995-3833